PRAISE FOR *MOTHERTRUCKER*

"Amy Butcher's *Mothertrucker* is a riveting book, a dynamic portrait of an extraordinary woman—a long-haul trucker, a mother, a survivor—whose company carries us into even broader explorations of friendship, trauma, renewal, and the collision of many kinds of precarity: environmental, economic, and emotional. Butcher's voice is tender, curious, adamant, grateful, and always, always searching for a more complicated version of the truth."

—Leslie Jamison, author of *The Empathy Exams* and *The Recovering*

"*Mothertrucker* is an unputdownable page-turner, the kind that asks you to listen more closely, behold each beauty, perceive every flicker of buoyancy or trepidation. This book is an adventure into the expanse of Alaska's wild, as luminous on the earthly plane as it is in the psyche—just as all good road trips are. Butcher's prose is a match struck in the dark. Readers will lean into each sling of the truck and know the cumbrous lurking of violence that shadows women into definition. Amy Butcher has crafted a tribute to a savior, and created one in its making. In short: I never wanted this book to end."

—T Kira Madden, author of *Long Live the Tribe of Fatherless Girls*

"Amy Butcher's *Mothertrucker* is both an intimate portrait of an unforgettable woman and a powerful exploration of how the author finds her way to a more courageous life. There's truth and beauty on every page of this gorgeous and gripping book."

—Cheryl Strayed, author of *Wild*

"This remarkable book is a polyphonic triumph of holy themes. It's a stunning tribute to the life of a brilliant soul. It's a social reckoning. It's a call to possibility. And it's a path to self-love. Healing is a journey, not a destination, and these pages allow us a passenger seat on Butcher's transformative ride of a lifetime."

—Alissa Nutting, author of *Tampa* and *Made for Love*

"I used to wonder what it would feel like to read a nonfictive piece of art that read like a literary novel, a mystery, a feature, the best of travel writing and welcoming theory. Now I know. A lot will be written about *what* Amy Butcher pulls off in this book. It's the *how* that is unsettling in the best way, the *how* that moves this book from remarkable to a gritty greatness we seldom experience in American literature."

—Kiese Laymon, author of *Heavy* and *Long Division*

"A beautifully written exploration of a woman's endeavor to let go of fear and open herself to joy. Can the divine be found on the most dangerous ice road in Alaska? Or is it through our own souls' journeys toward a most loving and merciful understanding of our own courage and pain? Or both and more? Amy Butcher takes us along for the ride with exquisite writing and heart-pounding yearning."

—Joey Soloway, creator of *Transparent* and *I Love Dick*

"This book should be required reading. Amy Butcher writes a wholly immersive and heart-stopping meditation on love, God, and intimate violence; I wanted to reach back through generations and hand this book to every woman in my family. May we all take this transforming ride on the most dangerous highway in America and become changed. We will be better for it."

—Chelsea Bieker, author of *Godshot*

"At once a gripping narrative, voyage of self-discovery, and manifesto of the power of female solidarity, *Mothertrucker* made me ache for all the women who have seen me, changed me, saved me. This book lights up the ways we as women lie to ourselves, even when we seem so strong, and recognizes that, more than any achievement or barrier broken, showing up for one another—being vulnerable with one another—will set us free."

—Sarah Menkedick, author of *Ordinary Insanity: Fear and the Silent Crisis of Motherhood in America*

"An extraordinary story about the power and solace of female friendship. Butcher's journey into the Alaskan Arctic—a place of danger and beauty—illuminates the complex psychic landscape of two women navigating domestic abuse through a deft blending of place and identity. Fearless, raw, and gripping. Butcher has written a necessary and urgent book."

—Jen Percy, *New York Times* contributing writer and author of *Demon Camp*

"Like her subject, Joy 'Mothertrucker' Wiebe, Amy Butcher knows the power of women's words, and the power of women's friendships to disrupt and dismantle cycles of violence and despair. *Mothertrucker* is raw, beautiful, and at times terrifying—not unlike the Alaskan landscape its gifted author describes. But what it is more than anything else is hopeful. This book is a gift."

—Cameron Dezen Hammon, author of *This Is My Body*

"*Mothertrucker* is a gorgeously written and immersive memoir that I binged in a day. I love this book, this story, and Amy Butcher for taking me along for the ride."

—Mary Miller, author of *Biloxi*

MOTHER TRUCKER

ALSO BY AMY BUTCHER

Visiting Hours

MOTHER TRUCKER

Finding Joy on the Loneliest Road in America

AMY BUTCHER

Published by Little A, New York

www.apub.com

Amazon, the Amazon logo, and Little A are trademarks of Amazon.com, Inc., or its
affiliates.

ISBN-13: 9781542014328 (hardcover)
ISBN-10: 1542014328 (hardcover)

ISBN-13: 9781542014311 (paperback)
ISBN-10: 154201431X (paperback)

Cover design by Nicole Caputo and Merideth Mulroney

"Dogwood" lyrics used with permission from Jenny Lewis.

Printed in the United States of America

First edition

For women,
and Joy, especially

In the springtime, in a little house,
I was determined to work it out.
Oh, in the springtime, in a little house,
the neighbors heard us scream and shout.

—"Dogwood," Jenny Lewis

Countless women are being told that they are not
reliable witnesses
to their own lives, that the truth is not their property,
now or ever.

—Rebecca Solnit

AUTHOR'S NOTE

In April of 2018, I embarked on a trip to Alaska—what I hoped would be the first of many—to meet and travel with Joy "Mothertrucker" Wiebe up the James W. Dalton Highway through northernmost Alaska. We spent six days together, and I left with a plan to return in August or September, when we hoped to do the drive again. Four months later, and several weeks before my planned return, Joy's tanker overturned on a softened shoulder along that highway, and I returned to Alaska—but this time, it was for her funeral and the memorial trucking convoy held in her name.

I've heard it said before that sometimes all women have are stories. And that because women are so often stripped of the power or the autonomy or the safety to tell their own, it is up to other women to share their stories for them.

This is the story as Joy told it.

This is the story Joy shared because she wanted the world to know.

Still, the hardest part of telling Joy's story is telling all of it. Some people, I imagine, will not want the curtain drawn open several years after that curtain closed. But my responsibility is to Joy, to the way she looked at me and said, "I believe God brought you to me." Said, "I believe God wants you to tell my story." Said, "You're gonna tell my story."

Her best friend hopes this book will be about how Joy brought people to God. Her sons hope this book will be about her spirit. I don't know what her daughter or husband expect. But for me, this story is about women—about the way we bend and love and listen, the way we forgive, forgive, forgive. The way we step forward for one another. The way we carry one another, even after death.

In writing this book, it has been important to me—above all—to tell Joy's story truthfully. I want to tell her story, and I want that story to be complete.

"They see me and they see all strength," she told me, "and there's some strength—heck, a lot of it—but there's a lot of suffering, too. That's the story of Joy Wiebe. That's the story, I think, of most women."

The material in this book is the result of lived experience, extensive research, interviews, journals, and ongoing inquiries. It is also based on memory—particular and private, impressionable and discreet.

Some names and identifying characteristics have been changed in the interest of protecting privacy.

PROLOGUE

The year that I met Joy was a consistently dangerous year for women in America.

We were killed in public parks and parking lots, on sidewalks and in our cars. We were killed, too, in basements and back bedrooms and on front porches while babies slept. We were tied up, tied down, kept hidden in secret rooms. We were drugged and dragged and beaten, yelled at and made afraid. Men moved around us like the weather, like things to be endured. We suffered at our workplace and we suffered in our bedrooms and we suffered at the hands of people who, in theory, loved us the most.

From my small town in Ohio, I began to think of women's bodies and the many places they should not go: the woods, for example, where three female joggers were killed in their own American communities in just one August week alone. Women should not jog alone, but also they should not walk alone, hike alone, camp alone, make their way across a parking lot alone at night or during the day or in the morning with too many bags or one bag or no bags whatsoever.

The year that I met Joy, an Iowa woman was strangled to death while out for an evening run among the cornfields, all honey-gold and shimmering, the sky like a pastel painting, like a Grant Wood tableau—America, and our American violence.

In Ohio, a woman was murdered while mixing a bowl of macaroni and cheese.

In Colorado, while putting her children to bed.

In Michigan, while shopping at Kohl's, and in New York City, sleeping, and in central Texas, gaming, and in Southern California, swimming.

In Pennsylvania, a woman from my hometown was murdered by strangulation and blunt-force trauma one week after beginning college. Her body was transported over a hundred miles and to three separate locations via Lyft—first in a blue plastic storage container, then a duffel bag, folded as if clothing, her body treated the same as a Gap T-shirt or Nike joggers—before police identified her attacker, a twenty-nine-year-old male who, when police arrived, was found cleaning blood from his apartment.

And in the Ohio town where I now reside, a woman two years my junior was found buried in a shallow grave at the entrance to the hills I like to hike.

"People don't respect human life no more," her grandmother told reporters. It was a crisp day, early autumn. "God gives it and people just take it."

There were many women who were never found.

There were many women found unidentifiable.

And there were a multitude of men made famous for the murders they'd committed against "their" women. A Colorado husband, for example, earned prime-time coverage for the murder of his pregnant wife, Shan'ann, and their two young daughters, Bella and Celeste. It was exactly the type of national coverage reserved for missing white women and their grieving, sullen white husbands.

"I just want them to come back," Christopher Watts told camera crews, incredulous. He stood on the front porch of his home. He shifted his weight from foot to foot. "It's like a nightmare I just can't wake up from. If they're not safe right now, that's what's tearing me apart."

It took prosecutors less than a month to determine Watts had strangled his wife to death and killed his two daughters through beating and suffocation, despite the four-year-old's coherent pleas, a detail the media lamented ad nauseam. He then drove their bodies to a commercial work site, where he dumped his wife in a patch of overturned earth, his daughters in an oil drum, all of this only hours after a backyard barbecue where the children paddled around a pool in hot-pink bathing suits, tiny pigtails matted against their heads.

He was texting his girlfriend as they swam, police later reported, perhaps even finalizing their burial sites and the manner in which he planned to kill each one as the girls did cannonballs and reapplied sunscreen and played pretend tea party underwater, their tiny hands cradling tinier teacups.

We read about the Watts family everywhere, but what happened to those girls and their mother is what happens to thousands of American women annually. Every year we are stalked and slaughtered, beaten and battered, snuffed out, slain. I knew this but didn't really know it until the spring that I met Joy, when the man I loved more than any other—a man who was good-natured, funny, *kind*—stood in my downstairs hallway screaming, looming over me, lunatic. In the months before that evening, Dave had backed me into a bathroom, yelled until I was on the floor, and screamed at me so violently in a vinyl tent in Colorado that I lay stiff the whole night like prey, wondering if and how he might kill me.

And I thought then, as I had several times prior, *This is how it happens.*

This is how we die.

1.

It is only in the Columbus airport a few weeks later, buffered by the sweet smell of Auntie Anne's and the particular fluorescence of industrial lighting, that I allow myself to consider what a ludicrous thing it is that I am doing: I am flying clear across the country to meet a woman I met on the internet, an Alaskan I've discovered on Instagram, an Arctic ice road trucker who goes by the handle "Mothertrucker." Despite my obsession, she is still mostly a stranger, no different from the men and women who idle beside me in the John Glenn Airport, coveting their premier spots beside the outlet chargers, or trying to secure their ten thousand steps, or complaining loudly about standby waitlists to smiling customer service representatives who have been trained to excel in empathy.

I, too, am trying to excel in empathy. I think this sense of openness—this sense of understanding—will help when I meet Joy, when we are alone in the cocoon of her truck cab for what Joy tells me will be fourteen hours, minimum, but could easily expand to forty-eight, depending, Joy says, on the weather or other truckers or the Sagavanirktok River, or even the road itself. The James W. Dalton Highway is the most dangerous road in America, 414 miles of gravel and occasional pavement that extends north from Fairbanks, Alaska, to the industrial town of Deadhorse and the oil fields of Prudhoe Bay. More drivers die on that road annually than anywhere else in our America, in no small part because its miles are subjected to the worst of Mother Nature. It is built on desolate, remote terrain that often gets washed out or slicked with ice or glazed so thoroughly by late-spring snow that the path ahead disappears, obscuring what is ground and what is air, what is road and what is tundra, and in that difference, sometimes, a life disappears, as well.

The truth is, I'd been looking for a savior, and Joy Mothertrucker came to me like a dream through the well-lit lens of Instagram, each photo another door that, at night, I'd escaped down and through.

Joy is an Instagram celebrity, though she'd never call herself that.

"They just like my photos," she told me the first time we spoke.

I found her account one wintry evening while scrolling innocuously past photos of perfectly plated pasta and beautiful children with sleepy cowlicks, well-designed white living rooms and handsome goldendoodles. Freshly fifty with the face of Kate McKinnon and a body like an exclamation mark—compact, lean, and somehow commanding the world's attention—Joy is the nation's only female ice road trucker, a woman who has built a life driving big rigs on the James W. Dalton Highway and documenting its beauty: rare and natural, snow-glazed and blue.

Joy calls that cold place *heaven*.

She says the highway is *downright holy*.

She seems like God to me.

That Joy strikes in me such envy might strike others as absurd. I am, by all accounts, exactly the sort of woman that American society is comfortable with: a thirty-year-old professor at a small college in Ohio, I write books and advise young students and teach a class in women's literature. I own my own home and till a garden. Each spring, I borrow a friend's pickup for Soil Acquisition Day, when I back the truck bed into the backyard corner and spread the compost with a thick green rake. Neighbors and friends and family are quick to note my independence. *Brave*, they call me. *Strong*. And yet I've spent the better part of three years privately tethered to a man whose behavior scares me, whose sense of power and sense of worth seem to hinge upon making me feel small. Dave is lovely, mostly, but when he isn't lovely, I feel terrified, stripped of all the strength I feel I have in all of the realms—professional, personal—that extend beyond him and our relationship. Over time, our love has become less a sense of liberation, an idyllic if compromising partnership, than a cage between whose walls I pace despite their minimalistic West Elm artwork, three-tier leaning bookshelves, and aesthetically pleasing accent paint in whatever color we'd agreed would reflect light.

Just leave, I think so often.

I never leave. It never happens.

Instead, for four months and through the worst of winter, I've watched Joy's world from my tumultuous home in gray Ohio, where the weather—and the man I loved—raged. But within Joy Mothertrucker's photo feed—those delicate, fragile cubes of color—the climate, the world, was manageable, the men hospitable and kind. Here was a woman who had built her home in a place of unfathomable fear and danger, in a landscape dominated by men and machinery, in an industry and a remote terrain whose googling returns mostly photos of house-high snowdrifts and 18-wheelers crushed and crumpled like pieces of paper, as if God took them in his fist and squeezed.

It didn't take long to track down her number. I scribbled the digits on a Post-it in Sharpie. I placed the Post-it on the refrigerator.

What took me longer was finally calling her. But when one evening Dave screamed at me in such a way that I gathered my body against the floor, felt it act involuntarily because of fear—when I realized, for the first time, what he was doing, how my state of shock, my state of paralysis, was exactly what he had intended, realized the many ways over the many months I had allowed his behavior to continue happening, to dominate our evenings, to *escalate*—I thought of Joy Mothertrucker. I thought of the word *escape*. I thought of all the American women who think violence and abuse won't happen to them until it does, and I looked at that square of Post-it as if it had been placed there uniquely for that very moment, when I would look up from the floor and see it, see the potential that existed, that waited quite plainly, in a space beyond all his terror.

The following morning, with Dave at work, I watched the clock until the hour seemed reasonable, and then I picked up the phone.

It was 8:00 a.m. in Alaska, and Joy was at her desk because of an injury.

I thought my words might catch in my throat, but instead they tumbled out easily.

"I would really like," I said, "to meet you."

~

My itinerary may bridge the divide that separates two strangers, bring our two very different worlds together, but as the airport terminal fills with people, I realize all I know of Joy is a series of stark bullet points I have shaped into a character.

I know, for example, that she is petite with long brown hair and looks like the kind of person who could make a very fine rustic soup—something with potatoes and red lentils, stewed kale and the half-moons of carrots.

I know she has a seventeen-year-old daughter, Samantha, and is decades deep into her second marriage.

I know her family lives outside of Fairbanks on a plot of wilderness with a mule and at least one horse and more dogs than I can keep track of in a cabin her family built together after the first cabin they built burned down.

Joy told me they chose the plot of land for its isolation and spectacular views. In the photos she's sent me—our occasional dispatches over the past two weeks since I placed my call and then purchased my ticket—her mule is teething against its bridle before a forest glazed slick with snow. A Samoyed puppy, a cloud of white, is bounding across a pasture, its paws stained green from grass. Joy's 18-wheeler shines in the driveway, freshly washed and waxed, a handsome blue.

It is in this truck that Joy undergoes her transformation, becoming a little less Joy Ruth Wiebe and a little more Mothertrucker—a name her son Daniel suggested as an Instagram handle but that became, in time, a lived persona followed by over eleven thousand Instagram users.

I have imagined much about Joy, but I know her highway better. The James W. Dalton Highway is the longest stretch of serviceless road in North America and a geographical landmark that has been documented at length, thank God, in books and on the internet, in television and in film. According to my sources—Wikipedia, primarily, but also Alaska's Bureau of Land Management, Alaska.org, the *New York Times*, and the very sexy DangerousRoads.org—it has been called "the most dangerous road in America" and "the most isolated road in America" and—what I am most interested in—"the loneliest road in America."

But to Joy, it is God's country. *His land* is what she calls it.

"Because you feel Him when you are here," she told me the first time we spoke. "And you're not beholden to any man."

Most people know the Dalton Highway from *Ice Road Truckers* fame: two dozen men and three women whose lives were documented, often outrageously, over the course of 138 episodes and eleven prime-time seasons.

I've never seen the show, and Joy has told me that I shouldn't watch it.

"Wouldn't want to give you the wrong idea," she said. "It's a carnival, plain and simple. I mean, some of those men on television? They knew what they were doing. But the women—I mean no disrespect, but I suspect they were hired by Hollywood. They were probably truckers somewhere in Canada, or on lesser Alaskan routes. But they had the, you know, big tits? And here I am, I'm fifty. I've been doing this road all my life. But I'm skinny as a string bean. I mean, let's be honest, I'm no spring chicken."

Spring chicken she may not be, but Joy is a veteran of that highway, and—as many men will later tell me—"the *only* female haul road trucker" and "a haul road angel, plain and simple."

For the past thirteen years, Joy has made a living driving that highway two to three times weekly; she has seen men die and helped men live. She has even raised her daughter, in some small part, in the cab of her 18-wheeler, where they talk about life and faith and family. Joy quizzes her on her spelling: "How do you spell *broccoli*?" They pull over at night to sleep beneath the mountains and watch the northern lights dance, electric, above the sizzling of pan-grilled rib eye and foil-wrapped potatoes wedged in the burning embers of an open fire.

Now she's offered to share that life with me.

You'll see what I mean soon about God, she texts. You definitely feel closer to Him up here.

And we will need to rely on Him, she says, because our drive will be rife with risk: blizzards and misfortune and terrain that punctures tires, or forces trucks into wrecks or worse. *Worse,* Joy explains, because there is no cellular network or Wi-Fi on the Dalton Highway. No data coverage, no police call box, no McDonald's at a highway rest stop. Most of the road is without barriers. All of it is without pavement markings. The highway features potholes the size of cars and stretches that can reach zero visibility. There are 16 percent inclines over steep cliffs and sharp drops with no delineator posts to hold you in when you're doing sixty-five or more, or when your brakes give out, or when you hit ice.

And while most of America may call it the Dalton *Highway* or the Ice *Road*, like in the show, the state of Alaska recognizes the route more properly as "a rural principal arterial," because while integral to Alaskan industry—it's the only supply route catering to those who work the largest oil field in North America—the landscape's harsh climate and severe isolation mean the state Department of Transportation can't possibly keep up with maintenance the way state roads require.

So one travels, in other words, at one's own risk.

Despite this, an estimated 3,700 large trucks travel the road each month, driven by hundreds of men—and a single Joy Mothertrucker—who make their living hauling goods north to Prudhoe Bay. These loads include structural materials and metal piping, wall coverings and twin-size mattresses and all the creature comforts necessary for an isolated but predictable Americana: Famous Amos cookies, lunch-box-size bags of Cool Ranch Doritos, Fruit by the Foots, Gushers, T-bone steaks, and instant gravy.

"You're going to die out there," a friend warned me when I told him my plan to go meet Joy.

But I wanted to drive the Dalton Highway. To sit shotgun in Joy's truck. To dive into the Arctic Ocean—just eight miles from where the highway ended—in what I imagined would culminate in a dramatic and truly lived Alaskan experience. It was still sufficiently early in the spring to think we might glimpse the northern lights. I imagined them crackling pink over chuffing chimneys, over forests packed tight and white with snow, and my body bobbing alone out there in the darkness, solitary and independent, the Arctic Ocean cold but exhilarating, the neon light above the water like God had swirled the sky with a metal spoon.

It's otherworldly, Joy had promised. *When you see those lights, you know: God is there, and He is watching.*

"Seriously," my friend said, "this is a capital-*T* Thing Not To Do."

He'd seen the lights many times and suggested I fly to his apartment in Portland, Oregon, instead, where he'd buy us a bottle of whiskey and an expansion pack of Crayola crayons and we could color them in, drunk.

"It's pretty much," he said, "the same."

Except, of course, it wasn't.

But what he meant was that such a trip wasn't safe. It was unwise for anyone—much less a woman—to fly alone to Fairbanks, Alaska, to ride alongside a stranger on precipitous, snow-packed roads, through canyons and valleys and tundra, until the yellow glow of industry dispersed to clear night sky.

"I mean it," my friend said. "My apartment complex has got a pool, and I'll get us the top-shelf-variety whiskey. You'll have a dozen shades of Crayola green."

But I was tired of men—men I knew, and men I didn't—telling me where my body did and did not belong, what I could and could not do with it, where it was and was not safe.

I've been doing this for thirteen years, Joy had texted me a few days prior. *So don't get cold feet on me now! I've seen it all, done it all! You'll be driving with a legend!*

I will be safe in the company of Joy Mothertrucker.

It is more than I can say about my own home. For what I've been learning lately is the same thing that one in four American women will learn at some point over their lifetime: what it feels like to be bulldozed, bullied. What it is to live in fear. What, precisely, a man can do when he cows your body into bedroom corners, or behind a toilet, or against a tent, or beside a creeping pothos housed in an Aztec planter I bought with him on a New Mexico vacation where I'd spent the night before in a La Quinta Inn, awake and sobbing. For months, Dave has been operating from what I consider to be an increasingly darker and more dangerous place on the imaginary axis of masculinity, and he is becoming comfortable—becoming fluent in—invoking my fear to get his way. At thirty years old, my life has become a case study of the hots and colds of one man's anger, a particular kind of terror that has moved, in these most recent months, beyond degradation or condescension or comments about my worth to his body moving toward me despite my own body backing away.

It has become clear I have two options: I can choose happiness and safety, or I can choose Dave.

And while I want to believe that my presence inside this airport—sitting at my Alaskan Airlines gate, awaiting the first leg of a three-leg journey—indicates my commitment to happiness, my commitment to safety, I am anxious with the knowledge that this is only the first of many steps I am not confident I can commit to making, or at least I am not confident I can make them with the consistency necessary to solidify change.

I choose to distract myself. I retrieve my phone from my jeans pocket and return to my text thread with Joy: her optimism, her hope, a photo she'd sent me earlier of a moose lifting its head and ashen, weather-worn antlers as it crossed the Dalton Highway just west of Livengood, its muscles sleek and definite.

Not yet moose-hunting season, she'd texted, so I'm just here to admire his beauty!

It's 2:00 a.m. in Alaska, but she is eager to know how I am doing, if my flights are still on time, if I've avoided early complications, because there will be plenty of them, she jokes, in the days to come. She wants to know how I'm feeling, if my boots are waterproof. She tells me what she bought us earlier—HotHands air-activated disposable hand warmers, and fire starters, and packaged cocoa.

LIQUID HEAVEN!!! she writes. I don't know what it is, but hot chocolate up in the Arctic is gooOooOooOood!

She wants to know if I've changed my mind about sleeping in her basement.

STILL THINK YOU SHOULD STAY WITH ME, she pleads as I clutch my boarding pass, fold and unfold its white, worn edges. It's the fourth time she's brought it up—I've said no three times already—because it seems like one thing to disembark from a quiet life in the heart of the American Midwest to fly to Fairbanks, Alaska, and meet a woman from the internet, but another thing altogether to commit to staying in her basement in a house I've never seen, in a city I've never been to, with a woman I do not yet know.

So sure, Joy is still mostly a stranger. But here is what I'm thinking as the flight attendants turn on their intercom and call Boarding Group A, then B, then C, as I cross the jet bridge and board the plane and take my seat beside a window: I would rather risk my life with this stranger than with the reality I have come to know.

I'm sure your plane is ready to depart about now, Joy writes. Dear Father in heaven, please take care of my new friend Amy. Thank you for the wonderfully awesome and amazing time you have set up for us together. We know you have brought us together for a reason. Please give her a safe trip here. We love you, Lord, Amen!

Amen to that, I write. Then, Can't wait to get my hot cocoa on!

In truth, I can't wait to be beside her, can't wait to have a foamy moustache of dehydrated marshmallow. I can't wait—for however briefly—to be anywhere but my own life.

SO GOOOOOOOD, she repeats, and then she sends an emoji of a mug of coffee, and it's as if somehow, together, we are placing our tenacity and an impressionable, unfathomable hope in two imaginary mugs of cocoa and a fistful of melted marshmallows, their shapes like bloated buoys I think, however foolishly, might save me from my own world.

The plane lifts up and off, and I imagine I'm lifting up and out of my old life. I raise the flimsy plastic of the window shade and watch as our plane's shadow floats between the peach-pink morning and the rooftops of old warehouses, of schools and banks and churches, of soccer fields and baseball diamonds, green and shimmering in early spring. It is easy to say goodbye, and to make an inventory of all of it, like I'm a character in a children's book: *goodbye, house; goodbye, trees; goodbye, boyfriend who screams at me.*

2.

The first photo I snap upon my arrival in Fairbanks at 4:00 a.m. is of a taxidermy polar bear glinting from behind a glass enclosure, its fur more a Bavarian cream than the snow white that I expected, and its teeth wider and denser, pointed fangs the size of adult thumbs. Someone has decorated its plaster snowdrift with two distinct shades of glitter: a standard silver, which plays it safe, and a surprising iridescent pastel that turns pink or green or purple depending on the light and the angle of the viewer. The second bear—a taxidermy grizzly—is wholly unremarkable.

It is disorienting to arrive anywhere at four o'clock in the morning, but my disorientation feels more pronounced by the alternate universe that is Fairbanks, Alaska, where snowbanks still line the curb and taxis blink white and red like a string of Christmas lights. Colorful tiers of glossy brochures turn under the hands of tourists, each promising some spendy package of Arctic sensationalism: a soak in the nearby Chena Hot Springs, or an authentic dog-mushing experience, or a signature apple martini served in a martini glass carved from ice. I idle by the baggage carousel, awaiting my suitcase, which I've packed with what feels practical from my life back in Ohio. My body throbs with adrenaline.

Our plan was for me to rest. This was my idea. After twenty-three hours on three separate airplanes, I'd imagined I would need it. Instead the baggage conveyor belt whirrs and the people around me move closer, expectant, while I scan my phone restlessly, wishing Joy would wake.

"We're nervous—period," my parents had told me the week before this departure. Never the type to be prohibitively protective, they'd insisted I draw a map prior to leaving for Alaska that charted my intended whereabouts.

"It's just Arctic wilderness," I said. "There's nothing to put down."

Still, I did my best to appease them, cropping a screenshot of the state of Alaska and drawing tiny lines along the Arctic Coastal Plain.

We'll be camping out somewhere here in her truck, I wrote over a two-hundred-mile swatch of nothingness.

I drew a tiny arctic fox. I added two stick figures in an embrace.

They didn't find my humor funny.

"How are we going to feel," they asked, "if something awful happens?"

Something awful was happening—with increasing frequency—but it wasn't happening in the Arctic.

And yet here, in Joy's state, finally, I wish I could go to her, wish I could sleep in her basement bedroom.

It'd be cozier here! she wrote. Plus I've got all these puppies— the six newest additions to the Wiebe family since Woody Wiebe, the Samoyed, gave birth the week before. I could take three to bed, and so could you!

I grab my bag and wheel it outside, feeling stupid for booking my hotel room with its Continental breakfast and in-room kitchenette and free airport shuttle, careening east.

Upstairs in the SpringHill Suites, I spread out on my second bed— "the snacking bed," a good friend calls it—and scroll back through our text message conversation, worrying that, by declining Joy's invitation to play tour guide and host, I've unwittingly insulted her.

I'M HERE!!! I text her. I attach the photo of the taxidermized bear, like the thousands of tourists who have come before me, then worry immediately that I'll wake her. But moments later, my phone pulses in my palm.

I can't sleep!!! she writes. She's tossed and turned so much, she tells me, that her husband, James, told her to take it to the couch.

But with the puppies! she writes.

The photo she sends next is the kind of cute that should be off-limits: a wad of black fur and fluff, the tiny pink curl of someone's tongue, her pajama top made of thin gray fabric above which half a dozen puppies doze, dopey-eyed and dreaming.

Outside, Fairbanks is rising slowly. Cats flick their tails in sleep and tired mothers scoop coffee grounds. Spring here is colder, darker, and pinker than Ohio. The sun looms over the low-rise buildings and the roofs lined with frozen snow.

Listen, she writes. I don't know how you feel, but we're heading to church in a few hours. It'd take a bit to get to you, but we could come scoop you up if you wanna join!

Church for me is complicated. Still I say okay.

We'll be the real dirty red pickup, she tells me.

In the parking lot a few hours later, all the trucks are dirty, coated in winter's worst, and nearly half of them are red. Still, I find her easily: hands flailing wildly inside the cab of a big red Ford F-150, big teeth white and shining. Her husband, James, is at the wheel, and her elderly mother and father wave to me from the back seat. They are dressed in their churchgoing best: her father wears a tie and her mother a neon-pink parka over a green dress.

Joy cracks the door while the truck's still moving and jumps down from the cab, pulling me close to her. She is shorter than I imagined, skinnier even than in photographs. She is the portrait of Alaskan couture in a fur-lined, knee-length parka half zipped to reveal a heavy blue sweater dress, black tights, and tall black riding boots.

She is beyond beautiful.

"Hiya, finally!" she says to me—the first words we've exchanged in person. Her arms wrap tightly around me, and her chin nudges into my shoulder.

"Hiya, finally," I say back.

Hiya, finally. It is the greatest understatement.

~

Golden Heart Christian School is a red modular trailer set on cinder block stilts beside a church. The parking lot is gravel, pocked and puddled with tire-deep holes. Inside the glass lobby, everything smells of warm feet, of macaroni and Elmer's glue, the same smell as every other elementary school I've ever been in anywhere. Joy tells me the school is home to three separate classrooms, and in each there's a different Bible study: one designated for men, another seemingly for young couples, and ours, which has no distinction as far as I can tell but is always, she says, led by Martha.

Joy always goes to Martha's classroom.

"She really *gets* it," she explains.

Martha's Bible study is already underway when we slink in, so we move quietly, our shoulders hunched as if no one will see us. We take our seats in foldout chairs that form a circle around Martha, who wears an airy cotton dress and tells us to flip to Matthew 21. There are twenty of us—mostly middle-aged men and women, some older, everyone clutching Bibles that look like long-standing family heirlooms: covers creased and bent, pages folded back and marked. I scroll to the Holy Bible app on my phone, something I downloaded months ago at Dave's insistence but use only intermittently.

Bible study here is a collaboration: we each take turns reading aloud from Scripture at Martha's kind command. One thoughtful man raises his hand to ask, every so often, a series of polite philosophical inquiries.

If Jesus were one of us, he posits, *would we even recognize him?*

No, we all agree. We'd be too busy sizing up his political party or estimating his net worth, judging him for his bumper stickers.

Joy reaches for James's hand, gives it a little squeeze. She whispers to me that she'd never put a Christian bumper sticker on James's truck because he drives too fast.

"Unchristian-like," she tells me. "He drives around like a bat outta hell."

James rolls his eyes, as if to say, *This woman.* He is a short, dense man with a strong jaw, warm eyes, and a shirt buttoned to his neckline. A man, so far, of few words, but when I smile, she slaps his shoulder and he squeezes her hand and smiles back.

"And all things," someone reads, "whatsoever ye shall ask in prayer, believing, ye shall receive."

"Do we believe this?" Martha asks. She lets the silence stagnate. "Do we believe God answers our prayers?"

The question goes largely unaddressed. To me, the answer is obvious. What others take as a test from God—a test of faith, or will, or patience—I have always understood to be proof of His utter absence.

My earliest experience of God began not with a light but with an angry boy hanging upside down from a tree. Seven years old, he hung there and told me with a conviction well beyond his years that my brothers and I were going to Hell because our family did not believe in God. His mother had told him this.

It was summer, very hot.

He was only allowed over, he said, because we had a swimming pool.

I know enough of faith now to understand this boy is not exclusive to any one theology. His flaw in compassion is inherited; his sense of knowingness spans the globe. The faith, the rules, the scripture might change, but the idea is always, more or less, the same: *Follow this faith or else.*

In Ohio, religious evangelists try to insist on a near-daily basis—
through billboards and mailings and flyers tucked under windshield
wipers—that God lives in all of us: in the mountains and the riverbeds
but also these inner, sacred spaces, in Martha's classroom, set on stilts
in this modular trailer filled with strangers. I have been told often that
God takes up real estate inside my body, that He has made a home
within my heart, but I fail to find Him there and most days feel, instead,
quite foolish, sitting still, trying to sense Him.

But at Golden Heart Christian School, I squint my eyes and pretend, less for me than for my company. It is important to me that Joy
and James feel comfortable. I want to assure them they have not made a
mistake. I want to prove that I am easygoing, that I am open, that I am
a friend. Martha speaks, and I fixate on the interior of the classroom. A
bulletin board in the corner holds a series of pastel construction paper
hot-air balloons, fanning out as they ascend, each marked with the
name of something a child is most grateful for.

God.

My mom.

Oreos.

I look to Joy. Her hair is down and fluid, blowing in the forced
air. I am thankful for her, and for James, thankful even for this woman
Martha, who asks us to set down our Bibles and settle our minds for
prayer.

Outside, I can see only trees, their branches holding the weight of
heavy snow.

"Lord, we thank you," Martha begins, "for meeting us here this
morning."

She thanks Him for His presence, and for the sacrifice of His son,
and most of all for His love, boundless and endless as it is. She reminds
us our God is a good God. She reminds us He is with us even in pain.
Then she encourages us to think and pray and ask for what we most

want to receive. For me, the request is simple: I want just Joy, her intrepid spirit, her generosity, her bravery.

The illusion—if not the fact—of her utter strength among men.

I pray to be open to this moment, to be open to this experience. To feel, forever, the calm of her blue sweater. To hold on to the feeling of peace each time I take her in.

"God, make of us your instruments," Martha instructs from the center, "and sharpen us as tools."

Sharpen me toward Joy, I think. I try not to think of all that dulls me.

Then, all of us, in unison: "In your blessed name we pray, amen."

~

As we stack our chairs in clean, neat rows, Joy tells me that Saturday Sabbath is her favorite part of each week.

"I just love it here," she says. "I never miss my Sabbath."

That Joy and her family belong to the Seventh-day Adventist Church is unremarkable in and of itself. But as a child, my family vacationed each summer in Washington, New Hampshire, a tiny New England town with just over a thousand people, a series of rugged green mountains, and thirty rural and mostly uninhabited lakes. Washington features a church and a little gazebo and a corner store that sells fried-egg-and-cheese sandwiches on paper plates and Styrofoam cups of back-yard bait. Years ago, I moved there, lived for sixteen months amid its nearly nothing, and now my parents have retired there. They spend their days reading and observing wildlife and generally speaking to no one else for days. In 1862, in that very town, the first Sabbath-keeping Seventh-day Adventists founded their faith. I know nothing about Joy's faith except that it is truly *the only thing* Washington is known for.

I pull Joy into me, gush, giddy, into her ear, "Your faith *was founded in our small town.*"

Joy's entire body seizes. She throws her hands into the air.

"Martha," she says, "Martha!"

Martha, too, is rhapsodic. She and Joy and several others circle me, lean in. Even I, despite great skepticism, have to admit it feels a little engineered by something greater: the odds that I would sit in an Alaskan classroom many thousands of miles from Washington and listen as the women and men praise a faith that has roots deep in the heart of who I am. Two years ago, Martha tells me, their Bible study even organized a trip to Washington to walk the Sabbath Trail, a winding loop I didn't even know existed. Martha pulls up photos on her phone to show me. I recognize the church in front of it, the view looking toward the road.

The men and women all around me—they've lifted fish from those very lake beds, hiked the mountains I often hike, walked through the general store's small aisles, and ordered a fried-egg sandwich with extra cheese.

"Remarkable," Joy says.

"Remarkable," I repeat.

Not for the first time, I begin to imagine Joy as God.

"You see?" Joy asks, her face wild and animate, her head nodding in easy reverence.

There, as the radiator hums quietly, she nudges me with her strong elbow, wraps an arm around my neck.

"I *told you* this was God."

~

In the pews an hour later, James leans into me, heavy.

"It's all," he says, "a little *crazy*."

Meaning that I flew here from somewhere, nowhere, joined them for church this morning, and then revealed within the hour that I have spent much of my life in the town where their faith was founded.

"Truth be told," he says, nudging me in the pew, "I didn't think you'd be one for faith."

East Coast, young, a professor—he tells me the boxes check themselves.

"It's a little complicated," I say.

James is thoughtful for a moment. He folds his hands over his travel mug.

"I wasn't particularly into faith until I met Joy, either," he says. He was forty-one when they met; she was twenty-eight. "I was," he says, hands fluttering, "a bit of a mess back then. But she fixed me up, she really did, and it'll be twenty years married come June. She got my head on right."

We watch from our place in the pews as Joy moves around the pulpit, flanked by the pastor and five other men. This morning is the first time Joy is helping with communion, and while she's excited to lend a hand, she missed last week's practice, "communion dress rehearsal," as James calls it.

"She was riding her exercise bike," he tells me. "Completely lost track of time."

We watch as Joy moves around the men anxiously, fluttering in and out, arranging and rearranging the tiny wafers.

"We forget the message of loving," James says in a moment that surprises me. "We forget the message of loving one another, I think. I believe whoever you are, you are welcome. That's what my faith is all about."

"Mine too," I say quickly. The words feel generous. Most experiences I've had with faith have been marred by faith's opposite: less loving-kindness than cruelty, blunt and outrageous and outright. Judgment, dissociation.

The man I love is also Christian. He's been trying to scream his faith into me.

"I think it's easy for people," I say, "to forget that truth."

We're silent for a moment, watching the big projector in the front of the room flash the great work Seventh-day Adventists are doing in places like Mexico City and Cuba and Haiti. One girl smiles from within the radiating orbit of a neon-pink Hula-Hoop. A young boy at a desk clutches a pen and offers a toothless grin.

"I don't know if you know this," James says, nodding again at Joy, who is arranging neat rows of Christ's blood in cups, "but that little lady is a legend."

I tell him I have that sense. I ask if he's ever done the haul road.

"Heck no," he says, defiant. "I've got no desire. Too risky, too treacherous."

Joy stands back, inspects her Dixie cup blood tablescape.

"Do you ever worry about her?"

He looks at me like I'm stupid. "What do you think?"

Service begins, and Joy glides over to offer us our wafers, our tiny cups of blood, both of which we hold to our chins but are careful not to consume. It's not the first time I've taken communion, but it feels like the most meaningful. I think of Christ's blood becoming mine, mixing inside my body into something altogether holy. The pastor prays, and I swallow the sweet juice, grin at Joy at the front of the room, who flashes two thumbs and a grin. Eventually, she takes her seat in the pew beside us, glowing, her whole body upright because she knows her job was indisputably well done.

James squeezes her tiny thigh.

This morning, the pastor is preaching from Matthew—a sermon on healing those in sickness as a way to prove His might.

"And the blind and the lame came to Him in the temple," he reads, "and He healed them."

Joy leans into me. "I'm lame," she jokes. "I'm lame!" She presses her palms together and looks up, hands clasped in showy prayer.

The pastor asks us about Jerusalem, if the city, as it is biblically rendered, reminds us of a place we know. Are we familiar with our own blind, our own suffering, huddled masses? And are we familiar with our own den of robbers, the thieves and the vile evil only God Himself can eradicate?

"What would it look like," he asks, "if our love of God alone could drive evil out?"

I think about driving evil out. I think about all the times I've prayed for this. I pull my phone from my pocket and load the last text conversation I had with Dave, when I'd told him I'd arrived safely in Alaska and he'd written back, simply, Good.

He doesn't understand why I am here, but I assume he has suspicions. Still, I must be some sort of fool, I think, for thinking any amount of prayer can drive our evil out.

I rise beside James and Joy to sing a praise song I don't know.

"Be strong, be strong, be strong," we sing, "and of a good, good courage."

Joy's voice lifts up and over everyone, and I think about all her courage, how this song feels tailor-made. I think about what it takes to drive an 18-wheeler, what it takes to drive it alone, all the extra bravery one must muster to be one of so few women in an industry—in an Arctic *landscape*—that's saturated with confident men. And to remain, somehow, undaunted, impervious, undeterred.

Be strong, be strong, be strong, I think, *and of a good, good courage.*

I am in desperate need of courage: not only for the road, but for the life that awaits me back in Ohio. Three years now in the Midwest, and it never ceases to devastate me how quickly a sky so blue goes violent with the grays and blacks of a summer storm, or from the anger of one mad man.

And of a good, good courage.

~

The only feet I've ever washed are mine, but when the pastor tells us we are committing ourselves today to washing the feet of others, as the women washed Jesus's feet, Joy takes my hand and leads me to a tiny room filled with metal basins. Young girls in floral gowns and braided hair take turns ladling lukewarm water to fill the basins. Joy leads me to a foldout chair and instructs me to sit as she rolls down my Smartwool socks. I'm embarrassed by my legs, which I haven't shaved in weeks, and by my stubby, too-short toenails, the pink paint flaking at the tips.

"So this is what we do," Joy says, oblivious to my embarrassment.

She slides her soft palms over my feet, moving in slow, sweet strokes. The water feels good along my calves, pooling and draining down my ankles.

"God's always been there when I needed Him," she says, cupping the water and releasing it. She tells me that her brother died several years ago from cancer. Worst hurt, she says, of her life, and she doesn't like to talk about it too much now, but God was there when it was hard.

I tell her that while I haven't experienced that type of loss, my mother has. Her brother died young as well, just a few months before I was born. His death was sudden, too.

"He was gay," I add. "He died during the AIDS crisis in the 1980s."

I tell her the details passed down to me by my mother: how I am the only one to have his yellow eyes, how he was a creative type like me, how he wanted to be a writer. I don't tell Joy that a woman in my mother's office wiped the receiver down with bleach after my mother took a call from him. Or how, while I was working on an angsty rendition of *Rent* in an English class as a tribute to my uncle, a blond classmate turned to me and said, "Your uncle was gay and deserved to die."

God's plague is what she called it, is what so many people have called it.

I tell Joy instead that my mother wept so hard, so severely, she asked the doctor if her suffering could harm her baby.

"Human beings," the doctor told her, "are toned and tuned for pain."

"Amen," Joy says, nodding. She pushes her palms into my feet, massages the toughest tissue. I haven't had my body washed by someone else since childhood, and I am in awe at how such a simple gesture can feel like a gift.

I want to give that gift to Joy. We switch positions, and I refresh the water from the young women who look like angels. When I make my way back to her, Joy is sitting in the aluminum chair and rolling up her leggings to reveal her tiny feet. I cup my palms and let the water drain slowly over her ankles. Above her calves, there are swipes of scars, long and parallel, like from an animal.

"My surgery injury," she announces, "obviously."

For a moment, I'd forgotten. Several months earlier, while hauling what she called, simply, "a heavy load"—pallets of a hundred thousand pounds or more—she'd kneeled a little too quickly, or popped up a little too fast, and immediately reeled back in pain at the sudden dislocation of her right kneecap.

She thought the injury would resolve itself, and she didn't want to take time off. And she thought that any injury would be proof of weakness, especially in a woman.

"They couldn't know I was hurt," she'd explained to me on the phone.

So for three weeks, despite her injury, Joy performed as normal: two or three trips every week, until one afternoon, when headed south toward Fairbanks, Joy felt her right kneecap buckle against the brake, slide in and out of its joint.

"The most pain I've ever felt," she'd said. "I knew then I had no choice. I couldn't keep ignoring that I was injured."

Going on medical leave and parking her big rig in the driveway for an unknown amount of time was *terrible*, she said. *Beyond.*

In December, she underwent surgery—a medial patellofemoral-ligament reconstruction procedure, used to correct serious and recurring dislocation of the kneecap—because her kneecap, the doctor told her, evidenced a prolonged history of injury and abuse.

"You have to take it easy," her doctor had told her, hesitant.

"'Take it easy,'" she repeated to me. "Does he know who he's talking to?"

What she'd hoped would be a few weeks' leave had blossomed instead into many months of physical therapy and pain management and evening physical rehabilitation exercises—waiting on her doctor to give her the all clear. The all clear hadn't come, so we'll be taking her pickup when we travel the Dalton Highway, instead.

The scar is long and angry, and I take my time, moving slow, letting the water flush over her legs and heels and toes. I cup and release the water, run my hands gently down her shins.

How much of this world's hurt, I think, could be remedied by such simple kindness?

"I know I said this," Joy says, "but I think we're soul sisters."

I picture our insides, wet and braided, our heartbeats beating in wild tandem.

"I like that idea," I say.

I take longer than I should to rinse the spaces between her toes. She wiggles and smiles at me. When we've finished with the footbath, Joy takes my hand, squeezes, and looks me in the eye. "Let's say a prayer," she says.

Wait, I'm thinking when she leads me to the windows. But once we are sitting, facing each other, our knees overlapping, the closest we've yet been, I am surprised at how close I feel to her.

"Blessed Father," she says, "we want to thank you for bringing us here together. It is a blessing, our connection, and we ask you to watch over us on our trip. Keep us safe and help us bear witness to your land and holy beauty.

"There is no beauty," she says to me, "like the beauty of that road."

Then we bow our heads, and I feel the squeeze of her hand enveloping mine.

I think, *Thank you, thank you, thank you.*

I can't tell if it's God—or Joy—I'm communing with.

"In your name we pray," we say. "Amen."

~

I take it easy the rest of the afternoon—a *True Blood* marathon, Taco Bell—and when I wake the next morning, it's not yet light, not even in Fairbanks. A church spotlight blinks in the windy darkness. I stand before the window and peer out over the town, the blue-lit jukeboxes of the bars still playing music, their patrons standing out on the sidewalk, shuffling, smoking. The Midnite Mine, the Arctic Fox, Soapy Smith's Pioneer Bar—all these places named for glory feel sad and dim in the pale light of morning.

You're doing this, I think. *You've come so far already.*

I start the coffee in the minipot and wake my laptop from idle sleep. In my inbox, there's a video Joy sent at 1:00 a.m., long after I'd gone to bed.

PLAY WITH THE SOUND ALL THE WAY UP, she wrote. *This will give you a good sense of what we'll be seeing.*

The video is of her truck parked along the Dalton Highway, barely visible beneath the snow. All around, a fierce blizzard blows snow in walls, obscuring the architecture of the truck, rocking Joy's heavy vehicle from side to side.

This was from last December! she wrote. *It was blowing harder than I'd ever seen it! I was scared that if my truck shut down—it was threatening to, the engine kind of sputtering—I wouldn't be able to get myself and my little dog up the road to my friend Angel, who was in her truck and could get us out of there!*

31

I watch the video once, and then again. I've never seen anything like it.

To think people do this on purpose, that they have chosen this path over any other, that they risk freezing or falling to death, their futures and families.

I can't do this, I think, at last acknowledging aloud the seed of fear Joy planted ever since dropping me off after church, when she leaned in for a goodbye hug and whispered that she'd packed Mace, flare guns, a pistol.

"I hope you're not antigun," she said as James and her aging parents blinked blankly at us from the pickup. "It's different for us up here in Alaska."

The gun I am okay with, mostly—there are polar bears, after all, and they won't be mounted, won't be superglued and stuffed. They're known to reach speeds faster than Olympic sprinter Usain Bolt, and I am not fast, not coordinated. I am, in fact, very clumsy. Still, her words served as confirmation of a secondary fear I'd been harboring all along: that while my trip across the country may have bridged the physical divide that separates our two bodies, there is no easy remedy to close the gap of our experiences.

This is made all the more evident by a text waiting for me on my phone, where—at some point in the night—Joy explained the need to pack incidentals: cans of food and nonperishables and blankets, so many blankets.

Don't wanna get stuck out at Atigun Pass, she wrote. That's an awful place to be cold or hungry.

Atigun Pass is the most dangerous pass on the entire stretch of the Dalton Highway, Joy wrote, a place where the road cuts between sharp mountains through sudden curves and climbs and offers unique dangers depending on the season. Spring brings washed-out roads, she explained, whole gravel stretches that slip like pebbles down a cataclysmic, thousand-foot slope. Winter offers tier-three blows that make the road altogether invisible. The people who fall down there? she wrote. They never get hauled out.

Of course, this makes me curious. Of course, I google for verification. The images that surface immediately make me realize that Atigun Pass is the sort of dramatic landscape Nintendo's Mario Kart might digitize. It's a slick road with steep climbs, winding curves that make maintaining control over a vehicle impossible, only we won't have an extra set of lives, no turtle in a cloud to retrieve our truck from its plummet and return it, safely, to the road.

What the video underscores is that I have fears; I have lots of them. I worry about my capacity for the unknown, for discomfort, for cold, for pain. I worry about polar bears and grizzlies, which are so plentiful in some parts of this state that ecologists estimate there is one bear for every square mile. In my backpack beside the bed, I've got an industrial can of bear spray, the back of which reads, excitably, *Be prepared to respray to adjust for wind, or cold, or more than one bear, or a bear that charges, or a bear that retreats and charges again, or zigzags, or circles.*

I stand before the hotel mirror, imagining the darting I'll do from bears.

I plan to get so good at darting.

Then, of course, there are moose, whose thick chests and barreled stomachs are precisely windshield height and who outnumber bears nearly three to one in Alaska, wounding five to ten people annually in this part of the state alone.

I worry, too, about Joy, who, despite her experience, is in an unprecedented physical state, by her own admission weaker than she's ever been. The pickup is just fine by me, and I know enough of her now to know that I will take to Joy Mothertrucker.

What worries me most—my real fear—is that Joy will not take to me.

Her world, just like her Instagram account, has given me the sense that there is no inauthenticity, no posturing or strategizing. My account, on the other hand, is highly prescriptive, performative, meant to contain exactly the sort of images you'd expect from a thirty-year-old Ohio woman: picture my beige suede flats, pointed inward on a sidewalk strewn by pointillistic autumn leaves. The books on my bookshelf arranged by color. Spring's first dandelion—a pop of yellow punctuating an otherwise well-manicured suburban lawn.

A hibiscus donut from a bakery in Brooklyn, fuchsia frosting nearly neon.

A cappuccino's fern-shaped foam.

The pictures and stories I've posted could've been taken by anyone, and I've thrived off this illusion, off the carefully curated sense that my life was exactly the same as every other, that I was not in danger, that there was no monster inside my home.

Sometimes, I'll admit, I thought about photographing my world exactly as it was: Here, the public places where Dave and I had sat crying. Or the meals we cooked but did not eat. Or my eyes so red and raw from sobbing that it hurt to wipe my lids with Kleenex. Despite the fact that he'd never outright hit me, I had never—in all my life—known tending to skin to be as painful as the skin I tended to because of Dave. Increasingly, I fought urges to photograph Dave moving around the house—screaming, looming, raging, or else packing up all his things, threatening to leave my life forever. Instead I only ever posted what would happen upon his return, when Dave would show back up in my life and driveway in his navy-blue sedan with some new piece of furniture he'd made for me, or my favorite takeout from the Chinese place, or a tiny raccoon figurine holding a sign he'd made from construction paper.

I LOVE YOU! it read in Sharpie.

Those moments were documented. *Those* moments memorialized, placed in careful frames on my bookshelves and my campus desk to convey the sense that nothing was amiss. Each month, each week, another tribute of his love, so much so that even those outside our relationship were wooed. As one of my best friends told me once, "I couldn't get that kind of love from my boyfriend *if I tried.*"

She didn't know how much it took—the *trying*, and the love.

The truth was it was taking everything; it was taking all of me.

But the world of Instagram, of course—and Joy—knew nothing yet of that worry, of the way I feared it was escalating. Instead of his red-faced screaming, a budding green bean sprout. Or the pinkest of our planted zinnias. The first pepper plucked from our garden—a gorgeous green Anaheim, curved with flesh as smooth as butter, proof of a backyard that could've been anywhere in Gardening Zone 5 or higher, could've been enjoyed by anyone, could've been tended to by people who did not live inside our mess.

If likes are validation for the way our days are spent, my existence seemed best defined by a photograph of our dog dressed in a taco costume made of cheap nylon and airbrushed cotton that came directly from a warehouse in China. I'd purchased the costume one Halloween specifically for its resemblance to a taco—the eight separate strips of orange foam meant to represent ribbons of shredded cheddar, its swatches of green to denote iceberg lettuce, its little lip of red tomato. I thought, which is ludicrous, *What abuse could possibly happen in a home with a dog dressed like that? What anger could escalate in the presence of such frenetic yipping? Such adorable high-fiving and taco-dog hybrid spinning?*

This one misconception about abuse most women know but I was still learning: abuse is not deterred by social class, by economic or financial privilege, by sexual orientation or race. These things undoubtedly influence how easy it is to leave—and to be successful in that endeavor, to be supported and safe and even believed—but they are in no way a barrier to abuse.

I thought the taco costume might help us. I thought it might make Dave laugh. And so I posted my dog wearing it, dizzily spinning, to the tune of a hundred likes.

"Cute," he said, and that was that.

Joy's life—on Instagram, or here in Alaska—was not hibiscus donuts, not privilege or its facade. It was proof of the rigorous and daily work of bringing other people the things they needed, and I worried that my presence—and my life, by approximation—might strike her as superficial, insubstantial. For months, I had considered myself not a *follower* of Joy so much as a *connoisseur*; her content made me feel giddy, *capable*, created a sense of emotional expansion. Her life made mine feel possible, which is to say quite simply that for all the differences shared between us, Joy gave me a sense of hope. She demonstrated every day the way a woman could put herself fearlessly out into the world, and I envied that strength, that courage. I thought it might rub off. I spoke eloquently to friends about the stranger I'd found online, how her rugged world felt transcendent, and I described her photos in layers: first the bevel of a blue hubcap, then the windshield marred by bugs, then the stiff peaks of a mountain range plumped like gray meringue and glossy in the Arctic sun.

In every photo Joy had ever posted, I could sense the legitimacy of a life lived well and defined by a fierce commitment to independence. Here, a photo of Joy feeding a donkey in eternal summer, eternal sunshine, midnight in Alaska.

Or a Samoyed puppy in a light-pink towel.

Another photo, an Arctic mystery: a big rig hauling a forest-green golf cart with brown leather upholstery.

Golfing in the Arctic? she'd captioned the photo in playful whimsy.

It is one thing to be deemed inadequate, insufficient, by a man. But it is another thing altogether to be sized up—and to come up short—by the woman I aspire most to be. In my final moments before our journey, here it is, my greatest fear: that I will survive our trip, the Dalton Highway, only to find I am not the woman Joy is capable of being every day.

3.

When Joy meets me in the hotel lobby at 5:00 a.m., she's wearing her Carlile Driver's Appreciation hat and a blue T-shirt that reads *HAWAII*. She's leaning across the desk, chatting with the receptionist about the right kind of window wiper fluid.

"I have to admit," the woman behind the desk is saying, "I'm partial to the blue. I don't know what it is, but I don't trust it when it's orange."

I linger for a moment behind them, trying hard to be polite.

Joy sees me and slaps my shoulders.

"Shall we?" I ask. I motion toward the Continental breakfast bar in the carpeted corner of the hotel lobby. "Come on," I say. "Big day."

The breakfast bar is beyond bountiful, with not one but two Belgian waffle makers, a pot of simmering oatmeal, a bevy of omelet fixings, and the soft, smooth roundness of bagels. There's a setup of ramekins heaping with sliced almonds and dried cranberries, agave syrup and chocolate chips. I fill my plate with scrambled eggs and waffles and a tiny single-serving packet of Nutella while Joy looks on, uncomfortable. She slides into our booth with empty hands, not even an orange, and whispers to me she's not allowed.

"What do you mean?" I ask. I sprinkle Tabasco all over my potatoes until Joy finally takes the bottle from my hand.

"You're going to hurt your insides," she tells me, suddenly serious. She looks back at the buffet and then at my plate.

"Come on," I say. "Get some breakfast. You're my *guest*. My suite is reserved for two."

This isn't entirely accurate. It's actually not accurate in the least. Still, my thinking here is simple: we are about to embark together on what will prove to be *at minimum* a fourteen-hour drive, during which we'll pass only one restaurant that serves hamburgers and fries, and even that is six hours away.

The buffet overflows.

"It's fine," I say. "You're *fine*."

Joy bites her lip and gets up, moving timidly: an apple, a scoop of oatmeal. Then the almond slivers and agave syrup, a squirt of honey, a rounded muffin. Behind her, a breakfast attendant replenishes the dairy options, and Joy, realizing she's Latina, attempts to say hello. She's been practicing Spanish with Duolingo: *te amo, buenas dias, cómo estás, gracias.*

She says something I don't understand. The woman smiles and says something back. That ends the conversation, and Joy smiles and bows demonstrably before settling back into our breakfast booth.

We finish breakfast, and I slip a clementine into my pocket. Joy tells me she wants a banana but is too scared.

"Look," she says, and points. A sign clearly prohibits what we are doing.

It speaks perfectly to her character: this is a woman who will drive the deadliest highway in America, but she's too law-abiding to pocket an unripe banana from the hotel's Continental breakfast bar.

I tuck her banana into my pocket.

"God, it wasn't me!" Joy says, throwing prayer hands to the sky.

Then she shrugs and laughs and leads me through the hotel doors, where the world—and her pickup—awaits.

~

In the parking lot, Joy prophesizes.

"The next time you're up here," she says, "my knee will be healed for sure, and I promise then we'll take the big rig."

"I'd like that," I say, but I feel distracted by *next time*, giddy that already she envisions me returning, imagines the future of our friendship.

She likes me, I think. I grin.

I throw my luggage in the back—a carry-on roller filled with a couple sweatshirts, two pairs of jeans, a dozen pairs of socks that reach my ankles. It was hard to know what to expect from this adventure or how those expectations translate into clothing. I'm well versed in the art of camping, but this is no state park. So I bought a pair of Carhartt overalls, mostly because Alaskan women on Instagram seem to wear them often. I brought beanies—a lot of beanies—in electric colors to offset the snow. I packed gum, cotton gloves, a couple Band-Aids, Raisinets.

"If we hit a blizzard," she says, and pauses. "If we hit a blizzard," she continues, "we hit a blizzard."

Joy drums the steering wheel and turns the key in the ignition. The truck cruises slow, slow, slow through early dawn in Fairbanks. But when we hit the Steese Highway north of town—past the Walmart and a row of hotels and the last red light we'll see for days—the pickup picks up speed.

"Gonna get wild," Joy says.

"Wild."

I feel my fear subsiding, feel a hard pearl of confidence take its place. It is surreal to see Joy in her element, in real life, to be so concretely taking matters into my own hands and to be making this trip happen. I should feel nervous, I think, but I don't. I should feel cut off, isolated. Instead my life's in Joy's hands, and in the road that she feels called to.

The view outside is wilderness, far removed from Fairbanks' commerce. Trees twist against the embankment and follow the contours of the valley. We have one last stop, Joy tells me, Hilltop Truck Stop—a gas station, convenience store, and diner all in one and the last business establishment before the Dalton Highway.

"Their official slogan," Joy tells me, laughing, "is simply I BRAKE FOR PIE."

It is here, Joy explains, that truckers load up for the long drive ahead, ordering plates of thick French toast and hash browns and pancakes and sausage, biscuits and gravy, fried chicken, ribs. We park and hop out, and Joy leads the way, holds the door open for me. Everything inside is soft light and sweetness, the smell of oil and eggs and sugar. In the corner, in a glass display case, tiers of homemade pie rotate—Butterfinger and blueberry, coconut and three berry. There's sweet potato and peanut butter and apple and Dutch apple, plus a kind called XXX cake, and another named Fatman.

"You've got to see this," Joy says, leading me to the back room, where meal tickets fan out across a wall. There are dozens, maybe hundreds. Those who have found themselves lucky enough to be stuck on the Dalton Highway—in snow, in ice, in washouts, with blown-out tires or a dying engine—and saved by another trucker have a habit of paying it forward via meal ticket vouchers written on empty order forms. Twenty or forty or a hundred dollars.

"This stuff *means something*," she says, pointing.

A Hilltop voucher is the best way, Joy tells me, to thank someone for lifesaving assistance out on the Dalton Highway—appreciation made tangible by way of BLTs and cheeseburgers, by baked beans and sausage links. By an endless mug of coffee and a bowl of chili and shoofly pie à la mode. I read a few.

Gary Huff: I AM ALIVE.

To Gary Huff: THANK YOU.

Tony Bensote offers twenty dollars in food to Lonnie, and Tim Oate has been gifted forty dollars.

Thanks for the slide help back in May, Jim Connor wrote. Then, beneath, as if a necessary afterthought: *I might not be here if not for you.*

You saved my life, reads another.

GOD BLESS, reads more than one.

We're silent for a long time.

"Wild, yeah?" Joy asks finally.

"Where's your name?" I ask.

"I don't have any up right now." She points. "Because, you know, my knee. Would like to be out there helping! But it's been a little while."

She sighs, turns to make her way past me, and it's then I spot dozens of gold placards adhered to a wooden frame—these commemorate the deaths of haul road truckers. Between them, the carved silhouette of Alaska, and a big rig bursting through its interior.

Grieve not, an inscription reads, *nor speak of me with tears, but laugh and talk of me as if I was beside you there.*

There are almost three hundred placards, so many that they spill onto a second and third wooden mount. I run my index finger over the grooves, then over the carved names of oil and trucking transport companies that compose a frame of industry.

Joy has moved on to the expansive candy aisle. She's studying a Starburst package and making *hmph* sounds to no one.

"Full of crap," she mutters.

For months, Joy has been taking a plant-based nutrition class with Cornell University's online learning system. From her place now beside the chocolate bars, she tells me she wants me to do the same.

"It's really helped me to see what's bad for me," she says. "Before, I ate mostly Hot Pockets from Sam's Club, you know? I thought they were healthy because they had this variety called 'cheesy broccoli.' Once I found one under my seat, and it had been there who knows how long, but I opened it up and it smelled the same. Sort of like, you know, a Twinkie?"

She kicks my boots in jest.

"I didn't eat it, but the point is, I probably could've. So loaded with preservatives. Before, I couldn't really think of why I shouldn't eat something," she continues. "I knew I shouldn't, maybe, but I never really knew *why*. So I just made poor choices. And when you're making little choices all day long—I mean, look at how many decisions you have to make on this road. And then what are you going to eat? Fatman cake? The big cookie right there at the register when you finally reach Coldfoot Camp?"

She laughs, and I laugh. A big cookie would be big delicious.

"Point is, I feel like my body is finally *healing*," she says, placing a Snickers back on the shelf. "Healing from all life's hardships, and healing through my learning. Not just my knee. My *whole being*."

The sweet Starbursts are beckoning. The Milky Ways make their siren call. But I consider Joy's advice and buy, instead, a few jugs of water, some sunflower seeds, a Nature's Valley granola bar.

We split the cost of three canisters of gas, climb back into the truck.

"Time to send our final texts," Joy says, settling into the driver's seat. "We lose service another mile up the road."

Last cell phone service for a while, I write to my mom, my dad. Love you all. I'll be safe!

Hitting the highway now, I write to Dave. Hope you're well. Thinking of you.

From her place beside me, Joy begins to laugh. DON'T EAT THE LAST OF THE MOOSE! she reads from her text to James. I want to share that with Amy when we get back!

"Would you like that?" she asks me, turning. "Would you like to try our moose? Samantha and I shot it back in the fall."

"Of course I would."

My eyes flit over my phone, where well-wishes have already arrived from my parents, but not from Dave, whose words have always mattered most. It's not that I didn't expect his silence. For months now, he's been in and out—of my life, of my home, even in terms of presence to me as his partner. I never expected him to understand my need for this trip, to get away, to have a moment to myself far removed from our dysfunction, and I'd felt protective of Joy, keeping my plans and my reasoning to myself as much as possible. It's no surprise, then, that he's not responding, but it still stings a little, or stings a lot.

Joy is still speaking, telling me how she'll cook her moose—slow, like a roast, with beets and carrots and purple potatoes. It sounds lovely, but I can't stop thinking about Dave, and now with the panicked feeling that surrounds so much of what I feel for him. I am rattled before the trip has even begun; I am rattled all the time. I want to leave on this adventure with Joy, but not before I've heard from him, not before I've gauged his feelings, not before I've secured his response, even if it is distant, because the truth is that I love him. *I still love him.* Looking out at the wilderness that dives and dips in the shadows all around us, I wish Dave could love me the right way back.

Joy turns the key in the ignition. I put my phone away.

"So this is it," she says. "Time to commune with God."

Heaven awaits us, the Alaska I have been promised.

"Ready?" Joy asks.

"Ready."

4.

The road to heaven is neon blue and paved only in places. In the corners, the tundra buckles, and then the earth turns back, unfolds within itself to reveal a layer of bright-blue permafrost, dipping deep into the earth, shining wet and nearly electric. Elsewhere, it is forested—neat rows of black spruce and pine that dissolve into denser, darker depths—until the highest elevations, where suddenly the trees grow short and then thin out and then disappear altogether.

It's exactly what she pictured, Joy tells me, as a child growing up in Arizona, where she dreamed—always—of winter: log cabins erected from knotted pine, the footprints of wild animals leading her through dense forests, tree roots frozen stiff inside the ground. She dreamed of ice cracking—heavy, underfoot—and slipping in whole sheets from rooftops, like it does the first warm day of spring. Mornings in her desert bedroom, Joy scribbled mountains on construction paper scaffolds, tracing their sharp peaks up and up and up until they extended across the entire width of the paper. Outside, the Arizona wind blew hot and arid. Scorpions moved amid the brush. Joy rode a bus to a one-room schoolhouse where the sun beat onto the pavement, cooking everything in waves.

This is life in Camp Verde, Arizona, a city whose official website advertises itself as "a quiet, safe place to raise your children" with a "small-town atmosphere" and "a friendly, relaxed, no-pressure way of life where practically everyone knows each other."

In Camp Verde there is an annual corn festival.

A pecan, wine, and antiques festival.

And every June like clockwork, the good people of Camp Verde come together at picnic tables to don plastic bibs and take up tiny hammers for their annual crawdad festival.

"I never went," Joy tells me. "Know what I call them? 'Ocean bugs.'"

Camp Verde, Arizona, according to its tourism bureau, is the "Center of It All," and indeed there is a distinctively outward-gazing, adventure-seeking quality to the attractions the city offers, something Joy seized upon even in youth. The Out of Africa Wildlife Park, for example, places tourists in tall metal cages secured atop yellow Hummers and shuttles them out into golden pastures where they drive past giraffes. As part of the Predator Zip Lines experience, miles away, one can don a harness and zip from tree to tree over heat-fatigued tigers and rhinoceroses that kick the dusty earth.

Forty-some years removed, Joy commands her truck with confidence. The world rolls out beyond our windows and pings against our undercarriage. The road is gray and mostly tree-lined, not altogether different from all the other roads I've ever known, but it is bumpier, full of potholes, mostly straight until aggressive turns. Joy's truck's cushions barely cushion; our coffee spills from our thermoses to the floor.

"Just so we're clear," she says, "from now on, if you have to go? You're going to have to squat roadside or hold it."

I tell her I have no problem squatting. I say, "I can pee off-road like the best of them."

I spent my summers camping, collecting kindling beside my brothers. Nothing has ever made me feel more powerful than working physically beside them.

"That's my girl!" Joy laughs, popping an edamame from its shell, for while this is the most remote region in the country, still we have, in bags between us, edamame and tortilla chips, organic black beans and whole ripe avocados, because—Joy told me earlier in the supermarket, scanning the ingredients on a bottle of kombucha—women know well enough to plan ahead.

"You eat Fritos, you become a Frito," she'd explained when she caught me eyeing their orange bag in the grocery store, as if the danger inherent in a single Frito was a greater threat than the Dalton Highway.

It explains, in some small way, the Instant Pot manual tucked inside the door, the cans of refried beans rolling around underfoot, the scent of Indian spices lodged deep in the truck's upholstery. Joy tells me that sometimes, when she's in the big rig, she uses the twelve-hour drive to simmer curried lentils, and beans are high in fiber, she reminds me— necessary for so much sitting.

"At my age," she says, popping another edamame, "and maybe your age, too, you have to protect your body."

The empty pods collect in the cupholder, spill over and around our feet.

Outside the window, tiny crosses surface from the soil like morbid mile markers—whole lives lived and lost memorialized in chipped white wood, wreaths of polyester and wire cloth. *This* is the Dalton Highway: less a testament to survival than a presentation on human fragility, on the many ways one can lose a life.

Joy points to a barren crevice beyond which the Trans-Alaska Pipeline glints, a silver vein running between matte mountains.

"It's beautiful," she says, "in an industrial sort of way."

Beautiful because of capitalism, because of commerce, because this pipeline has the capacity to pump two million barrels of unrefined crude oil south daily. It's part of an 800-mile journey that lifts up and over 579 specialty animal migration crossings and traverses thirty-four major rivers, three distinct mountain ranges, numerous earthquake fault lines, and enormous stretches of Americana before at last reaching Valdez, where the oil is pumped and primed and shipped throughout the country, to our men in wraparound sunglasses, our teenagers idling beside their cars, our softball moms clicking acrylic nails impatiently at the pumps.

"That's where Spud died," Joy says. I follow her gaze toward a ravine, which descends sharply into a valley. Above it is a tiny cross someone thrust into the soil. Women do it, Joy tells me, every spring, though by the end of winter the markers are largely gone, blown away or blown to shreds. Weather here spares nothing, least of all memory.

The cross is white and small and bordered by the soft lavender of dehydrated flowers.

"These are the toughest people I know," Joy says.

They work this road until they can't, or they work this road until the road takes them. Sometimes, both those things in tandem.

We pass another cross.

"The best piece of advice I ever got when I first started driving a truck?" Joy says, "'When you least expect it, a truck will be there.' These little hills"—she points—"they're misleading, and they hide trucks. That's just how Spud here died. A truck came up and he didn't see it. Startled him, spun him around. He was hauling long pipe, I believe."

She really liked Spud, she tells me. But she really likes everyone.

"That's terrible," I say.

"Well, at least they found him quick," Joy says. "Some men, it takes crews weeks."

I imagine bodies heaving in the tundra, the way men die in films, with sounds of suffering no one can hear. From the window, I watch a moose—no more than fifty feet from the shoulder—lift its head and stomp, sending mosquitos scattering. Joy slows so I can snap a picture.

"So, the thing about being a woman out here," she says, seemingly apropos of nothing, "is I'm always the only one. So it's sorta strange to have you here."

I ask her if this is what she pictured for her life, all those many years ago as a child in the desert.

"Yup," she says. She nods. "I always saw Alaska as the sort of place you could pretend was all your own, because no one else had changed it."

Joy pictured Alaska as a place for everyone: for those with and those without. In Camp Verde and nearby Cottonwood, where she later lived, the discrepancy in wealth was palpable. Like everywhere in America, it evidenced itself in name-brand sneakers and distressed jeans and the metal mouths of children. When in middle school Joy was fitted for braces and a retainer, her friends thought it was cool how her teeth caught the light, the way her silver shined, how her braces' bands—tiny loops of nubbed, colored rubber—became an accessory, reflecting the seasons or an impending holiday. Red and green in winter, pink and purple in February. A little ode to Christmas, or Valentine's Day, or Halloween, right there along your teeth, flashes of colored rubber that caught poppy seeds and broccoli florets and sharp slivers of tortilla chips.

Her best friend, Shannon, confided her own parents could not afford them.

"So you know what I did?" she asks. She turns to face me, knowing the road is straight and flat for miles. "I collected all these paper clips, and I bent them, right? So she'd have a retainer. I even fit it to her mouth—it was a little bulky, but we made it work—and really, when she grinned, you couldn't tell the difference. It made me *creative*," Joy says. "A *problem solver*."

Joy had no real reason for the pull she felt to Alaska, for its salt-slicked roads and caribou and the unfathomable open tundra. She had an aunt and uncle who lived in Kenai, a small Alaskan city, but she knew them only by way of stories: peanut shells, her uncle had told her mother once, lined the floors of a local restaurant, and there was a man who shot rats with guns. She listened—her whole childhood, she listened—tracing lines in the shag carpet, imagining Kenai as a place so far removed from Arizona, so different in every way, that she imagined every day would be a new kind of challenge. She set it in her sights that someday, she'd toss peanut shells on the floor herself.

Then at fifteen she met a boy a few years her senior at a religious retreat in the mountains outside Prescott, a place—her friend will tell me later—that offered canoeing and hiking and prayer worship but also boys, and lots of them.

"I told her, 'Go on a date with him. It's not like you guys are gonna get married,'" her best friend told me.

Then Joy was pregnant, engaged, married.

She had a home birth at seventeen with a midwife she and Jake paid for with firewood.

"Even trade," she tells me. "Also all we could afford at the time."

Joy tells me Jake had no money, no job, and no skills, so he decided to join the navy, and together with their son Andy, they shuttled across the country but only ever to destinations east: first to Mississippi, and then to Massachusetts. When Andy was old enough for day care, Joy decided to join the navy, too, taking a job as an equipment manager with the construction brigade.

"The Seabees!" she shouts. "*C-B!*" she spells.

Joy, in fact, was the reason the naval air station in South Weymouth, Massachusetts, had to designate their first-ever female bathroom.

"The lieutenant, he tells me, 'You're kidding,' when I call to tell him I'm coming," she says. She slaps her thigh midcackle. "He didn't think the men were serious when they said a woman was on her way! And there I am, like, 'Hello, sir!'"

But for Joy, it was never about challenging gender norms. She valued the rigorous sense of discipline, the long hours, the physicality of the work, the way her body was uniquely different from the men's, feminine and yet altogether capable. In time, she earned her colleagues' and superiors' respect. Still, she pined for remote Alaska. Her marriage was rarely good. As she bounced her young son on her knees, Jake would tell her she was fat, or would tell her that a woman shouldn't work. He finally told her, "You choose: me or the navy."

"I should have chosen the navy," she says. "But then, of course, I wouldn't have had our Daniel."

Our Daniel, a man I know only by photograph—I follow him, too, on Instagram. Daniel lives in Hawaii with his young wife, both of them dog loving and gorgeous. They take stunning photos of the ocean, sparkling at the edges in the sun, sometimes capturing the smooth, whipped curl of a particularly sea-green wave. They look like people I'd get along with, people I'd like to accompany as they snap their way through the jungle, hot and lush and wet.

"My Daniel," Joy muses. "He's something special. He's my guy."

Back then, she tells me, a woman could terminate her contract with the navy if she was pregnant, so that's exactly what Joy did.

"I listened to Jake," she says. "I'll be honest: I didn't know how to handle myself back then. I mean as a woman, but also as a mother, as a wife. I just listened to what he said. Yeah, I left the navy. Yeah, I had our baby."

Eventually, Joy got her way: Jake requested to be stationed in Alaska, and they made the move together along with their two young sons and a five-hundred-dollar tax refund Joy imagined might get them started. They'd never considered an urban life in Alaska—only snow and endless evenings and lives spent living off the land—but Joy did her best to picture Anchorage's buildings, big and blinking, and their life of half a year in light and another half in darkness.

That picture, however, was expensive, riddled, she found, with problems. The only apartment they could afford was a one-bedroom on the edge of town, and Joy worried that the landlord wouldn't allow them to rent something so small as a growing family—two children, two adults, such a cramped and tiny space. But when she called to inquire gently, the landlord only laughed. The DEA had come a few weeks prior, he told her, raiding the apartment. He didn't care about their children, so long as *children* wasn't code for drugs.

"But I made up my mind: we weren't living in a drug den," Joy tells me.

So they put in a request to transfer to Kenai, which they hoped would prove safer, less expensive, less developed. From the plane, Joy saw only wilderness, woods, and mountains, only mountains and, every now and then, a light.

Joy thought, *I want to live here forever.*

She remembered her uncle's stories about the restaurant with the peanut shells and the man who shot rats, but her aunt and uncle no longer lived there, and she couldn't find the place. Joy and Jake were all alone. Jake had unrealistic ideas about marriage, and Joy knew he could never stay in one place for long, so she made a promise to herself: she would stay there once he decided to leave. They rented a trailer for three hundred dollars, and four months later, when they broke up, she kept her promise. Jake returned to Arizona, and she settled in with her boys for the winter.

"Jake was happy, he was jolly, but I married him at seventeen. It was a cute wedding atop a mountain. And I loved Jake, I really did, but we were on totally different pages. And I didn't like where his page went. He wanted to have more than one wife, for one." Joy laughs. "That made it easy to say no. But he could also . . . like I said, he wanted to control me. Let's just put it like that, okay? And I couldn't have my boys see that. They were growing—growing up. They couldn't be raised in a house with a man like that as a model, thinking to be a man is to control a woman. That's not how you treat your wife."

She looks out at the mountains.

"Jealousy, that's *one thing.* But he believed a woman shouldn't work, should just be having babies and raising babies, and maybe that's okay for some, but me? I couldn't stand that quiet, all that sitting inside all day. What kind of life is that? For a woman, for *anyone*?"

A life starkly different from this, I think, gazing through the glass. Outside, the road has given way to yellow gravel, rocks kicking up beneath the wheels. There are no animals, no birds, only the distant smudge of mountains. It is twenty-one degrees outside, according to the temperature gauge on the dash, but it is toasty inside our truck. The sky is wild-berry blue, a color like candy, or like the crayons I imagine young Joy clutched, sprawled out on the carpet in Arizona.

When we round our first sharp curve, I adjust my seat belt across my chest.

There are questions I want to ask. Mainly: Was there violence? And what I *really* want to know is how and when she knew a man who wanted to control a woman wouldn't change.

"Were you upset when the marriage ended?" I ask.

"No," Joy says gently. She turns her gaze to the mountains, the biggest I've ever seen. "I had my reasons," she explains. "Heck, I had lots of them."

~

Our culture doesn't talk easily about abuse, and neither do Joy and I. But the root of our shared problems is simple: bad love never announces itself as bad.

The last time I was in Alaska, I was sitting cross-legged on a cold stone harbor wall while Dave, the man I'd later come to love, told me he'd waited all his life to find someone like me.

"Smart and independent," he said, "and cute, with a love of family."

I clung especially to that word *cute*. I was twenty-seven, one year out of graduate school at the most competitive writing program in the country, and I'd recently accepted a tenure-track job teaching creative writing at a small private college in Ohio. I had my first book under contract and a series of essays in the *New York Times*. Still, I could not deny the validation I felt when affirmed by a man.

Dave and I were both in Alaska that summer because of our professional success; we had been hired by the director of a prestigious Alaskan educational camp to share our love of music and writing with teenagers in fluorescent rain jackets from Homer or Seward or Ketchikan.

"All of these students have a passion and an interest in the arts," the director told us during orientation. "Still, their art may look different from ours. The students from Anchorage, okay, they might know what they are doing, because they're coming from a pretty rigorous high school setting. But it's not uncommon for some of our students here to come from more remote Alaskan villages and find themselves—for the first time—watching someone perform ballet. Or using a darkroom. Or writing a sonnet."

For two weeks we drew curiosity from our students and instilled a love for the creative arts: visual, performing, musical, or literary. It wasn't difficult. The students arrived in our Alaskan classrooms with the same blunted bangs as the teenagers I worked with in Ohio, the same faded crew cuts or rudimentary ballpoint ink tattoos scattered across their forearms, only these teenagers knew how to sliver the bellies of salmon, kayak against a current, and smoke fish in wooden shacks they'd built alongside the ocean. A few showed me photos of the glacier they hiked on Sundays. The plane they were learning to pilot. One, an Indigenous Alaskan student from a particularly remote village, showed me the musk oxen jacket her mother had made her by stitching together fur scavenged from last winter's hides.

It was my favorite job I'd ever had, a place where the end of a day with students was marked only by a shift from one captivating group to the next. In the faculty lounge, I stayed up for hours listening to my fellow teaching artists explain their choreography work for Cirque du Soleil, or how they'd filmed an undercover documentary on the humanitarian crisis at our southern border. A Tsimshian wood-carver walked us to his woodshop, where a totem pole he was carving with students lay, big and orange, across a table. He pointed to a set of tools, adzes and chisels and carving knives.

"I have to remind the kids"—he laughed—"to keep both hands on their tools."

Another artist—tall and handsome—showed us photos of the nine life-size ceramic mariachi band figures he had made, each playing an instrument and dressed in traditional Chicano clothes.

One woman—quiet, subdued like me—revealed only after we insisted that she had hand-drawn a quintessential scene from Disney's *Beauty and the Beast*.

"This was before CGI. Picture it," she told us, and we did: her hand cramping, sore, as she gave life to townspeople throwing open their wood-latched windows and yelling down to Belle.

I didn't believe I deserved my place to teach among these people. I struggled with imposter syndrome. Despite whatever success I'd garnered as an emerging writer, I always felt like someone misunderstood to be far more accomplished than I was. Everyone else was more talented, harder working, sharper, more creative, *smarter*. Still, sitting among my colleagues each evening, watching them perform on stage for several hundred fervent young Alaskans, I felt humbled and more than lucky that this job I loved so much had brought me across the country and to Dave.

All week, I had followed Dave around like I was his shadow, always a few steps behind as he chatted on the morning walk into town for coffee with the Disney animator, or spoke of his life performing music at prestigious venues in San Francisco. Sometimes, we'd sit alone in the faculty lounge in the lull of afternoon, and he'd tell me about the synth music he was helping his eight-year-old nephew make. I was not infatuated so much as fascinated; Dave possessed an outrageous, inexplicable intelligence about how to get people to take their walls down, how to make them feel comfortable, insisting through his quiet, understated humor that you were safe and in good company. To know Dave was to love him. It really was that simple. His brain pulsed with light and optimism. He spoke with presence and conviction, but privately he told me that he often felt as though life was unfolding all around him in ways he didn't always understand.

"I just want to be open to everything," he said. "I think it's important I be open."

I took this to mean he wanted to be open to his place in the world, his future, to any decisions that were too important to make without intentionality. Both of us were approaching thirty, and Dave and I shared the sense that life was becoming a giant game of musical chairs: the lilting music softening, the tension palpable, the people all around us sitting down with whomever they had and with the promise of permanence.

"I want to pursue the things I *want*," he said, "rather than convince myself to be satisfied with what I have. Does that make sense?"

It did.

On the last night of camp before our dawn departures—Dave back to California, and I to central Ohio—we sat on the harbor wall above the swirling gray of sea. The stone was damp and smelled of cockles. We could hear the music from the students' dance, see their bodies move in the shadows.

A soft rain began to fall. But any sense of impending romance was refuted immediately by the smells the rain ushered in: fish and the thick, rotting knots of seaweed in the rancidness of the recessing tide. Still, he kissed me, taking off his blue rain jacket and tucking it around my shoulders. The kiss was gentle, and then he asked if we might kiss again.

Yards away, I could feel the bumping bass of Katy Perry and the looming sense that everything important was coming to an end.

"I guess I'm going to have to come see you in Ohio," he said.

"Sure," I said. I laughed. "And I'll come to California."

I didn't believe we'd really do it. This was all I deserved: one night of kissing and one moment of meaning. The ocean slushed around us, the lights from the anchored fishing boats bobbing endlessly, like phantom buoys. The next morning, on the airplane, I felt giddy, as if my body housed a secret. Instead the wheels tucked up and in, and I curled my fists, still damp with nerves. Alaska swelled beneath me. Forest gave way to rock and then to swirling, blackened ocean.

He called me shortly after I landed, and that night, we talked for hours, despite the jet lag and exhaustion. These elements only made his magnetism more distinguished, more intoxicating. My whole life, I had excelled at everything except romance, and here was romance in a man who loved children and inviting joy. I wanted nothing so much as him. The following morning, in an attempt to demonstrate intentionality, I booked a ticket to go out to see him. Three weeks later, on a night in August, Dave picked me up at SFO and drove us to Bayfront Park, where the velvet of blue sky met the satin of the bay's blue water. He spread a blanket across one of the park's many benches and we watched the planes take off, their hulking bodies soaring, their windows sunlit and shining, slicing through the sky what seemed like just feet above our heads. We made guesses as to where they were going.

"Hawaii," I said. "Honolulu."

"Florida," he quickly countered.

There was no place else I would rather be.

Dave was a music teacher at a school in San Francisco that catered to the children of tech geniuses. They were some of our nation's best-dressed twelve-year-olds. I thought that because he taught the oboe, the cello, to children, he was, without question, good. The following afternoon, after his school's hallways emptied, I watched for hours from the back of his classroom as he meticulously cut and bent corrugated cardboard, shaping first the trunk of a tree and then the limbs and then the roots, knotted and gnarled.

SCHOOL IS—it read—*TREE-MENDOUS*.

The cardboard construction was six feet tall, and together we stapled it to his classroom's wall and hung little ornaments of his students' faces from the branches at various levels, trying to target a certain well-balanced aestheticism, hanging and rehanging, working diligently to ensure that Ensley and Everly and Ezra all hung uniquely and independently, bright red apples of prosperity.

It was a metaphor, I thought, that tree: how diligent he was in displaying his students' faces, how diligent he would be as my partner in life.

On the bookshelf in his apartment in San Francisco, he showed me a small doll a student had made him from the cardboard husk of a toilet paper roll, some blue sequin eyes, and brown bristled yarn. He said it reminded him why he did this, even on the toughest days. I imagined our future toddler, the frenetic art she'd make for him with neon pipe cleaners and googly eyes. I wanted a child more than anything, and I trusted he would want one, too. He showed me the framed invitation to his brother's wedding, which reminded him that everyone had a match, he said, though it took some more time than others to finally find their person. I imagined a framed photo of our summer together, a stormy black-and-white of the Alaskan harbor he had taken during his free period and with the photography teacher's permission.

He'd rigged his own darkroom in the closet of his apartment, complete with a blackout curtain on a curtain rod, to process photos. His first attempts at developing film hung on the wall: an eclectically arranged series of tiny plastic men handing off tinier paper airplanes, or helping one another up a cliff that, upon closer examination, was just a patch of crumbling sidewalk. The photos made me laugh, but there was such tenderness in their careful positioning, in the angles of their painted plastic expressions, such art in their minuteness. I wanted to see my life as Dave saw his; I wanted to see the art in our everyday.

In the hallway leading to his bedroom, he had a ukulele, the curved body of yellow wood glossed by the Sharpie signatures of his three nieces, who had pooled their money together to purchase it as his Christmas present. They lived in Maine, he told me, where it snowed most days of the year and they wore moccasin slippers with hot-pink beads.

In the fridge, he kept spinach, still-firm zucchinis, a pint of blueberries.

In glass jars along his counter, oats and whole coffee beans and peanut butter Puffins cereal bought in bulk.

Dave was a musical prodigy, a keen and knowing expert of more instruments than I could count. They lined the walls of his apartment's hallway or were kept in satin cases inside his closet. In high school, he'd played lacrosse and taken his team to nationals, held that year in a Florida city. He was good at everything, *passionate* about everything, and at times it was almost as if I could see the gears of his mind turning behind those brown eyes and thick-rimmed glasses.

I thought that these things, small but cumulative, spoke unequivocally to his character, his value system, his sense of what was important. That unlike the man I'd been in love with before him—who often drank until he stopped speaking, or else disappeared down dark alleyways and slept with a series of lithe, thin poets—*this man* would be kind to me.

Standing there that first, second, and third time in Dave's San Francisco kitchen, I thought I might die of swooning. He was tender with everything. He even handled coffee mugs with care, hand-drying them with a towel before hanging them carefully from hooks. He never seemed to cut himself while shaving. He dressed every morning in cotton shirts with buttons, which he insisted on fastening up to his chin.

It made him look like a librarian, I told him, and then I thought, briefly, of the apocryphal quote commonly attributed to Margaret Atwood: *Men fear a woman will laugh at them, but women fear a man will kill them.*

Dave's face softened at the edges. He wasn't insulted. What was so wrong with books?

He said, "Isn't that your forte?"

He asked, in his best librarian voice, if he could help me find what I was looking for.

"Have you tried," he asked, running his hands through his black hair, then gesturing to an invisible back corner, "our circulation desk?"

~

What I remember of our early days is love, love, love, and little sticky notes with reminders of where and how this love manifested. *Here's a note to say I love you,* read a mint-green Post-it edged between the bristles of my toothbrush, *to get your Monday started right!* Our love, our adoration, tucked inside the coffee beans, waiting in the pantry, rounded in my favorite mug.

In California, when I would visit—one weekend a month, using airline miles that had accumulated over busy years in graduate school when I hadn't the money or time to go anywhere—we toured the homes of famous entrepreneurs, imagined life in Silicon Valley, and stood in line for tacos *al pastor* carved from fluorescent-lit spinning spits. Those nights were among my favorites, the scent of sizzling meat seeping into our skin as we waited in parking lots behind parents holding their children's sleep-fatigued bodies, their little limbs outfitted in fleece pajamas. We watched as fathers fed them torn-off tortilla and talked lovingly in Spanish.

In Ohio, when Dave would visit, we ate tomatoes pocked with sea salt, drank beer from chipped white mugs, watched lightning snap across the sky to become a strobe light beneath the trees.

We spent those early weekends together, young and in love, in the rickety white rocking chairs my parents had bought at a Cracker Barrel when they, too, were young and in love. We turned chicken legs on charcoal grills and drank beer from Mason jars. Beneath the pink of dogwoods, we spread a blanket—a family heirloom—and read together. The blanket was given to my grandfather to use during his service as a Korean War medic, and along the surface of its fabric it held the scars and familial markings from two generations: burns from where fireworks had landed prematurely one July when my mother was a girl, sand from family camping trips along the dunes, an imprint of my body, wet and suntan lotioned, when I was six and on vacation in northern Virginia.

My childhood had left its mark upon that blanket and that blanket had left its mark upon my heart. Every time we laid it down, I thought, *I want to add our memories to this.*

I imagined it accumulating the dried dairy stain of picnic cheese, the sticky residue of our child's candy.

There was just one element of our pairing that suggested that future might not come easily. Dave was Christian and loved his faith; I was agnostic and loved my own. I felt lucky for my secular childhood. In the wilderness of rural Pennsylvania, on the plot of four wild acres where I was raised, we gathered around a well-worn kitchen table, and, in lieu of prayers, we discussed our days. My father was a chemist, my mother, a high school French teacher. Sundays were pancake breakfasts and rings around the reservoir, looking for owl pellets, tracking the footprints of wild animals lodged deep in a lake's silt embankment. We visited churches, but only for their parking lots: my brothers and I learned to ride our bikes in those empty spaces on Sunday evenings. Those properties were sacred, but because of my mother clapping in the distance, my father running alongside us in cargo shorts.

I believed then, as I did with Dave, in the quiet beauty of two people who loved each other despite their differences. My parents voted differently and often had passionate debates about the future of our country over spiral ham and mashed potatoes. But always afterward, my mother would stand at the kitchen sink, rinsing the dishes clean of their macaroni, and my father would be next to her, faded dishrag in hand. I came to see the benefits of a mismatched pairing.

So I felt proud, in those early days with Dave, to love someone so different, so *other*, to look to my partner not as a carbon copy of myself, my beliefs, and my ideals, but as my complement. It felt thrilling in many ways: the intellectual challenge of our differences, the separate philosophies that governed us. Whatever gaps we had, the other filled.

But one fundamental disagreement bothered me, and that disagreement was over our bodies or, more precisely, what we should do with them. Dave was saving himself for marriage. I wanted to have sex. It was the only reason, initially, I thought we might not make it. When he'd first explained that he was a virgin, I hadn't taken it very well. I took it, in fact, quite poorly—laughing, rolling my eyes, saying immediately, *No.* Stronger than my refusal to wait until our wedding was my desire to know him in this way and in those impressionable, early days of building a life together.

Still, we loved each other. *I'll give this time,* I thought.

A few months later, Dave told me he wanted to try, that he had prayed and prayed about it and felt ready to give himself to me.

"I don't want you to do this and regret it," I said.

What I meant was *regret me.* He told me he was sure. He loved me, he said, more than anyone.

It was late fall when we were finally naked together. He undressed me slowly, tenderly. Later, we lay on our backs as the space heater vacillated. The trees were full of orange leaves.

"How do you feel?" I asked.

He rolled onto his side and held me, one long muscle against my body.

"I feel good," he said. "I feel great."

~

We had sex those next few weeks everywhere: in the kitchen and in the shower and on the couch in the living room as birds dipped for birdseed beside the window, their happy sounds our soundtrack, their beaks flexing in playful song. I found a confidence that felt uniquely adult and feminine. Sex became fun—*new*—less a transaction between two people, as it had been for years before, as a way to squeeze affection, as much as something sacred, sweet, and *holy*.

Every muscle ached with want.

I'm certain that our life together in those days wasn't always joyous, wasn't always so carefree, but of those early months, when we visited each other frequently, I recall only happiness, and the fields, and the fog at night, and the cicadas chittering in the darkness.

Autumn escalated into winter. The hours accumulated. Our world felt so beautiful and full of love that I could almost envision God reaching a hand down every night to fold one wet, white corner of the earth against itself. Nights, I dreamed of entering Dave's bloodstream, of taking a job as a tiny mechanic tending to the inner workings of his heart. I was responsible for its pumping. I held a tiny wrench. I dreamed of living inside him; I dreamed of living as half of him.

I wanted to make every decision with Dave in mind, to encourage in him that same kind, gentle person I felt he was encouraging inside of me. But whatever peace I felt in those moments registered intensely in Dave as shame. He was ruminating on my body, on the way desire had undressed it.

Sometimes, it hurts to remember how fiercely we were in love, and how love—like listening—began to become a commodity, and how, like everything of value, it began to slip away without our notice, as if it were water, or time, or air.

～

On the Dalton Highway, Joy explains, everything is something else: cars are called *four-wheelers*, plows are *blades*, Joy is *Joy Mothertrucker*. When, eight miles in, she pulls the truck over along the shoulder, I worry she's turning back—that already this drive we're undertaking has proven too intimate—but she says no and points instead to a row of bulbous trees just off the highway.

"Candy Land trees!" she tells me. "Because they look more lollipop than tree!"

I counter with Dr. Seuss, but we both agree they're strange.

These trees are Joy's favorite. Everywhere, and on every branch, snow hangs in packed, tight circles, almost comically.

This is the boreal forest, Joy tells me—a stark departure from any other forest I've ever known, a place where trees grow relatively uniform in height but vary endlessly in width and shape. The forest looks like a patchwork, stunted spruce alternating between tall aspens and open space, the result of the way sunlight is always shining at an angle in the Arctic landscape, a dramatic difference. Each spring, the top layer of permafrost thaws only long enough for new roots to take hold, and then everything freezes up again, settles in for winter. The stunted growth is dramatic, gnarled and topped—on this particular morning—with perfect scoops of snow, like dollops of mashed potatoes.

We hop down from the cab, and I ask Joy if she'll take my picture.

"That's the point." She laughs. I slip across the icy gravel and climb the wall of snow that has been erected thanks to the highway plow. I struggle in the wild wind to remain upright and unrounded. Joy laughs and snaps my picture.

"Again," she says, stepping forward. "I think your eyes were closed."

I want this as proof—that regardless of any fear, any sense I don't belong, I have traveled to Alaska to sit within Joy's truck cab and observe the place as she promised.

We've only traveled eight miles, but already things feel different, foreign, as if this part of Alaska is part of another America entirely. I am the wild and lucky recipient of Joy's impossible generosity, and when she looks at me and laughs, I feel something warm inside me, like an animal, tight and burrowed.

We climb back in the truck and Joy points just up the road, where men's deaths begin to announce themselves with frequency. She points and tells me Handlebar was crushed by a pipe at this shallow pass just beyond Graveyard.

"It sounds like you're playing Clue," I say.

"It does sound like that," she admits, and then she rattles off some more names. Moustache spun out around Gobbler's Knob, and Elixir died after a medical emergency caused him to crash his snowplow near Oh Shit Corner. She tells me Donut was one of the lucky ones; he survived after being buried alive in a sudden avalanche as he was descending Atigun Pass last winter. There was low visibility, she explains, so crews had to search for him via grid formation, charting with unique precision the endless expanse of snow-white earth.

"This area," Joy says, sucking at her teeth, "it's not like the rest of Alaska. Here, storms come up so quick, so fast, and suddenly you can't see anything."

I think of how much of life is like that: *good* until it isn't.

Outside the window, there's another cross.

"I think about it a lot," Joy says. "How they all thought they were getting home that night."

Elixir and Moustache and Handlebar, Buck and Spud and Cactus Jack. Getting home to their wife or to their children or to a heaping plate of chicken pot pie. To linen stretched over a tabletop, a tumbler of milk neatly sweating. To *Jeopardy!* or the evening news.

It makes her a better driver, Joy tells me, a better member of this community. She releases a squeeze of windshield fluid and pivots the wipers from side to side. She tells me these men didn't expect to die, to go through their windshields, to collide head-on with another truck, to be crushed or burned or smashed. I listen, scared to be beside her—that much should be obvious—but it's a different kind of fear than the fear I've felt for years.

Which is to say, quite simply, I do not fear Joy's company.

Still, it is unpleasant. No one wants to die. I can't help but think of what my handle would be, what they'd say when they found my body.

"I'd call you 'Spice Girl,'" Joy tells me, "though I promise: you won't die. But the way you doctored up those breakfast potatoes earlier? The way you seem to doctor up everything?"

She nods down at my backpack, where the cap from a travel-size bottle of Cholula pokes out.

"Me? I try to help everyone I can whenever I can," she continues. "Like a guardian angel of the highway? There's that idea, 'Do unto others . . . ?' I try to truck unto others, you know, the way I myself would want to be trucked."

I think of all the verbs one might replace with *trucked*. *Loved* is chief among them. What would it look like if we all *loved* right?

"I've always got spare parts in the back, and extra food, blankets, matches, you know? All you need?" Joy continues. She rolls down her window to let a mosquito flee for the mountains, its black body sharp against the clean blue sky. "I don't care what it costs: my salary or my own schedule. You save a life if there's a life to save."

She's silent for a moment.

"You're going to think this is crazy," she says finally, "but I've always felt God made me to put me here. I think He built me to tend to this landscape, specifically."

I want to tell her I agree—I do, in many ways—but I also wonder what it says about the men who've lost their lives out here. What was God doing there?

Everywhere I look, the world is an open wound.

Instead I look to the console, where Joy's phone lights up the space between us.

"I thought you said we'd have no service?" I ask.

"*You'd* have no service," she clarifies. She points down at her phone. "GCI," she says. "They're an Alaskan cell phone company, and they've been installing a couple towers up here these past few months."

"The American wild isn't so wild anymore," I say.

Joy frowns in slight acknowledgment. She picks the phone up, studies it. A man by the name of Jim Rocker has sent her photos of his petunias. The flowers fan out, hot pink and yellow, across the screen.

"Text him for me, ask him to show me his bean shoots," Joy says. Then, "Not a euphemism!" She laughs. "There's something special about his soil."

She gestures again, and I take her phone and am surprised there is no passcode, surprised all the more by the wallpaper that blooms across her screen—the sherbet orange of a tundra sunset, as if she can't get enough of this place, not ever.

I type out her soil inquiry, writing, Let me see those beans!

The morning sun warms the inside of our cab, and I feel overcome by a sense of ease. For a moment, I feel willing to concede that maybe there is a God, and maybe He did create this place, but maybe we aren't the point, the heroes in this story. Maybe we are simply postscript, because God knew his creation was worth a witness: the stars and earth and mountains, the emptiness of this expanse, how it's the lack of human spoil that makes this place so goddamn gorgeous.

~

A year after we met, Dave decided to move to Ohio. He had been considering it quietly, he said, for several months, but only when he gave voice to this did we both realize the inevitability of his relocation; the possibility of proximity made another year of distance feel impossible. I offered to move near him—albeit reluctantly—but he said he respected my tenure-track job, which was nearly impossible to get elsewhere, whereas teaching jobs were plentiful. He wouldn't let me abandon a position most spend decades trying to secure, and while he loved the opportunities California offered him to perform, he felt hungry for seasons and simplicity, for snow and his first real girlfriend.

He packed up his apartment a few weeks later.

I wanted nothing so much those first few weeks together in Ohio as I wanted to protect him, but as with any move, the mishaps were abundant. First the moving truck was delayed, then he realized that he'd packed his social security card and birth certificate in a filing cabinet that was traveling on its truck bed. Without proof of identity, he couldn't get a driver's license, so no landlord would approve him. The jobs he'd been interviewing for would not hire him. Dave was fundamentally resistant to living in my home because of the strict parameters of his faith, but he had no other option while the truck teetered closer and our bank accounts grew slim.

I assumed but did not fully comprehend how living together—even briefly—put additional stress on Dave's faith. I focused on what he had told me: that he had moved across the country out of an abundance of love and respect. I did not know the way he saw it: that his move was an experiment, one concession to geography given willingly in the hopes I would compromise on faith.

I was distracted, reveling in his proximity. Some nights, we played music. Some nights, he spun me around the living room. We liked to watch ourselves in the width of my mantel mirror. However silly they might have looked, I loved those people—loved their love, and generosity of spirit, and the kindness they summoned within each other.

We made plans to form a family. We made plans to buy a house.

We got a dog instead, a rescue, one of thirteen extracted from a hoarder an hour south. That August, our new puppy at our feet, we planted zucchini and green beans and tall, thick stalks of tomatoes, their yellow blossoms blossoming outward, higher, reaching for the sun.

I loved him more than I knew I could love anything.

He felt holy to me—beyond holy.

Dave shopped around for apartments. When finally the truck pulled up, we settled him into an apartment three doors down from mine. That summer, time was abundant, and so when we weren't together, we took up new hobbies whose mastery benefited us both. I baked pastry—layers of butter and dough swathed with fresh berry jam, snapping from the oven's heat. Dave took up woodworking in my backyard—a hobby the small apartments and expensive real estate never permitted him in San Francisco. I loved to watch his forearms and the way he worked the wood, the way that golden sawdust caught in rays of the summer sun. Each afternoon, when he came inside, his skin smelled of orange oil and cedar shavings as he stood at my kitchen sink, drinking cold water from the faucet.

It was then, in that first fall together, that I began to think—for the first time—of prayer. All my life, I'd only known faith as a wall erected to create distinction. But with Dave in Ohio, I wanted to see faith as good.

The first time I prayed, we were on a busy stretch of Columbus highway, on our way home from breakfast. There was a man fumbling outside a stalling vehicle. Dave pulled my car over to the side of the road. It was one of the most dangerous places to be: outside a vehicle on the shoulder, just inches from the highway. The second most dangerous spot was where I was: inside a vehicle on the shoulder, observing, outrageously, precariously, helplessly. With each car's approach, I closed my eyes and prayed.

Never in my life had I wanted to summon forth a God and then will Him to protect the man I loved as much as I did in those moments. Each word I prayed made me want to continue, and it felt natural, *secure*, in some ways the calmest feeling I'd ever known.

The prayer—or the act of wishing—made me suddenly certain of our safety. I know how wild it sounds. I'm also certain of how strong I felt it. For months, I had watched Dave sacrifice his safety and schedule in pursuit of helping others. He was so giving of his time, of his absolute attention—through daily acts, through love he afforded strangers with nearly absurd and routine frequency—that it was easy, in those first few Ohio months, to accept his Christian faith. It felt so refreshingly foreign from the crooked version of Christianity I'd glimpsed as a child.

It's true—it remains true—that what I saw in Dave's early actions was what he spoke of as the grace of God.

I prayed, and then I watched Dave help the man push his car up an embankment to safety, and soon a tow truck appeared. In the months that followed that morning, I began to pray everywhere and without discretion: for a coworker's impending operation, over dogs tethered to stakes in lawns, once on a dark, snow-covered road when I was certain I'd lose control of the car until a snowplow emerged from nowhere, guiding my path with its light and salt.

Eventually, I began to see even our coupling as the result of God's long, thin finger, as if He had reached down through Alaska's clouds to nudge the two of us together. As if God knew somehow despite my skepticism that Dave would help me find Him through him.

~

Everything we saw began to take on a certain significance. The wild-flowers that grew between gravel stones, the California-style taqueria opening in our Ohio town, the sudden job advertisement at a nearby private elementary school—everything seemed to indicate a knowing nod at our intertwining lives, a celestial signaling only we could see.

This idea of double meaning—this sense of *signs from God*—had always been an integral part of life for Dave. In one of our earliest conversations, he told me he'd once ridden his bike through the streets of San Francisco asking God which way he should turn and where. Initially, I thought I'd fallen in love with someone whose stability I'd come to question. But over time, something about his conviction felt tender, open, and endearing. Where was the harm in a young man on a bicycle, pedaling around San Francisco at dusk, the palm trees still against the sky? I came to love the image of his smooth, stubbled cheek craning upward, his ear a soft receiver sifting holy dispatches between clay-thatched houses and thick humidity.

I pictured him as he asked, *Now what, God?* Now *what?*

He thought I might be his *now what.* I wanted to be it, too. Being near him made me happy. It really was that simple. I wanted everything to do with him, so I decided to try to share his faith.

Later, I would describe him as both the kindest and the cruelest man I've ever known.

But like Joy—like so many women—I came to know his kindness first.

5.

Beneath the backdrop of steel-blue midday, between the rising ridges of Alaska's Brooks Range, Joy teaches me how to read the road. She points to the rocks that line the highway's edges, proof of recent rain, predictors of washout or avalanche. She points to the horizon and its clouds, the way she's come to learn their names, the way she's come to understand which hold moisture and which pretend. She's no meteorologist, she jokes, but any Joe or Jane can learn their language—how, when read in conjunction with the time, or the temperature gauge inside the truck, the clouds and their density, their colors, can warn of incoming snow or fog or sleet or hail or lightning.

"I always look for animals along the shoulder," she says. "I ask myself, 'Are they standing up? Are they bedding down?' Everything tells you what's about to happen, and it doesn't take God for you to listen."

She points even to the objects inside her truck, the objects rolling between our feet along the carpet—the bear spray and the flares, the space blanket and the kerosene stove.

"Everything tells you how to use it," she says, "and men are like that, too. Now, men aren't objects, obviously." At this she laughs a little, squints, and eyes my notebook. "They don't come with a set of instructions, no sticker you have to pull, no pamphlet that takes up space, but they come with warnings sure enough, absolutely—indicators, however small, that something's just not right."

With Jake, Joy tells me, it was a penchant to manipulate and control her: in the home and in the workplace and in the machinery of her body.

Have another baby.

Give us another life.

"He'd made it clear I could have him or the navy," she repeats, "and I listened to him, because what did I know?"

I look out across the tundra. My warning sign looked different. My warning sign, if indeed there was one, was Dave's increasingly fierce desire to amend and alter what he perceived as my flawed worldview and his insistence that I be malleable.

In San Francisco, when I'd visited, I'd always joined Dave for worship service, held in a hipster megachurch that featured neon lights, a swoony pastor, and a leather-clad worship band. The women who sang were beautiful San Franciscans—long-haired daughters with bright lipstick, succulent tattoos, and suede heeled booties—and the men were tanned with edgy haircuts they pushed off their foreheads as they sang His name. The pews were stadium seating. The baptismal baths were made of rustic wood. Everyone raised their hands to feel the glory of our God under rave-like, roving beams that felt like spotlights searching for souls to save. After church, we'd walk across the street for ramen, saying very little about the sermon, choosing instead to slurp *tonkatsu* with handmade noodles tangled in the wet globes of soft-boiled eggs.

In Ohio, church was carpeted, stained with instant coffee, and always dark. The pastors were good, earnest, balding men with bellies full of bratwurst, Arby's sandwiches, and casserole. The lighting was uneven, the music was homely, and the drive home took us past two sad Burger Kings, a quilting store, and a PC and iPod repair shop. I knew Dave wanted to share his world of faith with me, but I felt afraid to speak, afraid that what was unfolding inside my chest was more a love and admiration for a man than a recognition and understanding about Jesus.

I wanted to sit each week in church with Dave.

I wanted to believe in God.

But in those early days of fumbling my way through faith, I felt inadequate and counterfeit, uncomfortable in my own skin. To pray felt good but always suspect; to offer grace was to offer gratitude—not to a God or Christian faith but to the flesh-and-bone man sitting across the table, to our love and how it made life matter, to his warmth and gentle kindness. Increasingly, I knew, I was forcing it; I was forcing my faith to try to keep a man. But maybe, I thought, with a little more time, I could get to where he wanted me to be.

Each night, I sat beside him on the couch, bowed my head, and said those words.

In your loving name we pray, amen.

But each prayer only brought into stark relief the sense that I would never match the fervor of a faith Dave had been taught to love all his life. I worried almost daily that no amount of time would ever make me as confident or sure of faith as Dave was, and that he would leave me when he found this out. I tried to talk to God, but I was a small girl in a room trying to earn my keep in a conversation Dave had been having since before his birth.

~

Less than four months after moving to Ohio, Dave sat on my couch one night, worn leather Bible in his lap, slumped, sullen, fearful that he was failing God.

"Because we didn't wait for marriage," he said. "I can't stop thinking about it."

"God loves you," I tried, moving my hands along his shoulder.

But increasingly, I was coming to understand that for Dave, my body—which he had touched and, in his touching, made impure—had become a reminder now not of our love but of vile, repugnant, foul temptation. For weeks, shame sunk its teeth into him, plunging him into an emotional geography he had never explored before and for which he had no map. What else could he do but rely on the moral framework that had otherwise guided him all his life? And yet Dave's Bible was one in which women were mostly objects, their bodies instruments: tools of labor, punishment, or temptation. Women washed the feet of Jesus, or women gave birth without sex to the son of God, or women were prostitutes who sometimes helped men by hiding them in walls. The Biblical women were always subservient. They did not teach classes on contemporary feminism. And although he claimed to respect my work, Dave increasingly began to resent the words I wrote, to find my ideas trite and superfluous. When one morning the BBC called for an interview about a piece I'd written on the need for professional female emojis, which had inspired Google to create and implement thirteen pixelated working women, including a chemist and a doctor and a plumber and a pilot, Dave rolled his eyes and said he found my essay "silly."

A month later, an international committee met to introduce and adopt the new emojis as part of all-new iOS software globally, and they cited my article specifically.

"Whoop-de-do," he said, spinning one finger vacantly.

I was rattled to see him so mean. Most of the time, Dave could be respectful, but he often couched his complaints about what I did and the women I wrote about in terms of scripture he admired: how much *holier* the women were who served, how selfless, how sanctified. Those women, I was reminded each time I read from a passage he praised, were never equal partner, never counterpart, but subservient, submissive. Worse, the origin of my gender always circled back to a problematic narrative about an overcurious temptress who'd wronged Adam out of paradise, which I pictured not unlike a temperate San Francisco, where Dave had remained a virgin, craning his ear to God.

I thought frequently of Eve, how it was difficult not to interpret a serpent whispering temptation into a woman's ear as a woman allowing an idea into her body.

And I was a woman with a lot of ideas.

The more Dave turned to his Bible, the more his great shame swelled.

The more he took that shame out on me.

By late fall, we ate as three: there was Dave and there was me and there was his palpable disgust, like a shadow attached to us. It made me think of the antidrug commercials of my childhood: the personified addiction always present, always looming, a shadowed figure whispering, *I need, I need, I need.*

Only it wasn't drugs Dave was seeking; he sought my body, virginized.

And yet I had stood beside him in my upstairs bedroom and told him I was ready—that if he wanted this, so did I. Now, months later, I was sin. He saw spoil where I saw love.

I could call it what my friends called it: misogyny, pure and simple.

Or I could call it a terrible shame spiral I had faith he would pull out of.

Or I could call it a breakdown, or an existential or spiritual crisis, or the beginning of a deconstruction of what it meant to be a man of faith.

Whatever we choose to call it, Dave began to scream, to rage, and it seemed I was always held in his shameful center, in the wild fluctuations of his temperament, resented—and then *disgusted*—for my body and the things we had done with it.

~

There is no way for me to accurately describe how much I began to hate my body because I felt Dave hated it. And there was no way for me to say—after several dozen iterations, several dozen variations on a theme—that having sex had not changed me, or if it did, that change was beautiful, a natural step in a progression of a more evolved relationship.

It was hard as an outsider to Dave's faith to help him sort through his shame and resentment. I didn't understand how he could feel as though he'd let down God when God had made him in His image, had allegedly made *me* from *his rib*, had put the two of us together on that sleepy fishing island in Alaska with the hope we'd find one another. The more I tried to meet Dave where he was, the more intolerant and fundamental he became, as if intractability was the only way to alleviate his shame. We disagreed about sex, but increasingly, we disagreed about everything.

Sin, Dave argued once, was the bed and the foundation of gay marriage.

Children should not be raised with values outside the church.

And women were in part to blame for rape or sexual assault if they were drunk or in a fraternity house or wearing clothing that was "too showy."

"I *work with* these students," I said. "How could you ever say something like that?"

I am embarrassed I did not leave, but I felt responsible for his education, responsible for his reeducation. I wanted to get through to him for me, but I also wanted to get through to him for everyone. I felt like a fumbling Christian, turning passages over in my head, dog-earing pages from his Bible, hoping those pages, their stories, might save me. If I could only find proof of my thinking in Jesus, I thought. If I could only get through to him with his own language. We became two people set on changing each other, making each other see our truths.

I looked to his Bible as evidence, the stars he'd marked in the margins proof of passages that gave him strength, or the questions he'd asked God, or the ideas he was mulling over. I wanted to know what his private conversations with God were like, how he saw God guiding him, or us.

But everything registered in a language I didn't speak, and I increasingly worried I would never understand it.

Still, I threw everything I had at prayer. We began to pray together, often several times daily, because never is the need for God as great as when you feel you should be punished. The midwestern sky was too vast for Dave, too open. He worried God was always watching, and out here, He saw everything. So we prayed in the light of early morning, and again as the night closed in. Sometimes even at midday—hunched into our cell phones on our separate noon-hour lunches, Dave idling in the car between job interviews, my office door closed to students.

I never knew what to say, but that didn't keep me from trying.

In truth, in those early days, my prayers were mostly apologies.

But regardless of how much I prayed, regardless of how much I got on my knees and said those words, I was failing to find a home for myself in Dave's religion. Mostly, I felt sorry. I felt sorry and very sad. I still thought Dave's shame, his sense of godlessness, was something I needed to be forgiven for. So I folded small notes into his pockets. I tucked his favorite candy bar inside his bag. I got up with our crying puppy in the coldest, earliest hours of still-dark morning to stand patiently as she did loops around the dark backyard, in no clear rush to pee.

"Go potty!" I'd yell, shivering, exhausted in more ways than one.

The dog's name was Oosk, named after Alaska, that tiny fishing port where we had met, fallen in love. We'd wanted a word that represented our place of origin. *Oosk*, from the Alaskan native language Tlingit. The word, a Tlingit friend had told us, was unlike any we had in English. Put simply, it meant *cute* and referred specifically to the faces of baby animals and people, but add an *a*, he'd laughed, and the word became *evil, sin.*

It was the word's sense of duality I liked—how one thing could represent two altogether different factions with just the littlest modification—and I enjoyed, too, the way that word felt as it rolled off my tongue.

Oosk, running through the newly scattered midwestern leaves in our backyard. *Oosk*, seizing crab apples in her mouth and, later, barfing them up into the heater grate. *Oosk*, kicking her hind legs out in sleep as she dozed and dreamed in afternoon sunlight.

Oosk, Oosk, Oosk, our new family, our emergent love, our Saturday mornings spent in bed, a daily exercise in love and kindness as she pawed at the comforter, and at our noses, and at our love for her, and yipped.

But the word was not without a reminder that any one thing could be both good and bad.

"Oosk or Ooska?" I joked with our new puppy every morning as she padded around our living room, tail wagging, eyes big and shining, but bladder threatening, I joked, a dam-like release.

Will you attempt your first sweet howl, or will you poop on your mommy's pillow?

Oosk or Ooska? Which puppy are you today?

But, with that same frequency, I began to wonder about Dave.

Who was I to him? The woman that he loved, or the mark of sin, of evil?

~

On the Dalton Highway, climbing fast, Joy tells me the dangerous part of life with Jake was she was only ever around Jake.

In those Alaska days, she had few friends. And Jake accompanied her everywhere: the grocery store, the mall, the gas station, the post office. For years, she had done everything in his company, and now—newly separated—her life was lonely. Her children cried with youth. Winters were long and dark—six hours of daylight half the year—and in summers, the mosquitos swarmed until the family's skin buckled in angry welts and she had to move the kids inside.

"But I had to leave him," she says. "I really did. It escalated, you know? And I could take it, it wasn't *awful*, but I had this sense that, if I let it, that abuse would become learned behavior. We had two sons, after all."

She pauses but doesn't turn her head to look at me like I expect.

"I'm so sorry," I say, "I'm so—"

"It was important to me then," Joy interrupts, "not to let my sons grow up thinking *this* is how you treat a woman."

So she left Jake. But it wasn't easy.

"Not just being a single mom," she explains. "Everybody *loved* him. I mean *everyone*. When we first married, people came over to see me just to see *him*, you know what I am saying? He was just that kind of person. Magnetic energy. People felt *drawn*."

Then she left and people blamed her.

"When you don't have a lot of money, and you have to divorce a controlling husband," she begins, "well, you're sort of like a stereotype. I don't know. I think it makes people uncomfortable. Because if it could happen to you . . ." She stops.

So friends began to visit less often. Others looked at her, looked at her children—her kids, young and wild, wrestling in the front yard—and thought, *Woman, you are crazy.*

"But I'd rather be crazy," she tells me, "than be controlled in any capacity by a man. Except now I was poor. I'd quit my job because of Jake. I had two boys, and I had nothing."

Joy found work at the Fort Knox Gold Mine, driving a bulldozer, a job she tells me was indisputably *men's work*. She knew to make it through she would have to lean on God. And what better place than the state that remained—more than any place in America—exactly as He'd intended? Rivers running, glacial mountains, tundra soft as birthday cake—spongy and yellow and sweet and softening each spring underfoot.

"I wasn't moving home," she said. "That would've been easier, I guess, to have my parents near, but uh-uh, nope, no way. I refused to go back to Arizona, back to the Lower 48. I'd finally started a life for myself in Alaska, and I was hell-bent on staying put."

Still, as a Seventh-day Adventist, Joy wanted, more than anything, to keep Saturday Sabbath. She decided to make her pursuit of God her priority. So she took a calendar from the drawer and drew an X over every Saturday in Sharpie.

"Those were the days," she tells me, "I decided I'd no longer work."

But the mining company wouldn't have it. If she wanted to drive bulldozers at the mine, they said, it was on their schedule, and that included Saturdays.

"I think in some ways," she says, "God was testing me. Like, 'How bad you want this, little girl?'"

She wanted it very badly. So she took the only job at the mine that afforded workers Saturdays off, as a mechanic trainee, washing the very equipment that, weeks prior, she'd been driving.

"It was—what do you call it—a demotion in many ways. I mean both in terms of power and money. I made the least amount out of anyone."

She swivels halfway in her seat to grab a can of refried beans from the back, then procures a can opener from inside the dash and dispenses the beans into a red plastic bowl I had no idea she'd packed. She reaches around again: arugula, tortilla chips, cilantro. She begins to harvest the tender leaves with her fingers, which are short and smudged with bean.

This, she laughs, is a Dalton Highway healthy nacho.

A blue truck passes us, full speed, and Joy notes the transport company by color.

"Carlile," she says knowingly.

The driver honks his horn at Joy, raises his hand emphatically in a hearty *thanks*. She pulls the CB radio to her mouth.

"No problem, my man!" she croons.

She engineers another nacho. Beneath us, the blue truck careens, catches the light from the sun, and shimmers.

I reach for a tortilla from the bag between us, splash it with Sriracha. She hands me an avocado and gestures toward the glove box, where she keeps her pocketknife. She wants thin slices for this salad, the unspoken answer to the question I'd raised earlier in the supermarket: *How are you going to eat that on the road?*

It's clear to me now that she knew I'd help.

"But what it comes down to: I believe God sends us messages," Joy says as I hand her a wedge of avocado. "And I believe He's always testing us. He gave me that washing job, and when I kept it—when He saw how hard I'd work, how little I'd take if it meant keeping Him—He came up with a plan to reward me."

She pops the chip into her mouth, and I hand her another quarter moon of avocado.

"Yeah," she says, "mm-hmm, I think He knew exactly what He was doing."

~

If God was sending us a sign, Dave and I could no longer ignore His message.

We woke in late September to the backyard tree—formerly a vibrant, healthy elm—oozing black sap from knotted, dark welts on its leaves and branches. The trunk was infested with clouds of biting flies that bit our small, new puppy until pus-filled lumps surfaced across her back, her neck, and her fluffy thighs.

The tree was rotting from the inside, an arborist we called informed us, and would need to be cut down—a stump so big and deep the landlord wouldn't even bother to exhume it. I began to think of it as a backyard statement piece, a physical reminder that even internal rot surfaces eventually.

We tried everything to savor what was left of backyard weather, but our skin prickled with angry welts from flies still buzzing in confused circles, searching for their home. The welts itched most at night, which made it difficult to sleep, and each day, we grew more restless. When we did sleep, I dreamed of the flies burrowing inside our bodies. Dave dreamed of the whole house burning down.

Mornings were equally uneasy. Dave was a finalist for a position as a band director at a competitive private school. With his talents, the job was his, they told him, if he could transfer his residency. When one afternoon he went to the DMV to get his Ohio driver's license and switch the tags on his car, he returned with his head down, holding the license plate up for me in silence.

It read, insanely, *GPS 6666.*

The fourth six, he said, was incidental. The message, we agreed, was clear.

Your new coordinates: Hell.

I joked that the devil's locale was awfully full of polite midwesterners, Bob Evans buffets, and Quaker Steak & Lubes, but the joke was too close for comfort. Dave believed Hell was exactly where we were. The license plate was just another sign, like the rotting of our backyard tree, like the pus-filled lumps on our puppy's back.

I was exploring my faith, but clearly, I wasn't finding it fast enough, or I wasn't finding it with enough conviction, enough certainty. Part of me believed I would be better off without him, but another part of me was beginning to see the world as Dave did: signs in our lives were proof of our failure and subsequent punishment. That part of me felt real and dark, superstitious, paranoid. The only thing worse than failing to find God, I thought, was failing to find God and subsequently losing Dave, and lingering in that place of punishment—that place of darkness—alone forever.

And so my early reaction to Dave's increasing irritation, his increasing yelling and physical intimidation, was to see his rage, too, as a sign—a punishment in and of itself and, above all, proof of my own worthlessness, my sin, and my inadequacy.

~

"Here's another thing I like about this highway," Joy tells me, pointing. "These very same mountains you hug on your way up late one afternoon are the very same ones you'll see on your way back the next morning."

But we both know there is a danger in finding comfort in familiarity. You begin to find yourself stuck in patterns—in your history, in your relationships, in the men you align your life beside.

"Deep down," Joy tells me, "I knew Jake was a mess. Even before I married him, I knew. The problem is simple: people count on women to do men's work. Jake was a mess—a total mess—but he and everyone considered it my job to fix him up."

I relate to this entirely. Years prior I'd sat in a motel room beside a man I'd loved for ages as we watched live footage of a tornado three hundred miles south suck up homes on television, spit them out as shreds. I loved him and had told him so often, despite the fact that never in our five years had he brought himself to repeat those words. He loved me, I felt certain, but didn't know how to show it. He'd cheat on me, say mean things. Then, always, he'd return. That night, in the motel, drunk from too much beer, he looked at me and told me that he loved me. It was the first—and only—time he'd ever say it. He really hoped, he said, I knew.

On television, we watched plywood blister into debris, whole supermarkets gone, miles of highway ripped like scabs from the earth's flat body. I felt devastated for the people and could not bring myself to hear his words.

For five years, I'd thought that I could save him—from his drinking, from his past, from the dark and lonely undercurrent that seemed to saturate everything. But that night, as I read and he kept drinking, he flipped the couch over while I was in it, quick as the tornado and its violence. I felt my body float and then my knee whack against the edge of the coffee table. A bruise blossomed across my leg. I recognized it instantly: he was trying to elicit a response from me.

"I thought," he said, "it would be funnier."

It would take me several months to finally leave him, to find a man less like a storm, because I believed—I still sometimes do—that I was worth more when I was with him than I would ever be alone.

But make no mistake, Joy tells me, it's dogs, not men, women should spend their time rescuing.

"And a man," she tells me, "is no animal."

It was, in fact, animals that Joy and I first talked about in those earliest days: me, apologizing for my rescue dog howling in the background, proof of her fixation on a front yard squirrel, and Joy laughing, saying, *Oh, please,* telling me she was, at that very moment, bribing her Samoyed outside to pee by way of a Kong toy filled with peanut butter.

In fact, those first few years on the Dalton Highway, Joy told me, it was often just her and Bullet, the German shepherd who routinely joined her.

She looks at me briefly, and I want to tell her I understand that desire to fix a man. That I sympathize, *empathize.* That I have been there, too.

That I have been there more than once.

"I've had my share of Jakes, too," I start. "Only, we never had a child."

I think, *They never even married me,* and this should come as a relief, but still some deep-seated, self-loathing part of me cannot help but feel that this could be proof of my own inadequacy as much as it could be proof of theirs.

~

That fall, Dave built me bookshelves, and cleaved-log coffee tables, and tree-limb disk coasters with rings and years you could count.

Time made tangible, like his gifts.

But the first time he screamed at me, I cowered in our tent between the red rocks of Mesa Verde and the Colorado desert that stretched beyond. It was our first vacation together, our first time out of Ohio since his move, and the first time I worried about his anger. I found myself initially mesmerized, as if another person had entered his body. I couldn't believe this was Dave. But my fascination gave way, and quickly, to reality: I was a woman in a desert sharing a small space with a man in rage.

That night, I lay awake, perfectly still, trying to determine if he was finally sleeping, trying hard not to make noise. Never in my life have I made myself so small, a bird burrowed in the bushes. The campfire still smoldered just outside the tiny mesh flap, but we had both become someone else. When finally the tent swelled with the morning heat, it was as if night had taken the terror with it, folded it inside the sky with the rest of the evening's darkness. He turned to me, apologized.

"I don't know what," he said, "I was thinking."

It's a fluke, I told myself.

I wish I could go to that girl in the desert. I wish I could tell her it was not a fluke.

What happened in Colorado happened, too, in New Mexico, and Oklahoma, and on return visits to California, and it began to happen, with increasing frequency, in our small home in central Ohio, where we were just beginning to build our life. Picture our planters overrun with basil, our pantry boasting his local honey, our red plastic Adirondack chairs angled for conversation in the backyard beneath the bedroom window where, on hot nights, he'd rage at me.

One night, late, while helping me stretch new sheets on the guest bed upstairs, he started crying, screaming, told me I was a ruined woman, and he a ruined man, and that we had made a path to hell. Then he wept and prayed to God before bending over himself in exhaustion.

"I don't want to hate you," he told me mournfully.

A ruined woman, he repeated, as if I was a rotting fruit, a nectarine soft with flies.

~

Any time I try to explain what began to take shape after that first largely beautiful year with Dave, I think about a thundercloud I witnessed once from a plane.

Less shades of slate, less *obviously angry,* it was more a concentration of lightning pulsing through the clouds, self-contained. The lightning never struck the ground, never made contact with anything other than itself.

From the outside—from below—no one could feel our charge, the way Dave was splitting open and cascading, bathing everything in hot, white light, or the way my body had become—somehow, in his eyes—something tainted, filthy, vile, worthy of punishment. He grew colder, increasingly unknowable, distant, *hostile.* Some nights, he said nearly nothing. Other nights he spoke, which was often worse.

"I don't love you," he insisted. "I never did."

One afternoon, I took out the trash and found a card I'd made for him poking out from a bag inside the dumpster. I dug my hands through the plastic like a lunatic, feeling feral, feeling ashamed, until I came upon more mementos: a ticket stub from a play we'd seen, a photo of us at Christmas, my body slumped around his beside a tree. All of it was covered in eggshells and orange peels and the detritus of our days. I pulled each object from the trash, wiped each clean of coffee grounds.

I put them in my pocket, as if that might remedy the problem.

I can't say why he never outright left—or left *definitively*—but I suspect it was some variation of the shame that kept me calling him back: we wanted to redeem ourselves. Dave, for the actions he felt were sinful, and me for the judgment he'd made about me. I wanted to convince him he was wrong, that I was lovable, valuable, *worthy*.

I hated the ways in which I was bargaining. Dave's behavior—and my reaction to it—ran counter to everything I knew about the way women deserved to be treated. Had a friend told me she was in a relationship with someone who treated her this way, I would have insisted she break up with him. I knew no one deserved to feel so unloved, but I cared for Dave more than I'd cared about anyone, and his opinion of me mattered—mattered more than that of my friends or family, mattered more than that of neighbors or colleagues. And I still felt embarrassed by my own cruelty, the way I'd sat in his apartment in San Francisco when he'd first addressed his virginity and how I'd laughed and rolled my eyes. I hadn't afforded him respect in that moment, and now he would afford me no respect whatsoever.

Also, there was this: I thought I owed him a time of transition. Dave had moved across the country for me, and it seemed the least I could do was endure his outbursts, which seemed above all to come from a place of profound shame and self-loathing. By winter, however, he slumped away when I touched his shoulder, and I realized that I was justifying these violent outbursts the same way I'd spent much of my life justifying other violent outbursts. I no longer recognized him, and it was hard not to think about the many men I'd known who had been good men to me before—and sometimes even *while*—they were terrible to someone else.

~

Dave was not the first man to inspire fear. Like many women, I have feared for my safety and my body for years. I have feared, if we're speaking frankly, of what men might do to it.

This morning with Joy in Fairbanks, for example, is the eight-year anniversary of the night a close college friend—a man I would characterize as sweet, soft-spoken, calm, with a voice like a folk singer, fingers thin like a pianist's—walked me home from our regular bar and then returned to his own apartment, where he brutally murdered the woman he loved in an attempt to take his own life.

Emily Silverstein was nineteen years old, an on-and-off-again girlfriend my friend Kevin had called because he was depressed, and when she showed up at his apartment, he told her he was suicidal. He held a kitchen knife to his neck. When Emily lunged to intervene, he stabbed her twenty-seven times in the neck and upper torso. Then he wept over her body and phoned the local police, saying, *I am sorry,* saying, *Will you come?*

In the year that followed, I met—and intensely attached myself to—the unrepentant, wandering-eyed drunk responsible for my bruised knee. The man I dated after him was a nature enthusiast I'd met one balmy summer evening as I was stoking a bonfire with a friend at a local state park. He was camping in the site next to ours, and when I asked him about his life, he revealed to me suddenly that his former live-in girlfriend had been cheating on him for several months.

"I could no longer live," he said, cinematically, "inside her house of lies."

It was a beautiful line, ripe with poeticism, and I told him this, which made him smile.

We spent a few weeks together, and I thought of him with fondness, believed in some way that he had healed me, had served as a very necessary reminder that not all men want to hurt women. We spent those hot summer evenings outside restaurants and bars, amid crickets and heat and hotter pavement, ordering round after round, and suddenly everything good felt endless. We both agreed the world had brought us together in what could only be described as a dramatic show of tenderness and necessary respite and romantic grace.

But I later found out that he'd fractured a woman's skull in three different places just one month before I met him. He'd thrown her against a wall.

It took me two hours after I heard the news to work up the courage to call and ask him if it was true.

"I mean, yeah," he said, reluctant, "but you should know what she did first."

Never in my life had I felt so ashamed, as if I'd struck him as a woman who might entertain such violence as justifiable.

These relationships established a foundation Dave would later build upon. Those moments stretched back into childhood, to a shotgun-style prefab on the edge of the woods in Pennsylvania.

Set against an abandoned fire station and an abandoned restaurant and, beyond, an abandoned mill, my friend Amanda's house was located in the farthest corner of our school district, in a place the suburban sprawl had not yet reached, not yet bought up and bulldozed. We joked about it sometimes: how the very place where Amanda lived was a place no one else wanted to be.

"Including my own father," Amanda joked.

He left when she was just a baby.

But things were getting better—her mother had remarried, and Amanda's new stepfather, Tim, worked as a mechanic and built things Amanda's mom couldn't afford: a swing set and a backyard deck where, weekend mornings, she sunned herself in a hot-pink tankini, raising Virginia Slims to her sun-cracked lips.

It was nearly Halloween when Amanda invited me over for my first sleepover, and we made cut-and-bake jack-o'-lantern cookies sliced straight from the plastic tubing. The cookies tasted like garbage but were redeemed by their undercooked centers, which we snatched from the still-hot parchment, wadding the dough against our gums, biting off one eye and then the other until all that was left was a toothy grin.

Night came, and we sat on the plump, plush couch watching *Jeopardy!* while Tim and Amanda's mom chain-smoked cigarettes. The room was gray and hazy, and light bent like it does underwater, washing out the popcorn ceiling, giving the flannel furniture warm, dull edges. My eyes burned every time I blinked, and my tongue moved over gritty teeth. I had never before been around cigarette smoke, much less a small room full of it, and Tim seemed to have this sense. He kept looking over at me, observing.

Amanda and her mother were in the kitchen popping popcorn before the eight o'clock movie began. Tim slid closer beside me on the couch, my body seeping into his as he sank into the soft interior and placed one rough, large hand on the small of my rounded thigh. He squeezed it as if to see how soft I was, the quality of my meat.

"I am so excited that you're sleeping over," he said. It meant so much to Amanda, even more to him. A sense, he said, of normalcy.

From the couch, I swore I saw Amanda's mother in the kitchen, swore she looked away so as not to see me.

When they returned moments later, their bowls heaping with buttery popcorn, I coughed and said I hurt—something in my body, I was too shaken to think of what.

"I don't feel well," I said. "I think I need to go back home."

Amanda and her mother looked at me and grimaced. Tim looked at me intently.

I called my parents and cried: *I hurt, I hurt, I hurt.* I did not know how to put into language the violation that had just occurred, so *I hurt* was all I said. It was all I'd say for several decades.

Tim insisted he'd take me back, and he told Amanda that she should stay. He wouldn't want her to miss the prime-time movie, or the final round of *Jeopardy!*, that reveal of whose handwriting is least legible, that important question on the Ancient Greeks.

In the pickup truck, he put his hand on my thigh a second time. This time, he sounded angry as he spoke.

Is this because we don't have money?

Is this because we didn't go to college?

Is this because of our small house, our tiny couch, our television?

There were four miles between Amanda's house and mine, miles that traced wilderness and all we'd made from wilderness before we abandoned that as well. We passed buildings boarded up and vacant foreclosed homes. When at last we reached my driveway and my mother swung open the front door, I pushed past her and up the stairs. Tim shrugged and said something smart, scuffed his feet against the stoop.

Maybe another time, he offered. Maybe I was still too young.

I was—he was right—too young: too young to defend myself, too young to know how to condemn his actions, too young to understand that it's rarely the outside that harbors danger, rarely the strangers on our sidewalks who pose the biggest threat to our collective lives.

It's the men we date and marry, the men like Tim everywhere, and they're building swing sets in our own backyards.

~

With Joy in her truck cab, I don't know what's worth sharing and what's implied simply by silence.

"A man is no animal," I repeat, "but I'm just as guilty as you are when it comes to thinking it's my job to fix troubled men."

My relationships lined up like dominoes: one after another they fell. One experience of exploitation led to another and then another until, eventually, they consumed my life. For months, I'd fixated on Dave's goodness: my sweet boyfriend, a man who hand-pressed tortillas in my kitchen to mariachi music, who placed wry figurines around the house with little signs protesting work on Saturdays, or grading past 9:00 p.m.

Dave, I'd thought, *is good.*

But the distinction between *good* and *frightening* had collapsed entirely, and what had grown in its place was a hard pebble of fear.

6.

Outside the landscape is unfolding, trees thinning with every mile. We've risen up and out of nowhere to arrive at a place called Yukon River Camp, a tan modular unit adjacent to the Yukon River about 120 miles up the road. Thick patches of stubborn ice skirt the building's edges, and the parking lot is yellow dust, releasing clouds as we pull in. **FOOD, LODGING, FUEL, GIFTS!** a sign reads. The doorway is a bright turquoise.

Joy shifts the truck into park and whistles as we hop out. Dust immediately covers my boots' laces. I like the way they look. I am, in fact, so enamored by the sight of this physical proof of my trip with Joy that my eyes remain on the ground, admiring the dusty leather, so it's not until Joy holds the door that I notice the life-size bear butt painted across a boarded-up window.

"A bear broke in here once," Joy says, answering the question I've yet to ask. She points. "This butt re-creates the scene."

Inside, the world is warm and smells of cinnamon. It's midmorning in the Arctic, and someone is making sticky buns. After peeing in the state-of-the-art aluminum toilets designed with the Japanese in mind—metal basins that show our reflection, and automated everything—I meet Joy at the front counter, where she's sorting through packaged tea.

"Gotta get that herbal energy!" she tells me, seizing a bag of chamomile. I inquire about the spicy soup, advertised in looping cursive behind the register.

"Yeah, weird, right?" the attendant says. Her name is Ann, and her dark hair is tucked back in a high ponytail, save for two tendrils that curl around her face like fresh confetti. "We didn't used to do much food," she tells me. "Sandwiches, mostly. But we're a stopping point for ships coming up and down the Yukon River. Not to mention"—she smiles at Joy—"all you truckers, because you've got some kind of appetite. And now, of course, we've got the Japanese. So many Japanese. They're all about the northern lights, you know? Or seeing the Arctic Circle? So we started offering Asian soup recently. Thought a sign out front might stir curiosity. And spicy soup, let me tell you. It's been a real boon for us."

I offer a scale of one to ten, and Ann tells me their soup is an eleven.

"Perfect for you!" Joy prods.

I'm not hungry, but I order anyway, because who turns down ramen in the wilderness?

Ann turns and ladles fresh noodles and then fresh stock into a bowl, bathing everything in luscious broth. I am surprised, when she places the bowl on a tray in front of me, how full and hot and hearty it is, with delicate curls of authentic ramen rung around baby bok choy and slivered radishes.

"Aw, baby lettuces!" Joy croons, pointing at my bok choy.

I find a rotating carousel of condiments along the wall—Sriracha and red pepper flakes and a spicy chili oil. Ann tells me the tourists want their options.

"It's great, though," she tells me, "because we've had to up our game."

I add a little bit of everything. I can feel my taste buds tingle.

"SPICE GIRL!" Joy shouts from her seat by the wall. She throws her arms up in an awkward dab.

"Spice up your life," I taunt. I take my seat beside her, lean into her, heavy.

In the Yukon Camp, surrounded by postcards of shimmering fish and mountains stiff as peaks of white meringue, Joy blows into her chamomile, wafts the aromatic steam against her face, and says, "I've been beaten, knocked around a bunch. But it became important for me to get back up even stronger than I was."

I look at her and wait.

"My whole life," she says, "I tethered myself to men, thinking this is what makes a woman."

Less anatomy or biology than a certain kind of intrepid, dogmatic endurance.

"But when Jake left, it was only me. And for a while, I made that work. *More* than work. *Excel.*" She takes a sip of tea and runs her finger around the rim. "But I wasn't trained to think that way, that I could do stuff on my own. No woman is, I think. So when I met James—you know."

James—a fellow employee at the Fort Knox Gold Mine and the man who leaned into me at church, saying, "That little lady is a legend."

I like James very much.

Joy, too, liked him instantly. A recent divorcé with children of his own, James shared her lunch break and love of family. Joy liked that he brought his meals from home, rather than going out with the other guys. How sometimes he packed baby carrots, or grapes, or cherry tomatoes, proof that he was someone who took care of his body.

"I met James and I thought, *There*," Joy tells me. "Like he was God's way of honoring me after a bit. God saw what I had done—He let me slosh it out in the mechanic bay, washing things covered in grease, working hard to keep my promise that Saturdays were for worship— and He knew that time would make me humble. And when it did, I thought, *He brought me James.*"

With James's encouragement, Joy got her commercial driver's license. That way she could make her own schedule, they agreed, and earn a better salary, and anyway, she was made for something better than the work of washing things men used.

"He supported me," Joy said, "and wanted me out there in the world. I didn't know what I was doing, really, but there was this *one* other trucker woman—her name was Tina—and she was the only woman I knew in that line of work, so I just began following her around, studying. She said I'd get it, and eventually, I did."

With her new job in trucking, Joy was able to keep Sabbath, and now she brought James with her. They sat together in the pews and afterward went out for lunch. Usually spicy Korean, she tells me, grinning.

"I thought it was God," Joy says. "I thought it was God rewarding me—for my patience, and for keeping my commitment to my faith."

"Yeah," I say, but I'm unsure. On the one hand, I agree, but I also know from experience how dangerous it can be to interpret everything as God's reward or God's punishment.

"I met James," Joy continues, "and I thought God was honoring me for the hard work of leaving Jake, of raising my boys alone, of knowing what I deserved."

I picture Joy in those early days, some twenty years ago, sitting out at the mechanic bay picnic table. I picture Joy laughing, the first time in a long while, and how it must have felt when James asked her out, after so much solitude. The movie tickets and the popcorn, crunching beneath their feet on that theater floor. The joviality of their first date, and then a second, and then a third. Dave driving me to Bayfront Park to watch the planes pull up at such great angles, and how he drew my body into his, the air around us cool as it swept across the bay. How there was no place else I'd rather be.

"I understand," I say.

"But I see the problem in my thinking now," Joy says. "James—he was not without his problems."

"What do you mean?" I ask.

"I mean." Joy pauses. "I mean, as a woman, you get bumped around so much, you tend to think one kind of bumping is better than another."

She moves her hands quietly, struggling to find the words. Before I can ask her to clarify, she reaches for her truck keys.

"I know that to follow Christ is to suffer," she says, more as a reminder to herself than to me. "And it's not the suffering I have a problem with. It's distinguishing the *right kind* of suffering: Christ's suffering and man's suffering."

I don't want Joy to believe her suffering is a test from God. I don't want her or the rest of the world to view her abuse as the stuff that builds character.

What doesn't kill you only makes you stronger, but how infrequently this is the case, especially for those of us well versed in the world of intimate partner violence, or the millions of Americans who are marginalized, criminalized, exploited. It feels like a particularly prescriptive, conciliatory feminine mantra: we are uniquely strengthened by our pain, which the world is all too eager to dole out to us. Our bodies—dead, mutilated, missing—are the foundations of countless movies, books, the flashy openings of true crime television, and we are gorgeous as wounded women. We are prettified by our pain. More often, it seems to me, what doesn't kill you doesn't make you stronger but becomes a blemish you work your whole life to find a way to live with.

"I think the problem," I say, finally, "is that I don't come from faith, so I feel pretty darn capable of distinguishing."

Suffering is simply suffering. It's dangerous to glorify.

"And yet?" she asks me, probing.

"And yet I haven't acted on that distinction," I admit, "for quite some time."

Back in her truck, my body sinks into her passenger seat.

"I don't know what that's about," I say.

Joy takes a long sip from her Styrofoam. I wonder if she'll inquire further. Instead, she nods. "Amen," she says. "You're right, I think. You're right. And that's the burden of our gender—that we know better, *but we were built to love.*"

It's not the verb I would choose. Still I smile and I nod, and Joy nods and puts the key in the ignition.

We pull back onto the road, and suddenly Joy turns to me, her whole face flat, as if recognizing something very important.

"You know sometimes what I think?" she asks. "I think women are better off alone."

~

Happiness is a radical act, and I began to lose my capacity for it. Happiness was, in fact, the first thing to go. Once you are convinced of your lack of worth, you can't easily be convinced otherwise, or that you deserve to have something better, or that your suffering, even, really matters.

Back in the truck alongside Joy, I turn her words over in my mind.

As a woman, you get bumped around so much, you tend to think one kind of bumping is better than another.

I believed my bumping with Dave was manageable, and I burrowed further into our isolation—in part to protect myself, but largely to protect him. I skipped four weddings, three baby showers. For however convincing I might have been with others in the day-to-day of my tumultuous life, I knew that I would risk ruin if forced to answer probing questions from pretty young women in bridesmaids' dresses, or pretty young women at baby showers, holding up pastel blankets they'd knit. No one could know what our private life looked like, because if they did, they'd tell me to leave him. I worried I wasn't capable. So every night, I endured his shame and silence, and the physical manifestations that took place in my body as a result: grinding my teeth in my sleep— to the point of five chipped teeth in one year alone—and headaches that lasted through morning, and stomach pains so great they made my body curl as I absently pushed food around my plate.

On the way home from work each evening, I sat in traffic knowing I was driving home to a man whose mood I could not predict, whose anger I could not fathom, whose disgust for me in time had made me disgusted with myself. I found myself grateful for any red light, any minute *here* or *here* or *here* that would allow a little extra time for his attitude to readjust. Any word I said could set him off; any symbol might come from God. I couldn't help but think of Puritans: how they'd persecute anyone, everyone, over perceived "signs and wonders," how they beheaded women accused of witchcraft, how they hanged them until they died.

I was not without my head; I could breathe. I arrived home some nights to tacos—flank steak marinated in Korean barbecue sauce, tinged with rings of tiny scallions and spicy ginger and pickled peppers, the glistening kernels of yellow corn—sweetened gold for all my waiting. Other evenings, to his instability and the ongoing accusation that I did not know God. He'd yell and shake and scream and then isolate in another room.

"I'm not the man I used to be," he told me once.

I couldn't bring myself to disagree, and these admissions felt like breakthroughs, though he lingered on them only briefly.

Some nights, Dave threatened to pack up all his things and leave. Other nights, he did. And you would think I would have been relieved. But in his absence, it was only fear I felt. The news depicted an outside world intent on hurting and killing women, and it made aloneness something to fear. The screaming in my own living room was at least *familiar*, *recognizable*, and it always stopped before it got worse.

~

We've driven for half an hour in silence—ostensibly in awe of the natural world, the gray-blue everything outside our window—when Joy asks me what I teach, and I find myself in a preemptive state of censorship. I don't know how Joy votes, what political party she ascribes to, but I know my answer has the power to alienate us from each other.

"I teach writing workshops mostly," I say. "I teach students to write pretty things."

Joy smirks, smacks the steering wheel. "I always thought I'd be a good teacher," she says. "I love people—getting to know them, getting on their level."

I look at her with consideration. As an Alaskan, and an oil field supplier, Joy might have predictable politics, but she's also demonstrated—here, and always—that she places great value on her independence, in affirming her agency, her autonomy. Would Joy consider herself a feminist? Or would she balk and dismiss the term?

"Getting on their level is really great," I say. "Especially when you teach students the age I teach."

"Oh, I bet," Joy says. "I bet they look up to you!"

But what to say about all those afternoons back in Ohio that I spent teaching primarily young women in my contemporary feminist literature class? The way the light fell across their faces and how they took careful notes on what I said, because they seemed to believe that my education, my expertise, made me a strong woman, my own advocate?

I designed the course around women and nonbinary writers I loved and valued—assigned essays that explored intersectional approaches to feminism by Rebecca Solnit, Tressie McMillan Cottom, Lacy M. Johnson, Lidia Yuknavitch, and Terese Marie Mailhot, among others. That winter, as my relationship with Dave escalated, we lingered over passages whose truths I knew but pretended I didn't: that women are assaulted and killed most often in their homes, most frequently by men who know them, in 93 percent of all homicides by current or former intimate male partners.

Boyfriends, husbands, lovers.

We read the risks were greater for women of color, greater still for women who identified as LGBTQI+, greatest for those who identified as transgender—never mind what it meant to be more than one or all of those.

Thirty percent of African American women, we read, have been raped, beaten, or stalked by an intimate male partner.

Forty-five percent of Asian Americans.

Fifty percent of all Native Americans.

"And all of these groups at higher risk," I taught them, "are far less likely to seek human services or visit a hospital or women's shelter than white women, in large part because they understand that while the crimes committed against their bodies matter, the systems of power will insist they don't."

My students concentrated, scribbled things down. They wrote powerful essays about our culture, about the many ways violence against women was rampant, systemic, and, ultimately, all about control.

Each afternoon, I finished teaching and watched my students leave, and then I put my things away and prepared to return to my abusive partner. Perhaps even greater than my desire to overlook what felt like an increasingly fundamental schism in both my and Dave's moral fiber was my desire to believe I had not ended up in my circumstance despite the knowledge I'd spent years accumulating, despite the feminist texts I read and studied, despite the dynamic students I instructed daily who—Joy was right—looked up to me.

But as the Me Too movement gained momentum and the national news increasingly centered women's narratives, I began to find a foothold, a necessary bridge between my profession and the private life I shared with Dave. It became overwhelmingly clear to me why it was so important, so downright necessary, for our nation to witness women at every level and in every industry risk shame and consequence to point out their harassment, their abuse, and, above all, their abusers.

Dave, on the other hand, likened the Me Too movement to tuna fishing.

"Sure, you net some of the bad guys," he explained once—the *tuna*—"but you're bound to get a lot of dolphins."

And sometimes, he intoned, those dolphins were nice guys who'd just acted in the heat of the moment or weren't in their best state of mind.

"Everyone makes mistakes," he said. "Doesn't mean they should lose everything."

As if a woman who'd been raped, harassed, assaulted, a woman who had been stripped of her dignity or her autonomy, had lost nothing of comparable value, or should be held responsible for the repercussions of those crimes.

Then one night, during a particularly awful fight, Dave worried aloud that I would accuse *him*, someday, of rape.

"What?" I asked, incredulous, certain I hadn't heard him right, only of course—*of course*—I had.

But for Dave, an accusation of rape could be something women offered when they wanted to indisputably harm a man. Personally or professionally. Whether it was true or not.

Sometimes, he explained, *sure*, rape was real. But other times it was just a way for a woman to win an argument. The ultimate chess move.

"Okay," I said, blinking.

Dave's worry that I would falsely accuse him confirmed an intuition I'd long suspected: Dave did not trust me, or women. He considered me a dangerous live wire. His accusation simultaneously made me the most villainized type of woman and the worst archetype among us: a woman who would claim she was the victim of a very true and epidemic crime in a desperate power grab of petty revenge.

Dave never raped me.

But our conversation was a catalyst, the first moment where I began, finally, to want out, though oddly not for my own safety or well-being. All along, I'd been so buried in my denial that I still thought it was possible: that his goodness might come back, that he might stop screaming at me, that together we could raise a family: a daughter we'd practically willed into being when we first met, discussing the way we'd raise her, the things we'd teach her about the world. We'd joked she'd have the charisma of her father, the intrepid drive of her mother, and of course her own little whimsies, evident in plastic art she'd melt and mold for us.

But how could I ever build a life with him? How could we ever raise a daughter, or even a son, for that matter? I had reached a point where I barely valued myself, but I could see the value of our potential child. Only by looking outside myself—looking to something that did not yet exist—could I see how wrongly I was being treated. If Dave grew angry like this with me, the woman he claimed he loved most, and if he called me ruined and sinful, and if he screamed at me until I shook, what would prevent him from being awful, I worried, to any daughter we made together, or instilling in our son the same shame that permeated his views on everything?

What did it matter, how long this kindness lasted? How generous he was with others? What would he say to them, to *his own children*, about their bodies inside our house?

7.

The soup of the day at Coldfoot Camp—170 miles up the Dalton Highway—is spicy Cajun with red beans and rice and an occasional spoonful of rounded sausage. Camp is just this restaurant, itself just a handful of tables, and a row of rustic guest rooms across a dusty parking lot, where two hundred dollars a night will buy you a twin-size bed, a toilet and a shower, and eight hours of reliable heat. It is the anywhere of nowhere, and it smells like hamburgers.

"Here is a truth every Alaskan will agree upon," Joy says as we walk in. "To be Alaskan is to love your soup. Get out your notebook. Write that down."

At the restaurant counter, I meet Chelsea, a twenty-six-year-old with blunt brown bangs who moved to Coldfoot last May. Chelsea's job is to ladle soup, turn the hotel rooms over, and bring heaping plates of fries to truckers and chartered tourists. When I speak to her, she's arranging neat rows of chocolate chip cookies—the kind Joy warned me about—that are as wide and round as my face.

A few years younger than me in a town that boasts no residents, Chelsea has me wondering what she does with all her time.

"Other than work?" She laughs. "Because I work pretty much all the time. I hike. I walk. I stare. I don't know, I find things to do."

It's not much different from life in a city, Chelsea explains: you wake up, you work, you eat. One life is the same as another, and a day here is a day anywhere, except there's no bank or grocery store, no mall or Panera Bread. There's nothing commercial, actually, and also no town or church or house. There are only customers. They are always hungry and often dirty. They want coffee, coffee, coffee. They want to know how recently she saw the northern lights, or if there's any wildlife around worth photographing. They're always unpeeling layers. It's negative thirty degrees in the winter, forty if you're lucky in the heat of summer.

I ask her what she does for fun. Chelsea smiles. Sometimes? Hitchhikes.

"Up here, there's only two places people are ever going," she says. "Either back to Fairbanks or north to Prudhoe Bay."

The first time she chose to hitchhike, she couldn't stop herself from smiling.

"Like an idiot," she says. She spreads her lips wide like a horror film caricature of someone off their rocker, deranged. "Big dumb grin, like I'm being wild, you know? But people up here—you feel safer. Everyone is just here to work, and they don't want to risk their job by doing something awful to a woman. So I hitchhiked. I wasn't scared. I thought, *I'm going to the city.* I'd been isolated all this time. I had a weekend off. Why not re-associate with society?

"I went to the movie theater," she says. "And a couple downtown bars. It was December, and I'd been up here for a couple months, totally snow-stuck."

Then she went to the grocery store.

"I bought a bunch of vegetables. I'd made a grocery list before I left, sorted out all the things everyone up here wanted—beer, mostly, and snacks—and then I caught a ride back with another trucker, an old guy who had a hamburger and tater tots in his lap when he picked me up. He was really sweet, which is great. I get a little nervous sometimes hitchhiking—you know how it is."

I do know how it is.

I also know from my nights spent planning this trip that it is more dangerous to be a woman in Alaska than anywhere else in America. This is a state that routinely ranks highest among reported cases of domestic violence, and that violence is largely perpetrated against Indigenous Alaskan women. According to a 2010 report by the United States Department of Justice, as many as four out of five Indigenous Alaskans will be subjected to domestic violence in their lifetime, and as many as 50 percent will be raped, beaten, or stalked, a number that is more than double that of white women in America. This violence occurs largely in the interior and in small, remote towns or on reservations, which often lack police departments and, quite frequently, even access roads leading in and out. Reaching these women can take days and often requires boats or planes that are many times delayed by Alaska's weather. There is no 911 to call, no emergency Amber Alert. Community members are the first—and often only—responders to cases of domestic violence and sexual assault. It is for these and other reasons that Indigenous Alaskan women are far less likely than other races to receive medical care, access resources, or have criminal charges brought against their abusers.

Women rarely go missing on the Dalton Highway, but they go missing more frequently in Alaska than almost any other state. Poor data collection and reporting compound the issue, making it hard to know the actual number of missing and murdered Indigenous Alaskan women, but data gathered by the National Crime Information Center suggests at least 5,700 Native American women have been reported missing nationwide since 2016 alone, and that number is likely an undercount, according to advocacy groups. Thirty-one percent of cases involve Native women eighteen years or younger, and as many as one-third aren't even listed in law enforcement records.

"We were both from the Midwest," Chelsea continues, "so he and I had plenty to talk about. When he dropped me off back here at Coldfoot Camp, I unloaded my bounty, and everyone was so happy, because they hadn't seen Cheetos in months."

And anyway, she says, life up here beats life down there. Chelsea graduated in 2003 from a college in Wisconsin, then spent four years working as an exterminator.

"Bugs," she says, "all kinds of bugs."

She found her current job by searching one keyword—*Alaska*—and figured Coldfoot would be an adventure. So what if she was a glorified waitress, innkeeper, and maid rolled into one? She would be these things in *Alaska*. And anyway, it beat bug genocide.

"Every day up here," she says, "you meet someone new. Sometimes that someone is a tourist from another country—India, China, Singapore—and sometimes that person is a trucker you've seen forty bajillion times before, but it takes hitching a ride back north to realize all the stuff you've got in common. And sometimes"—at this she smirks—"sometimes that person is a moose or caribou, and he's just chilling in the parking lot, much to the delight of all the tourists. But every day it's something different. And you learn a little something from everyone."

~

They say the third time's a charm.

I say it's when I knew Dave could hurt me.

He had screamed at me in Ohio, and he had screamed at me in a tent in Colorado, but in early spring, in March, he began to use his body in unprecedented, physical ways meant to terrorize me into submission.

We were visiting his friends and family back in San Francisco, staying in an apartment I had booked for its white everything: white desk, white bedspread, white rug—all evidence of a couple who lived their days without our darkness.

San Francisco was a place of sunshine, eternal warmth, endless summer. It's where we went on our first date, where we'd sat on piers and ridden hand in hand on Ferris wheels. I'd hoped that something about us would be remedied by a visit, that our fights would not follow us.

One night, we went to dinner with Dave's friend—a double date at an Italian restaurant with white lights strung among the palms, votive tea candles, and sensible portions arranged aesthetically, each noodle's end looped elegantly on the plate.

The friend was a man Dave had met through church and known for years, a fellow follower of Christ who Dave hoped could mentor him in this time of crisis. I didn't want to go, but he'd begged.

"It would mean the world," he'd said.

I ordered the pappardelle. We were seated at a table set with white linen beneath the trees. No one touched the sliced baguette or the miniature jar of homemade butter. The man's young wife spoke to me about her career in interior design—the couches, the south-facing windows—while the man, two feet from my plate to his, warned Dave aloud about our relationship.

"This is an uneven yoking," he said. He nodded in my direction. "You have to be careful with a girl like this. She will draw you from your faith. Consider Calvin."

Calvin had proposed to an atheist. Now they never saw him. They were convinced he had turned from God.

"This girl," he repeated. "I do not see this ending well."

The young woman continued on about the antiquity of orange leather, the aesthetic of globe-domed lighting. I wanted to make a scene. Instead I simply watched as the man I loved nodded silently. Dave did not defend me, did not relay the ways I'd bent for him, our church services and daily prayer. Said nothing of my heart, nothing of my character, nothing of the woman I had *demonstrated* myself to be.

When at last they dropped us off at the rental house I'd hoped would fix us, I caved. There, in the middle of the street, I broke down.

"Inside," he said. *"Inside."*

Inside, I cried and he began to yell. I was wrong, he shouted, to interpret his friend's statement as callous, or cold, or cruel, wrong to criminalize his silence, wrong not to see the tremendous value behind such a simplified evaluation of our pairing. He screamed, gesticulating wildly with his hands, then backed me into a corner of the bedroom, and then a corner of the bathroom, and then finally behind the toilet, where my body began to shake, tremor, *seize*, because I finally understood that he might actually hurt me.

I shook, terrified. I looked down at my arms, my torso, at the way my whole body buckled, the way *he had made my whole body buckle*, and Dave—he watched it, too.

After a moment, he left without a word, slamming the door behind him.

Back in the bedroom, I sat on the comforter, unmoving. There were plenty of people I could call, plenty of friends or family members who would help to extricate me from the situation, but I didn't call anyone.

I'm okay, I told myself. *He just scared me. He was upset.*

When he returned hours later, it was early dawn, a white-pink sky punctuating the air beneath the palm trees. He showed me a photograph he'd taken of two trees twined together. Another sign from God. God hadn't given up on us, he said. We just had to continue working on growing together.

In his hands were two cappuccinos. On their surface, wobbling fern-shaped foam.

"I talked to God behind this dumpster," he said, as if these words made sense. "He told me that growing together often causes great discomfort."

He handed me my coffee. I felt his hands, warm, on mine. He always seemed to take such pleasure in taking care of me after he screamed, as if a showy display of tenderness might remedy the reason I needed it in the first place.

He sat on the bed beside me. I felt him reach for my arm, felt his fingers trace first my chest and then my collarbone and then my chin, stroking the skin he screamed at but never struck.

"That shaking was weird," he said finally. "I don't know why your body did that."

I knew from the texts I taught that this was exactly how abuse functions: in gaslighting your reaction, your abuser begins to control your story. Your relationship to the world. Sometimes your relationship to your own body. They begin to rewrite the narrative: *That was weird, what your body did.*

The white bedsheets billowed around our ankles.

That was weird, I thought. *That was a weird thing my body did.*

~

I find Joy at the back of the restaurant, idling beside the trucker table, a long, glossy wooden slab reserved exclusively—a sign announces in three languages—for truckers.

Joy is sitting with a trucker named Mike, who looks no more than twenty-five. He wears a ball cap and cargo pants and a black hoodie that reads, *Diesel.* He's one of what Joy will later call "the new men," the kind who grew up on *Ice Road Truckers* and flew to Alaska to strike it rich, to feel a part of a still-wild America.

"Nothing wrong with those guys," Joy will tell me later, "but they don't respect the rules of the road. Tend to push it a little bit, go a little fast, a little hard. And that risks the safety of all of us."

At the trucker table, Mike dips chicken tenders into ranch dressing. He tells me it's his second year, says he's never had a job like this, says he plans to retire never.

"I don't think it'll ever get old."

Behind him hangs a series of framed photographs, news clippings, and homemade, inspired artwork meant to celebrate the men who drive the haul road. These are men like Georgie Spears, the cover face of the October 2006 *Truckers News*.

Ride with Alaska's Drivers on the Dangerous Haul Road! the caption reads.

In the photograph, Georgie wears denim overalls and holds a gallon-size plastic thermos full of coffee that reads, *Filler Up*.

Over on another wall, I find a collage of postcards sent from travelers all around the world, fans of *Ice Road Truckers*, and some from seasonal drivers, including a series from "MudD & Franny," who've sent loving dispatches from Iceland, from New Zealand, from the Mojave Desert and Santa Clarita.

There are framed photos of polar bears, and framed photos of the mountains, and framed photos of patrol cars with their lights lit up to warn of caribou crossing the road. There are advertisements for transport companies and inspirational posters about hard work. In one photograph, two male hands grasp each other, white but slick with grease, beneath the words *Hands That Work*.

I will not get hurt today, reads a poster-size photograph of a truck owned by Lynden Transport. In bold letters beneath: *That's my pledge!*

Everything seems like propaganda meant to make men forget about the risks associated with this line of work. But it's a painting that stops my heart. In it, an 18-wheeler cruises through the dark night, a round, smiling trucker at the wheel, but the body of the truck blends into Jesus, who is pointing aggressively, dogmatically, onward. *Fear Not, I Am with You,* a plaque beneath it reads.

"Do you know where we got this name?" an older trucker swivels around to ask me. He wears a green felt hat and blue flannel and is well into his seventies. His gray hair is tied back in a ponytail that extends to a delicate, thin braid, and he has the kindest face I've ever seen.

His name is Rich, he tells me, and he's one of Joy's best friends.

"*Best* friends," Joy tells me, clamping an arm around his shoulder. "Man, I love this guy."

"The story of this place," Rich tells me, "is the story of men who got scared."

Founded at the height of gold exploration in 1898, Coldfoot Camp was originally known as Slate Creek, and it featured a gambling hall, two roadhouses, two stores, and seven saloons. But after mounting concerns about Alaska's winter, several hundred of those gold prospectors got cold feet and retreated south, with hardly any gold to show for it.

"A few of them stayed," Rich tells me, "and thirteen miles further, in the tiny town of Wiseman, they pulled gold straight from the riverbeds."

"As if sanctified for bravery," another man adds. His name is Donald, he's about Rich's age, and he's eating steel-cut oatmeal with blueberries.

"They've got breakfast all day," Joy tells me. To Chelsea, she says, "I'll have a vegetable omelet with jalapeños, mushrooms, tomatoes. But no bell peppers, please. I'll be bummed out if there's bell peppers. And home fry wedges, please."

I order sunny-side-up eggs with hash browns, rye toast, and chewy bacon.

"So don't go getting cold feet now," Rich says, motioning to Joy. I am reminded of the text Joy sent me back in the airport, how she'd used those very words. "This little lady says she's taking you north to Prudhoe?"

"That's what she says," I say.

"You're in for a ride," Donald says. "This lady, she hauls pallets that weigh more than her!"

Rich turns to me. "You're going to notice a bunch of road markers these next few miles that all have women's names. Creeks and hills and turns—they're all named for the women of Wiseman, the ones who stayed and made this place flourish. I hate to say *prostitutes*, because their job had a different connotation back then; they were a vital part of the village. But anyway, that's what they were, and folks named the rivers and hills up here for them."

"That's pretty cool, I guess," I say. I watch Joy tear off the cover of a creamer and sniff it.

"Rich," Joy says, stirring her coffee, "he was one of my first friends up here. Been working this road—what?"

"Since it opened."

"Rich practically helped *build* the road," Joy jokes.

"You helped me. I'll never forget that time. One of my vents froze up on me. I was already up on Atigun Pass, and I needed to get back down to the bridge. I had the whole road blocked—there was a line of trucks behind me, and you were the only one to help."

"I was."

"And I'll never forget that time."

"We needed to get by you!" Donald adds, stirring his oatmeal.

Rich smiles. He turns back around to face me. "One rule, since you're new to this? If you ever break down or roll into a ditch, make sure you have the whole road blocked so no one can get by, because that way you're guaranteed to get some help."

He laughs. Donald laughs. I can't tell if they realize this is something I will never do.

"I'll make a note."

"You better, because that's unofficial protocol," he jokes. "Only us old-timers know that."

Our eggs come and we eat them.

"This is good," I say to Joy.

"So good," Joy agrees.

Behind her, Fox News warns us about Democrats. The camera cuts to Donald Trump speaking from behind a podium. He's wearing a blue suit and a blue tie and speaks with his hands across his chest. A ticker at the bottom reads, in all red, *FOX NEWS ALERT*.

"I blame the people who were running America," he says. "I blame presidents. I blame representatives."

A younger trucker watches, his chicken tender hovering in the air. Mustard drips onto the table. I slit my yolk and watch as Rich considers the carousel of jams.

That Donald Trump is a hero among these people—truckers, oil field workers, Alaskans more generally—comes as no surprise. This is a place that uniquely benefits from Republican policies, a region where the majority values financial profits more than the consequences of exploitation: of land, of people, of policy. The towns that exist up here—and indeed, the industries—exist solely for the purpose of economic gain, and for several decades, those gains ballooned. Thirty-five years ago, Prudhoe Bay—two hundred thousand sprawling acres, beneath which lie an estimated 25 billion barrels of crude oil—experienced its peak in oil production, with nearly two million barrels of refined oil produced daily. But times have changed, the oil has been depleted, and daily barrel output more recently has slowed to 280,000. Prices, too, have declined, and there is renewed global competition.

A few years ago, Joy tells me, the Prudhoe Bay Hotel—where we've booked a room for tonight—was overflowing with oil field workers and the many cooks and custodians and cafeteria attendants whose job it is to cater to them. But increasingly the halls are quiet, the fitness rooms cold and empty, and there's no longer a line to take a shower.

"It's hard not to worry," Joy says, "because I mean, *sure*, no one wants to wait just to get clean. But it makes a person wonder. What will become of the oil fields when oil is no longer present? What will become of the men and women who only know this life? What will become of *me*?"

It's not just black-and-white, she tells me, oil or no oil. It's a livelihood. It's a way earnest, hardworking people make their living, put food on tables.

"This place," she instructs, "was *built* on the promise of fortune. What do you do when that fortune dries up?"

"I don't know," I say.

You recalibrate, she tells me. Refigure. You find new land upon which to drill.

"The Arctic National Wildlife Refuge," she says—a vast stretch of untouched acreage often referred to as "America's last great wilderness." This area, which spans an unfathomable 19.6 million acres, is home to one of the most fragile and ecologically sensitive ecosystems in the world and some of our nation's most treasured animals—moose and wolverines, caribou, polar bears, and countless migratory birds—but also an estimated 5.7 to 16 billion barrels of unrefined crude oil.

The land was officially declared a federally protected area by President Eisenhower in 1960, and in the decades since, numerous presidents and congresses have successfully resisted efforts to allow oil and natural gas extraction, in no small part because the landscape's inhospitable climates and short annual growing season mean any disruption to the area provides little time for recovery. In aerial shots of the refuge taken as recently as 2018, you can still see the scars from vehicles used for exploration and seismic testing in the mid-1980s.

They zip like track marks across the tundra.

Drilling on the refuge, however, has long proven a Republican priority, and so the land is thrown into uncertainty with every new presidential election. Now, Joy tells me, with the GOP controlling the Senate, House, and presidency, drilling advocates are salivating, convinced that they're the closest they've ever been to industrializing America's last great wilderness.

"I don't know if I like it," Joy says, "but at least it's something, at least we're not *pretending* there is no problem, and that Alaskans' livelihoods do not matter." She takes a bite of her omelet. "I get it both ways, you know? That land is obviously important. But these people are my people. Their right to a living matters."

I think about her term, *my people*, about whose livelihoods do and do not matter.

According to Alaskan Republican senator Lisa Murkowski, drilling in the refuge would result in incalculable job opportunities for Alaskans and up to $1 billion in oil and natural gas revenue over the next ten years alone. Opponents counter her plan would net only a fraction of the projected revenue at the cost of irreparable environmental damage; one recent analysis conducted by the Center for American Progress reported Murkowski's plan "fails to consider production costs and fluctuating market conditions—including, most especially, low crude oil prices—and relies on outdated resource estimates."

Even more importantly, the project would result in widespread, permanent environmental damage, jeopardize the area's wildlife and fragile ecosystems, and decimate the Gwich'in tribe—the group of Indigenous Alaskans who've subsisted on that land for several thousand years.

"We are the caribou people," Gwich'in member Sarah James wrote in *Caribou Rising*. "Caribou are not just what we eat; they are who we are. They are in our stories and songs and the whole way we see the world."

The Gwich'in people, in particular, are fierce defenders of the land and adamant protestors against drilling for oil in the Arctic National Wildlife Refuge. Oil extraction in ANWR, they argue, would undoubtedly decimate the caribou herds along with so much of what makes their life possible.

"It's hard," Joy says. "It's hard. Obviously, I don't want anyone to lose their home, their hunting ground. And the Natives were here first. I get that; I honor that. But what about the rest of us when those oil fields are dry?"

I look at her and Rich and Donald and all the faces whose names I don't yet know. No part of me wants their livelihood to be threatened. I think but do not say that the Gwich'in, Tanana, Koyukon, and Iñupiat have a right to live, too, and inarguably more than anyone. This *was* their land first. These are the very concerns they will have to manage exponentially when their food and hunting sources are depleted, when crucial migration patterns are disrupted, when their villages are destroyed.

Joy looks at Trump and smirks. "I don't know," she says. "I think he's doing good."

Chelsea pours us more coffee, and Joy dumps it into two Styrofoam to-go cups.

"We should push on," she says. "It's late afternoon, and the National Weather Service predicts clear skies through the evening. If we leave now, you'll see the empty tundra at sunset, and on a night like tonight, there'll be sun dogs."

I feel some shameful relief, grateful for the reprieve that is a change in conversation topic. I ask her to define a sun dog.

"A sun dog," Joy tells me, "is an illusion."

It's a term to describe the way the sun's rays hit the tundra, forcing little vibrant rainbows, which form a halo over everything.

"Bright lights," she says, "everywhere," as if God Himself was ushering you to the finish line.

I picture my tiny terrier, bounding across a white expanse empty as the moon. I picture her pouncing on permafrost, digging her paws into that magic blue.

"That sounds beautiful," I say.

Rich and Donald are headed south. They both give me a hug.

"I'll tell you," Rich says, big hands on my shoulders, "if I had a professor like you—someone who worked to know all *kinds* of people—I would've gone to college."

"You've done well for yourself," I say. "But this is some kind of classroom."

"Rich and I like to joke," Joy says, "we *are* enrolled in college. We go to Dalton University."

They smile at each other. I want what they have in friendship.

"Bye," Joy says, finally. She hugs them both. "Maybe I'll catch you guys later this month?"

"We hope so," they say.

Joy leans into me as we push open the door and the cold air blows in.

"Donald's dad," she says, "he was a writer, just like you. Erwin S. Bourne. You should look him up. He wrote seven books, and Donald is always talking about how he's never read them. Never has the time. When he retires—when he's done trucking—he says he's going to rent a cabin in the middle of nowhere and finally read them, and I hope he does. Because guys up here? They have big dreams for their retirement. They say they're going to do stuff. But the truth is, and this isn't pretty, that they often die before they ever get that chance."

We climb into her truck. She sprays windshield wiper fluid, rinses the glass of bugs.

"This one guy, Leon?" she continues. "He told me a few months ago he was going to retire and go out to a cabin to fish. Three months later, he fell off a blade—that's what we call the trucks plowing the roads—and died a few days later. You just don't know. You do not know."

I watch Rich and Donald climb back in their trucks. They wave tentatively, and I wave.

"I didn't expect their kindness."

Joy nods, draws her hand up to her forehead in a swift salute. "Yeah," she says. "Those guys. They're the nicest men I know."

I think, fleetingly, of James. Joy pulls her phone from her pocket, studies it.

"I've got a few bars thanks to GCI," she says, "so I'm gonna give home a ring real quick before we disappear again. James will want to know how we're doing."

She lowers herself from the truck, puts her hand on her hip, and squints through the dust and mosquitos. James picks up and I can hear her.

"It *better be* your hot darlin' wife!" She laughs.

Alone in her truck, I pretend it is my truck. I pretend it's the big rig and I'm Mothertrucker. I lean across the seat, place my hand on the steering wheel, feel the tight grip of leather beneath my fingers. I reach for her sunglasses on the dash, put them on my head.

"This is God's land!" I say.

Who is Joy, really? I flip through the contents of her door, find a veterinarian-prescribed anti-itch spray, a hairbrush, some black hair ties. There's a Colgate 360 toothbrush, an Australian Gold bronze accelerator.

Who would've ever thought Joy Mothertrucker would use bronze accelerator?

I find a package of bobby pins, a pink air freshener in Morning Fresh. There's a West Valley High School student parking permit for the 2016–2017 year—Samantha's—and a '70s Gold CD, plus a handicap sticker because of her injured knee.

From outside the truck, I hear Joy ask for Samantha, and then she squeals.

"Samantha!" she says. "Samantha, 16.8! You're never gonna believe what your mommy did!"

She is ecstatic over her mileage. I know from previous conversations that Samantha has her learner's permit, and they've been casually competing in the pickup to see who can get the best gas mileage.

"Not bad for the Dalton Highway," she teases. "Someday you're gonna have to try it."

I watch in the rearview mirror as she laughs, hangs up, holds the phone to her chest, and sighs. I watch her with her sunglasses on. Then she turns to climb back in the truck.

"James says it's going to start blowing up here tomorrow," she says, cracking the door. She grabs the sunglasses from my head.

"What's that mean?"

"Means you're in for a show!" she says. She slaps the wheel for emphasis. "We'll just have to take it slow, or maybe stay an extra night in Prudhoe, I don't know."

Her phone dings.

"Oh, looky looky," she says, "it's my buddy Lee Grace."

Every day, Joy explains, Lee Grace sends a group text to about a dozen people. She tells me it's spiritual.

"Usually, it's something I needed that day," she tells me, scrolling, "and here's what we got today: *Isaiah 53:5: But he was pierced for our transgressions, he was crushed for our iniquities; the punishment that brought us peace was on him, and by his wounds we are healed. Have a blessed Jesus-filled day!*"

"Every day he sends something like this?" I ask.

"Just about," she says. "I worry about him sometimes. Funny thing is, I don't know who the other people are on this thread. They're just random numbers to me."

"At least with something like this, you know Lee is okay?"

"Oh, that's true," Joy says, nodding. "I guess I never thought about it that way. But you're right. If he's texting, he's living." She exhales through her teeth. "Man, you know, I don't know what I'd do without Lee Grace. I don't know what I'd do. Makes me feel like God's in my truck."

I think—again—of the painting hanging on Coldfoot's wall, how Jesus's finger pointed north.

"I always write Lee Grace back, or I call—I do," she says, looking out the window. "You just can't be too careful. Never know when it's your last opportunity."

Then she starts to sing a hymn, one I've never heard, though that is true of most of them.

I try to imitate her tune, be a backup beat at best.

"Sometimes," Joy says, by way of explanation, "if I'm tired? I listen to rock and roll. But if I feel scared, I sing a hymn. My favorite one is this one, 'Precious Lord, Take My Hand.'"

She straightens and begins to sing, her voice washing the cab in gentle noise.

"When the darkness appears and the night draws near," she lilts, "and the day is past and gone? At the river, I stand, guide my feet, hold my hand, take my hand, precious Lord, lead me home."

I look at her, listen, smile.

"It can really be intimidating when you're up here by yourself," she says. "I don't work Sabbath, you know, so I'm usually leaving on a Sunday, and a lot of the guys don't do that, so I'm on the road by myself a lot. Don't pass a whole lot of fellas. So I sing whenever I'm nervous. I sing, I sing, I sing. The snow can get so swirly around the truck that, honestly, I get carsick. But you know? I'm not stuck, and I'm not dead. And I thank my God for that."

"How's it go?" I ask.

"Precious Lord," she hums.

"Lead me home," we sing.

"There you go!" Joy says.

"I've got it?"

"You've got it!"

And while she might trust Him absolutely, and we both might think she's brave, I watch as Joy looks out into the distance and begins to sing another hymn.

8.

We're somewhere near Rollercoaster—a series of steep hills that come in quick succession and are responsible for sharp increases in speed—when Joy asks me, out of nowhere, what I think about feminism. Only, she doesn't say the word specifically. She wants to know what I think about Dr. Laura Schlessinger.

"I know nothing," I say, "about Dr. Laura Schlessinger."

Joy knows everything.

"Oh!" she says, excitedly. "She's this tiny little Jewish woman!"

And this tiny little Jewish woman, she tells me, is an expert on men and women. She has a rule for divorce, for example, and it's easy to remember because it's the rule of A's: *Only divorce a man if there's abuse, addiction, or affair.*

"Dr. Laura says men are simple creatures," Joy says, "and women need to be smart and tap into that."

A successful marriage, according to Dr. Laura, is one where a woman commits to a man and to completing a few basic endeavors that ensure mutual satisfaction and equilibrium in the household.

"Men want a woman to make love to them," Joy rattles off, raising her fingers to count the rules as she goes, "and to make them feel secure, and to take care of the children, and to take care of the house."

Dr. Laura is not my girl.

I can tell by the way Joy responds that she subscribes to Dr. Laura's checklist: do *this* and *this* and *this*, and *a man will love you forever*. Of course a promise like that is enticing; I suspect every woman in America would bite if it meant securing her body's safety.

"Feminists *hate* her," Joy continues, "but she's a feminist in her own way, I think, because she believes women should be treated like queens. *Queens!* Dr. Laura, she's like, 'A man should want to bring you lemonade through shark-infested water—that's how good you should treat him!' And feminists can be mad all they want, because honestly, she's right about the stuff. Hate it or love it, but Dr. Laura is right. I started listening to her when Samantha was just a baby, but I wish I'd started sooner; could've saved me a little grief."

A grief she would have liked to save: if a man is an alcoholic or an addict, Dr. Laura says don't marry them for five years.

"'Cause it's a really hard thing to do," Joy says, "getting sober and getting clean. And Dr. Laura says it doesn't matter who he is; you shouldn't get into something with him unless he *means* it."

She looks out at the tundra, the endless white expanse.

"Women are dedicated creatures. They go in, and they're all in. So it's really important that a man *means it*. And that means *putting in the time*."

I can't tell if she means Jake or she means James or she means any man in between. Despite everything Joy and I are not saying—because we love our men despite their problems, or because we feel ashamed, or because deep down we realize we're still mostly strangers to each other—there is some sense of sameness between us. There is a collective collage of experience, a shared acknowledgment, however silent, that we are two women who have spent our lives catering to men who aren't deserving, men who have not treated us right.

There is so much we can't say, so much I'm afraid to ask, and I can't speak to whether Dr. Laura is right. But it's clear, through the way we both look out at the ashen mountains, and through the silence settled between us, that a little less attachment to men would've been good for both of us.

She makes me promise to listen when I get home.

"I will," I say. I'm lying.

Then Joy tells me about her dream—a dream Dr. Laura has convinced her she can attain. A horse, Joy tells me—a horse she found on Craigslist whose owners no longer want him.

"He's little," she says, "and he's white, and frankly, he's adorable. So I'm being extra sweet to James," she confides, "because I want that little white horse."

The little white horse is more beautiful than any horse Joy has ever seen, she tells me. She pictures riding him in the open pasture that flanks their cabin and the wilderness.

But he's more money than they've got, and his purchase would mean buying a trailer, and hooking it up to James's pickup truck, and driving it south to no-man's-land where the little white horse currently lives.

Still, her heart is set.

"Just have to convince James," she says.

Out there in their cabin, in their wilderness, I picture her making her husband breakfast, buttery pancakes with honeydew melon on the side, maybe a little bacon. Icing his knees after work, watching reruns of old war shows after dinner. I picture the sweat equity of a wife who wants to please a man she loves, even if that love is complicated, and the payoff her love earns: a little white horse she can be sweet to, feed carrots, and ride in fields.

"I'm going to get him," Joy says wryly. "James says we don't need him, but we do. He just doesn't know it yet."

I feel the tires slip beneath us as we ascend the first hill of Rollercoaster, and I find myself reaching for the dash. It's taken me a long time to differentiate between the fear of something new—a necessary discomfort—and the fear of my body in danger. But there's a key distinction. Sitting next to

Joy, the fear of newness is exhilarating. The truck bumps and jolts beneath us, and it feels as if we're flying.

"Woo-hoo!" Joy says, throwing her hands up to the sky. "*This* is the Dalton Highway! *This* is Rollercoaster!"

I let out a little yip.

"Come on," Joy says. *"Be louder!"*

She yells and then I yell. And then we yell with great abandon: a yell so loud and raw and animal that my body strains and my throat muscles stretch against my neck. Then I feel my whole body unwinding, everything inside me, every muscle going limp.

"Isn't this fun?" Joy squeals.

"It's fun!" I yell. And it is!

She's laughing, and it's beautiful. Her big white teeth shine bright.

I'm glad I have traveled four thousand miles not simply to meet Joy, not simply to drive this highway or be far away from a cruel man, but because I expected, in some small way, that this experience might rinse the fear clean from my body. I think of Dave and the men before him and how they've made me fearful—of everyone and everything.

Joy screams again, and I scream, and I can feel my fear flush out.

Our bodies bump and bounce and land, and for the first time in a long time, I love being in my body. I feel safe enough to submit to the moment. I imagine Joy on her little white horse, imagine me right there behind her, imagine us racing through fields of fireweed and purple lupine, through red foxglove and tundra rose. There is nothing hard about it, nothing to fear or fight or flee. The mountains beyond are smudged charcoal. The truck gallops beneath our bodies.

Another hill, another descent, and we are present for all of it.

~

Back in Ohio, days stretched into weeks and weeks stretched into months. Year one slid into year two, and the old Dave did not return, only became more taciturn. I tried to adjust to his behavior, to focus on the good, but often I was reminded of the crab apple trees that lined the neighbor's fence: the way their branches filled with fruit and drooped low, heavy as river stones.

The world, meanwhile, was abounding with gentle things, and I made it my work to notice them. Asters bloomed tall against the vinyl siding of our house and, on them, baby ladybugs still too young and light for spots. Swallows skimmed the midwestern fields, over golden poles of brittle corn, and each week at our small-town summer farmers market, women in green hand-sewn dresses sold curling peppers in tiny baskets. Our coffee was still hot on autumn mornings, our slippers soft beneath our feet, and we enjoyed these small joys together. Sometimes at night, I still found Dave's face so beautiful in the soft pink glow of an antique lamp that I had to reach across our gap and touch it.

It isn't easy to confess, but we took good care of each other in those moments when we still felt like caring. At times, I found phenomenal pleasure in our pairing: in folding his black socks, or hosing off our backyard patio, or preparing two sandwiches instead of one. Dave took pleasure in cleaning out my car, in preparing charcuterie, in broiling— one evening—s'mores because the sky had darkened, dampened, and rained on our backyard bonfire.

Another winter came, and we enjoyed its evening fires. Then summer, and Ohio's cool lake beds, and I found gratitude in this and everything, for all the small and simple things that presented an opportunity for love, for kindness.

I taught myself, in time, to become a woman who needed less.

But in the spaces between these pleasures lurked an anger I could not control, an escalation I could not predict. Any peace between us was only an illusion.

That's when I began to see her—a woman my same shape and size who flitted between the bedrooms, sunned herself in our backyard. She was a version of a woman I might become, the quiet and agreeable wife who publicly deferred to her charming husband and who, in private, feared him. She was a mother who knew only her children, a housewife who busied herself with chores, a woman who gave up all her friends and all her ideas and all her passions. Gradually, over time, I saw her world grow increasingly small and quiet and lonely. She tended to her husband, and she tended to their children, and she went to the grocery store and church and otherwise lived a life of female containment.

She was me, and she was possible, and, in short, she terrified me.

~

That spring, as the daffodils pushed up and the tulips birthed bright color, I began drinking heavily, and Dave began drinking heavily, and all the time spent between us became a series of small combustions—like kerosene, like fire.

At the suggestion of a friend, I started seeing a therapist. In our first sessions, I told her I drank too much, which was true, but not all of it.

"Why do you think you drink too much?"

"Because I don't feel anything when I'm drunk," I said, "and that makes everything so much easier."

I told her how I was concerned that everything was becoming patchwork: the man who'd walked me home and then killed Emily Silverstein; the man who'd flipped a couch over while I was in it, laughing at my bruise; the camper and his ex-girlfriend; how Dave backed me into a corner until my body began to shake and then returned with cappuccinos.

I worried I was carrying these moments with me; I was carrying violent men. They weren't simply men on my periphery, men I'd met or acknowledged or observed, but figures I'd *absorbed*, incidents I'd housed inside my body.

"And what about the man you're with now?"

"I stay with this one," I said, "because at least I know his kind of crazy."

She was quiet for a long time.

"But I'm worried I'm getting closer," I said, my toe dipped in a pool. "Like the ring of violence keeps encircling, closing a little tighter around me every time."

I was sad all the time, I said. I often groveled. I drank too much. I didn't recognize the woman I'd become. I'd compromised myself out of my beliefs. I told her about Dave and our increasingly hostile relationship—the worst of his rage, of course, but also the way he could be so gentle, how it seemed, I told her then, that he took pleasure in taking care of me after making me feel terrible.

"And then he leaves," I said, "and then, especially, I turn into someone I don't know. I plead into the phone. I beg him to come back."

It was as if I was so empty, I told her, so hollowed out, that I didn't even care which version of him greeted me upon his return.

"Half the time, he terrifies me, but the other half, I swear, it's like he's the only person in the world who matters. Isn't that insane?"

It wasn't, she said, insane. She told me of a study in which scientists determined that domestic abuse lights up the same neurotransmitters as gambling.

I felt addicted to pulling levers. I wanted triple cherries. Everything I did became a means of acquiring the kindness and generosity Dave afforded others, of trying to win one kind of love, of trying to avoid the other.

I thought this is what it meant to love: to hurt, and still to love, and to fear, and to love then, too.

"Think of it like a casino," she said. "You walk in there knowing you're going to lose, but there's this small chance that you might win, go home big, receive all you've ever wanted, and so it keeps you coming back."

It's what kept me coming back.

This, the very real, very tricky problem of loving a man who is cruel to you: you begin to think that the intensity of their outbursts indicates the intensity of their passion. That there is never tenderness without cruelty, and that cruelty, in fact, is not a byproduct but a symptom of their love.

"We're going to get you there," she told me, by which she meant *get you out.*

Each week, I drove to her office above a river. Gradually, I grew more comfortable, brave enough to tell her everything: the nice things Dave had done for me, but also the screaming, the intimidation, the way his words could be sharp as weapons. Each week, I heard her voice on the long drive home, keeping me company in those moments when I felt the terror escalate. Her words were fine-tuning me slowly, back to smarter sensibilities, back to health and back to safety.

One evening, Dave became so enraged that I locked myself in the bedroom. For the first time, I texted a friend, I don't feel safe.

I thought of calling the police. I thought of changing the locks. I thought of putting his things in storage and how good it would feel to tell my therapist that I'd done it: that I was through with him.

Instead Dave left that evening, as he often did, and returned home a few days later. I was preparing a roast chicken and root vegetables for dinner.

"It smells so good," he said.

His back ached from nights on his friend's futon, and he was disheveled. He told me he was sorry.

I told him about my therapist.

"She thinks this is abuse."

I waited for him to finally hit me. Instead he cleared his throat.

I saw in him the man I'd first loved. I saw who I wanted him to be, and who he had pretended to be, and then I saw the man he was now.

There would never be one without the other.

"I don't like it," he said at last.

"What?" I'd started crying.

"That you've been talking about me to her. And that you think that she can help you. And most of all," he said, "that the only side of this she knows is yours."

There it was: his truth, which he believed justified his behavior.

He peeled back a piece of chicken skin and ate it.

There it was, out in the open, as commonplace as roast chicken.

9.

The closer we get to Prudhoe Bay, the stranger the world becomes. Here, hundreds of miles north of the Arctic Circle, everything is bathed and glazed in a way that makes risk feel beautiful, that disguises the pervasive danger—the inhospitality—of this land. Frozen puddles and potholes glint, arctic foxes scurry across mounds of snow, and Joy reminds me that even the light is God, that He fills every space and barren crevice, that He is everywhere and anywhere, always with us, even in our fear.

"He's even in this truck cab," she says.

It's why she feels so lucky to call what she does here *work*.

"I get to experience His closeness," she says, "plus I make a lot of money."

But the *danger*, I implore.

"I'm safe as safe as can be," she says. She bats the air with her hand. "And anyway, it's not just me. I'm doing this mostly for my children. I miss them, I do, and do I want to be with them? Of course. I want to be with Samantha, especially—she's only seventeen, and I need to take care of her, watch out for her."

She chews the skin around her nail and checks the rearview mirror.

"But I know enough about this world to know that I also need to provide. As a woman, you must provide. I feel that very strongly. And the best way I can protect my children is to have money in the bank if something, if anything, goes wrong. This road—I drive it because I want to, but I also drive it because I have to. Do you know what I am saying? I need to know I have a way to care for me and mine."

So she trusts the Lord to keep her safe. She tells me she's rarely scared, that she can feel she's in God's presence.

"He's always with us," she says, "but up here, I don't know, I feel closer to Him than ever. All the other stuff—the *life* stuff—it doesn't get in the way. I can feel Him taking care of me. I can see His beauty everywhere."

I settle in my seat. It's true I feel a steady calm. I feel tucked in a cocoon. Is it God or is it Joy that makes the world up here feel a little softer, the colors a little brighter? Is it God or is it Joy that makes me feel like I am capable, that I am in control, stable, *strong*? The way I feel inside Joy's presence is how others articulate their belief in God. Joy is the feeling of warm pajamas, the sound of my mother singing me to sleep, the earth that held my body on the hottest summer days. Joy is the memories of goodness, of kindness, before new memories took their place.

"Whatchu thinking, Spice Girl?" she asks, and when she looks at me and laughs, I realize she's fueled a flame inside me that had grown terrifyingly dim.

"Nothing." I smile. I open a bag of Cheetos and put one in my mouth.

"Don't fill up on junk," she warns. "We'll be in Prudhoe Bay in no time."

I twist my body against the window, feel the stiffness in my joints. For as eager as I am to arrive, I feel possessive of this time, do not wish to share my Joy with anyone. We are just west of the Arctic National Wildlife Refuge, Joy tells me, and outside, the landscape is evolving. Every ten or fifteen miles, the earth takes on a new geography. What first looks like an ocean, all gray-blue with rigid peaks, shifts quickly to tundra, flat as arid desert. A few dozen miles later, we're on the moon.

"There it is!" Joy says, pointing beyond the windshield. "A sun dog!"

It is radiant and white, as if God Himself laid a halo, gold and glistening, above the Earth.

Joy slides the truck into a pull-off and promises we'll move fast. There's no time to protest; I race out alongside her to meet the tundra. Behind us is the shadow of a mountain, but in the field beneath, the golden light cascades. The sky is a yellow arch, shooting forth above and setting a prism along the ground, white and impossibly bright. Our whole world is like a snow globe someone shook, and we are standing in its stable center.

"Holy shit," I say.

The land around us appears empty, but I know it is full of life.

This is Gwich'in land.

I look east beyond the highway, toward fields that wind through Indigenous canyons and sunlit valleys, steep summits and downhill drops and the relentless flow of the Yukon River. In addition to the Gwich'in, the Alaskan Arctic all around us is home to the Tanana, the Koyukon, and the Iñupiat, all of whom migrated to this area several thousands of years ago, settling into the land, establishing varied and complex cultures, and prospering over time through the development of language and the study of migration and climate patterns. Some nine thousand Indigenous people still inhabit this area, dispersed among fifteen villages scattered throughout the Alaskan Arctic. We may not be able to see them, but that does not mean they are not here or that they are not affected—immediately and adversely—by the decisions we make.

"Quiet as quiet gets!" Joy says, and while it's true this area might look empty or uninhabited, it is "always already inhabited," a term used commonly by literary theorists and philosophers to denote things that have happened (already) and are still happening (always). Explains activist Andrea Smith in her essay, "Heteropatriarchy and the Three Pillars of White Supremacy," one of the pillars of white supremacy is the "logic of genocide."

This logic, she writes, *holds that indigenous peoples must disappear. In fact, they must always be disappearing, in order to allow non-indigenous people the rightful claim over this land. Through this logic of genocide, non-Native peoples then become the rightful inheritors of all that was indigenous—land, resources, indigenous spirituality, or culture. As [author] Kate Shanley notes, Native peoples are a permanent "present absence" in the US colonial imagination, an "absence" that reinforces, at every turn, the conviction that Native peoples are indeed vanishing and the conquest of Native land is justified.*

My thoughts return to Coldfoot Camp, to the arguments for drilling just beyond this place.

Joy squeezes her hand in mine.

"I don't know if this is cliché," she says, "but I always make a wish on sun dogs. Or a prayer if the spirit moves me."

She closes her eyes and folds her hands. I close my eyes and do the same.

Are we wishing, or are we praying, and might we do more than this? I think back to Sacred Heart Christian School, how Joy's own pastor asked, in earnest, how different the world would look if our love of God drove evil out. Why is it always God, amorphous, invisible, elusive save for the mind that houses Him? We, as people, are enough. We have the power to do so much good.

Joy lets go of my hand, and we stand together in silence for a moment, taking in the rich expanse, the sun dog and its bright white shimmering. I think back to those early, hot summer nights of my childhood, fireworks blinking in a field my father had let go to weeds. I think of my bare toes gripping river rocks in a neighborhood creek, pulling crayfish up from underneath to study their anatomy, their tiny bloodred claws grasping, eager to be released. I think that to be happy is to be free, and that the erasure—the ongoing exploitation and abuse—of the people who have long called this place their home requires a shortsightedness we cannot fathom.

I look back to the road, the white gravel dusty and built up along the edges. All day, I have seen and met and engaged with dozens of men and women who call Alaska home and who have made of this state their livelihood—truckers, and restaurant attendants, and oil field workers shuttling in on an occasional plane overhead—but they have built their lives in vastly different places, other cities, even other states. The industries their jobs support—and the industry that gives Joy's life so much meaning—is antithetical not only to Native politics, but to Native cultures, Native lives.

I am grateful for Joy, grateful most of all for this experience, but I've begun to feel guilty to be on this highway, to be sitting shotgun in Joy's truck, to further exacerbate a wound through a land that is not ours. The highway is a symbol of freedom for Joy, of security, but from our vantage point, this far out, I see the way it splits the valley like a scar across a body.

It happens not just here, but everywhere. The truth is, the very fact of American life—a life I enjoy, take pleasure from—insists on a hierarchy of profit that leaves the marginalized in ruin: communities disrupted, food and shelter resources depleted, landscapes decimated. Oil pipelines are erected to lift up and over America's poorest communities, neighborhoods already at heightened risk for environmental pollutants and the illnesses these pollutants cause. According to the NAACP's report "Fumes Across the Fence-Line," the Mountain Valley Pipeline, a three-hundred-mile pipeline spanning from northwestern West Virginia to Virginia, will disproportionately affect poor, rural, Indigenous, and Black communities, which already suffer from toxic pollution released from the industrial facilities that are often located in close proximity to them.

"These life-threatening burdens are the result of systemic oppression," the NAACP reports, "perpetuated by the traditional energy industry, which exposes communities to health, economic and social hazards."

It is for these very reasons—under the guise of "legal uncertainties"—that Dominion Energy and Duke Energy recently canceled a proposal for the Atlantic Coast Pipeline, a six-hundred-mile line that would have run from West Virginia to Virginia and then south across eastern North Carolina. And why, thousands of miles west, the Dakota Access Pipeline—the subject of massive, worldwide protests and sit-ins that included fifteen thousand participants—has been ordered to be shut down and emptied of its oil just two years after it was opened, following an in-depth environmental review that reported the United States government had failed to sufficiently study "the effects on the quality of the human environment." The pipeline charts its path through numerous sacred American Indian sites, including Sioux tribal lands and the Standing Rock Indian Reservation, and has leaked at least five times in 2017 alone, including most notably a 168-gallon leak near the line's endpoint in Patoka, Illinois.

I look out across the highway.

Time and time again, the industrialization of America relies on tracing the troubled fault lines of systemic racism, ecological ruin, and poverty. Whole communities are upended, ways of living disrupted, and lands and bodies poisoned while wealthy Americans just get wealthier.

I look at Joy, who looks at me. We are complicit in all of it.

"Hold tight," she says.

She races back to her truck, leaving me alone on the sunlit tundra, the earth like cake beneath my boots. I watch as Joy slides her phone up on the hood, exactly like I taught her, finding a piece of jagged ice upon which to lean it. The phone's glass glints in the white-hot sunlight. Then she races back to me, the camera counter counting down, the light flashing as I anticipate what it will capture: the sunset pink behind us, the sun dogs shimmying as the fog creeps in, two women, no longer strangers.

"Smile!" she says. "Quick!"

Her arm lops around my body so that in the photo I'll print later, two women will look like one, our worlds so different and yet so similar as we stand and squint strangely in this place we should not be.

~

Back in the truck, I lean my head against the window. Above, the daylight slips into the horizon, but still it's enough to wash the truck's interior in a gauzy haze. In this state, in this weather, time begins to pass without discretion, one moment folding sleepily, seductively, into another, as if the hours and days hold no meaning, as if the two of us are tucked into a tiny pocket of unyielding time.

At last, Joy turns to me. She wants to know how I'll tell her story to others who will ask.

"I'm not sure," I say. The question makes me nervous. If the past few years have taught me anything, it's the danger of committing to telling someone's story the way they want it to be told. For months, I've told a story about what it is to be with Dave that looks nothing like our reality.

"What's the story you'll tell about me?"

"My little professor friend," Joy says. "How God brought you here to me because He knew we needed each other. How He knew your heart and He knows mine. How He brought you here to tell my story."

Her story is the story of many women, which is to say it is about strength—not just in this male-dominated industry, as I expected, but in the way she has been pushed and shoved and broken, and how she's healed, somehow, regardless.

"I'm sure you'll know how to tell it," she says, "but it's most important you include my friends. They mean so much to me."

Because sure, she tells me, she's got stories, but what's one story over another? Especially up here. Every mile, she says, another story. Some miles, more than one.

The story she chooses to fill the quiet with is the story of her friend Rux.

"My friend Rux," she says, "he was this guy, really great—trucker— really funny, liked to gab."

But like so many people up here, she tells me, Rux developed a drinking problem.

"One night, I met him on this road, saw him at Coldfoot Camp, and I could tell that he was drunk."

Get caught drinking, she explains, and it'll cost you your job, plus a fine and who knows what else.

"Not to mention you're risking everyone's safety," she says. I can sense her anger, her frustration. "I mean, you're risking the life of people you don't even *know* who work this road because they have to."

It's selfish, plain and simple. But Rux never used to be a selfish guy.

"Drinking—it makes people selfish," Joy says. "I try to watch out for everybody, but drinking—that is its own kind of danger."

She tells me he died just a few months after she confronted him. He was returning home from Fairbanks, where he'd been helping a friend move. He was riding his motorcycle. He always kept a little dog strapped to the back of his bike, Joy tells me, and it had its own little black leather jacket.

"Can you picture it?" she asks. "Little thing in a littler jacket. Both of them in matching leather. They were a sight."

That night, she tells me, Rux had no helmet on. The roads were slick and wet, and his motorcycle spun out. Was he drinking? Joy doesn't know. All she knows is that it was a dark, cold, lonely night when her friend Rux died.

"But wouldn't you know it," she asks, "that that dog *lived*?"

"Who took it home?" I ask.

"I don't know," Joy says, "but I think God takes pity on the innocent."

I think about Rux, a barren road, the front wheel of his bike still spinning.

"I think God rewarded that little dog for being loyal," Joy continues. "I hope it lives in a big home somewhere with a bunch of toys and a big ol' bed. But I hope it still wears its jacket."

"I hope so, too."

Joy nods, stares out into the distance, as if that takes care of that.

"No one ever put a cross up for him," she says finally, "I guess because he didn't die on this road? Because he died down in Fairbanks? But I think it was this road that caused him to die. All those long hours with no one to talk to. All this loneliness, and no one around. No wonder he—and so many guys—get a dependency for booze. It's the road, and all this darkness—nothing to come home or back to. I mean, just think of all that quiet."

I do.

I think of a man alone in a truck cab. I think of these hours and this weather and this sense of impending doom and how it has all been buoyed by Joy's small laugh, by her stories, her companionship. I think of whole days without, and then whole months. All those empty hours and no one to interrupt them.

Joy's eyes form small, wet tears. I can feel the absence she feels from his absence. On one hand, I know, she is telling me the story of her friend Rux, but her story paints a bigger picture: that this road is dangerous, sure, but that its dangers are not confined to its steep descents and stormy weather, its avalanches and head-on collisions. Looking out at the space between us, I know Joy and I both learned early in our lives that a lack of love is just as dangerous as anything else this world presents.

In some ways, I think, it's worse.

My shoulder slumps against the window, the heaviness of the day nudging me to something like sleep. When finally I open my eyes, the light is folding in the golden curves and the shallow edges of Joy's face, in the soft flesh beneath her eyes, in her clear and luminous skin, stretched, pallid, pink.

"I think about him a lot," she says.

Were my eyes closed for ten minutes or an hour?

"Who?"

"Rux," she says.

And while she's glad that I dozed off, she tells me, she's glad, too, that now I'm up. She tells me she missed my company. And anyway, she says, she needs someone to hold her to it.

"Hold you to what?"

"Rux," she says again. "It's time I finally do it—I think about it, but I never do it. Rux was like the rest of us—he got caught up in something bigger. All of us truckers? I think we're running. I think we're searching for something more. And Rux was one of us, I don't care *where* he died."

"What are you running from?" I ask.

"Sometimes," Joy continues, a conversation she's having with herself, or God, "I think we tend to remember people at their worst because it makes missing them a little easier. But we should remember them at their best."

I see Dave, his dark arm hairs shimmering. The smell of his detergent. His fingers on my skin.

"I don't think I have that problem."

"Me neither," Joy admits, "and it's probably gotten me into a lot of trouble. But a lot of people forget, and they need to remember. I want Rux to be remembered for who he was, apart from what this highway made him. Do you hear me? I'm going to put up a cross. Rux deserves to be remembered."

"I'll hold you to that," I say.

Joy nods. "Yeah, okay, good, good, good. Because his story is of value, and we need to remember the lesson in his death. All the invisible ways this highway kills us. We need to remember our friend Rux, too."

The truck begins to slope upward, and I look out, steady myself against the dash.

"This is it," Joy says.

Atigun Pass is in our windshield, steep and terrifying. The road gleams wet and dark. There are avalanche signs that warn of danger, and just off the highway, on the embankment, I can see the eleven-foot-high guns the highway patrol uses to set them off.

Timed avalanches, Joy explains, keep the road more stable.

Joy hands me a stick of gum as the truck begins to chug up the incline. In a moment, she explains, we'll reach a summit of 4,739 feet, so I'd be wise to start my chewing.

"Your ears," she says, "are gonna *popppp*."

The earth here is dystopian, nothing like the colorful cliffs I'd imagined. We are so high now there is no sun, only the steely gray of clouds swirling around our headlights and fogging up my side window. I scan the rocky cliffs for mountain sheep, for caribou, for an avalanche—for a sight to thrill or kill us, which are both in wild abundance on this desolate stretch of treacherous highway.

"This is where we cross the Continental Divide . . . right . . . here!" Joy shouts. She points. "So that means all the rivers north of us empty to the Arctic Ocean, and all the rivers south to the Bering Sea."

I don't see any rivers, only the thick gray of gravel and clouds that hug the steep, dark mountains. The truck continues climbing, climbing, making a chuffing sound. I begin to worry about our engine. If it went out, would we slide back at an angle and come to rest along the road, or would we tumble backward and plummet to our death? My fingers grip my seat belt. To advance up Atigun Pass is to submit to the very worst part of a roller-coaster ride—all that anxious energy as your body is lugged farther up and farther up, blind to what is in front of you and the exact moment when you will drop.

"I'm scared."

"Don't look down!" Joy shouts.

But I don't know where to look. Where do I place my eyes?

"Look out the window!" she commands. "Watch for little Dall sheep!"

Dall sheep, she explains, will appear like little white blips on the horizon, invisible when not in motion. They'll look like a painter took a paintbrush and dabbed the mountains with his small, white tip.

I try to narrow my eyes and detect any movement along the cliffs. I am watching for Dall sheep, as instructed. But nothing moves except our truck.

"Maybe too cold for Dall sheep today," Joy concedes.

I try to yank my gaze back to the sky, but despite my best efforts, my eyes keep darting downward, a little farther every time, settling first on the window and then the upholstery just beneath it. When finally I do it—I look all the way down, and boy, *do I*—I can't even see the bottom, only a straight, steep drop that extends without any guardrail. There is nothing down there but gully. The truck twists and turns, and I feel our wheels struggle for control.

"Any icier than this," Joy says, "and I would have chained our tires. I probably *should've* chained our tires."

"Don't tell me that!"

Joy laughs and slaps my thighs.

"I'm kidding!" she says. "Kidding!"

But I don't find it funny. My fists dig into my thighs. The truck continues to climb, the clouds thinning to wisps of woodsmoke. I try to calm myself. I roll the window down and reach one shy hand out to hold a cloud inside my palm.

"See?" Joy says. "It's *fun!*"

The clouds curl wet around my knuckles, rise and fill the cab that contains us. I might not know exactly what a prayer is, but I know how to pay attention, as the poet Mary Oliver wrote. I know how to be idle and blessed. I, too, know what I plan to do with my one wild and precious life.

"Whoosh!" Joy says.

"Whoosh!" I repeat, looking up just in time to watch the road unfold in front of us, everything now downhill—the landscape on either side descending sharply into a sunlit valley.

I think of Atigun Pass as a divider, the sharp, stiff peaks a stark disruption from everything my life was before. Call it silly wishing, call it the weight Joy put into the pedals, but both have brought me to this place where permafrost peeks through cracked, dry earth, electric blue beneath the tundra. I want to get out and feel it, press my hands against the earth in thanks, but Joy tells me there's no safe pull-off and there'll be plenty of time for that in Prudhoe Bay.

Then she points to the mountains, quickly taps the brake.

"There they are!" she shouts. She gestures.

Dall sheep are out and trotting, small white pinwheels moving with the wind.

10.

The blow we hit thirty miles south of Prudhoe Bay is bad enough to shake the truck. There are four feet of visibility beyond our window; everything else is gauzy white. Night is finally approaching, and Joy ushers it in with a lullaby, tapping her foot against the brake to a rhythm I imagine thirteen years have trained her to hear.

"This is nothing, this isn't bad," she says.

She's popped open a carton of organic strawberries and nibbles one down to the stem. But I can tell by the way she sucks her lower lip in that this isn't *nothing*, that she is nervous. For the first time, Joy looks scared. She pinches another strawberry between her fingers and the tires slide beneath us, rock the heavy weight of machinery.

"It isn't *all that* bad," she clarifies. "Just enough to make you *remember*."

She means remember *to be careful*. She means *steady*. She means *death*. Her fingers grip the wheel, each a tiny fist, as if one small act of diligence might protect us from what we both know can happen here.

"So what we're looking at," Joy explains, "this is called an ice fog."

Ice fog is a ghost, ice fog is encircling our vehicle, ice fog frosts the windows, making the road invisible. Joy rubs her hand against the glass. Ice fog happens when the sun goes down and moisture warms and visibility drops rapidly. The air is cold enough that fog itself begins to freeze. Her fingernails scrape the glass, at the ice fog forming inside our vehicle.

"I don't like this," I say.

"Neither do I," Joy says.

The temperature on the dash reads three degrees, then negative three. Snow blows in front of us in thick white walls and accumulates rapidly along the road. From the CB radio, a staticky male voice warns us it only gets worse up ahead.

"Roger that," Joy says. Then she turns to me. "We don't really talk that way," she says, "but sometimes I pretend." To the radio, she adds, "Thanks, my man. Appreciate it."

This is what truckers do for one another, what Rich and Donald and all the others were talking about as they dipped their fries in ranch and why others wrote savior stories via IOUs.

This is what it means to warn, to protect, to ultimately save each other.

"Maybe no one's even in the vicinity," Joy explains, "but still you call out into the darkness because you really never know, and so you never know what those words might mean. My philosophy? If you're not in a ditch, you're headed for one. So you have to keep your head on."

"You're welcome," the trucker calls back.

My fingers clench. My feet dig into the floor. We slide into a wall of ice and Joy again picks up the transponder.

"You weren't kidding!" she calls. "This is pretty bad!"

I try to settle in my seat. I feel the wind against the window. It blows, sounding animal.

"I have another story for you, but this can't go in your—this can't go in a book! Not until I'm dead! Only when I'm dead can you tell this story!"

"Okay," I promise.

Her brave trucker facade has finally dropped, and in its place, I am expecting the story I imagined she'd tell eventually: her true account of what it's *really like* up here. I cannot imagine Joy doesn't hold a story of how this highway has hardened her, or at least the ways it's tried. The wind blows against the cab, and I prepare myself for a frank and genuine conversation about all the shit she's had to endure, all the truckers and the stuff they've said, all the crude and grisly ways in which men up here have made her feel inadequate, as though she has no place on this highway.

"This one time," Joy begins.

I steady myself.

"I really had to poop."

And here's the thing, she says: of course there was no rest stop, no bathrooms, and the porta-potties out here are far and few between.

"And honestly," she tells me, "porta-potties are so much worse."

I grin.

"So it's blowing really hard. And I mean, I have *got to go*."

She finds a spot where the highway widens and decides to park the truck against tundra, get out, and squat behind her load.

"I was hauling, I don't know? Pipe? Something big and bulky? So this way, you know, I figure I'm at least a little hidden if another truck passes by."

So she's pooping and she's pooping and then she sees a truck's big white lights.

"And I'm trying to finish up," she laughs, "but this poop, and all the *blowing*, you know, the pressure? I've got some kind of stage fright, and it's making it *really hard* to go."

"Stage fright?" I'm laughing now, too.

"Exactly!" she says. "Let's say I've got poop fright! *Poop fright!* And I'm trying to hustle up, I wanna pull my pants up off my ankles, cover my little derriere, but this truck, man, he just keeps coming. And of course he's gonna know it's me. He's gonna *look*, first of all, because he thinks maybe I'm in trouble. And then he's gonna see my cab and colors. And he's going to see my pooping butt."

Joy shimmies her butt in her seat in reenactment. I'm laughing so hard that I can't swallow.

"So I'm shimmying," she continues, "and finally I push the poop out and pull up my jeans, except *this poop!*"

Now she's hysterical.

"This poop of mine, it's caught in the wild blow, and it starts to tumbleweed, freezing as it rolls. Like a little Frosty the Snowman action. And then it *tumbleweeds across the road.* I mean *feet* in front of his truck!"

"A poop tumbleweed!" I'm laughing so hard I start to cry, and then Joy is laughing and crying, too.

"Exactly!" Joy says. "Exactly!"

Thick tears trace down her cheek as she struggles to catch her breath.

"And I've never said nothing about it," she continues, "but hoooo boy, he saw it, my big poop tumbleweed."

She looks at me and grins, tears flooding the creases above her cheeks. She's never looked more beautiful, her guard down, unafraid.

"He saw it and he knew. He knew *exactly* what that was."

She says, "Let me try again."

She wipes the tears from her eyes. "Okay, this story you can share."

She points to a mile marker, but we're moving too quickly for me to read the number.

"I was just about at this spot, and it was full-on, deep, dark winter. A big blow, I mean, *big blizzard.*"

I rise in my seat to try to make out the highway. Shards of ice cling to the windshield wipers, and I can feel sheets of densely packed snow grind against the wheels and break from the front hubcaps every time we bump over a pothole or shift in incline in the road.

"Not like this," Joy tells me, sensing my anxious energy. "This, like I said, Spice Girl, this is *something*, but it isn't bad. This is just ice fog, that's all it is. But the time I'm talking about—I mean, I was *scared*. I could see nothing. Nothing in front of me, nothing to my left, nothing to my right."

We hit a pothole and the truck slips. Joy steadies her hands against the wheel.

"Now, they tell you in trucker training that you ought to drive along the shoulder when you're dealing with low visibility, because you can't see what's coming at you, and you know, these are mighty big trucks coming in, and fast. But the edges are a problem, too, because the state of Alaska built them up. In some places, especially here up north, this road sits eight or ten feet higher than the tundra, because the Sagavanirktok River—'the Sag,' we call it—often floods, and when it floods, the highway gets washed out and no one can pass, sometimes for days. You're just waiting, watching movies in your truck. It's kind of like a big-rig campground, because we get out, you know, mingle with each other, share some snacks, that sort of thing. But you're talking millions of dollars of revenue lost for every day the highway's blocked."

"I read that," I offer.

"Right. So they built the highway up, no big deal, except there's no barriers. There's supposed to be metal delineators—big metal rods that are supposed to tell you where the road is, but they get knocked down in storms, or they weren't put in properly the first time. They're supposed to be every fifteen feet, but in some places they're every hundred feet or so, which is a crap way to save some money if you ask me. But anyway, there I am. I'm just driving and driving blind. I mean, I can't see a thing."

She shakes her head.

"I can't see where the highway ends and where tundra begins, so I decide to drive real slow down the middle, take it easy, try to be attuned to what's up ahead. Luckily, it's late—that's my God again, because that day I'd wanted to spend time with Samantha, so I got a later start than usual. I think it was that lateness that kept me safe, truth be told, because no one was out here with me."

"So you're all alone on the road," I say, "in the worst storm you've ever known."

"Yes. It's dark, it's bad, and it's spooky."

Certain nights, Joy tells me, you get the sense you're about to die. Something about the loneliness of the Arctic on those evenings—when there are no stars, no moon, just a hard, dark dome of sky—makes you think you're going to die.

On those nights, Joy tells me, you make amends with everything. You forgive everyone. You say a little prayer, she says, because you just know.

You wait for your time to come. You think God is testing you. You surrender yourself as one small spirit in a universe of spirits, your pain like anyone's. Your troubles, just the same. God has figured out your value, and He's ready to take you home.

"You actually get *kind of excited* because it means you're going to finally meet Him. You just resign yourself."

This, she tells me, was that kind of night.

"I thought I was going to die, so all this tension inside me snapped. I stopped the truck and I threw my hands up to God. And that's when I saw him."

"God?"

"No, no, no. This tiny fox, this little white arctic fox. He's maybe ten feet in front of me, and he's being pursued by three white wolves."

It was like a fairy tale, she tells me: a small fox covered in snow, his frantic footprints disappearing behind him, except this fairy-tale fox was covered in blood.

"Blood everywhere," she says. "I didn't know what to do. I really felt for the little guy—he was clearly hurting, and he was outnumbered."

Joy watched them. She thought she'd give him a witness. Just as he stepped out in front of her truck, he turned and stood perfectly still in her headlights, the wind whipping in all directions around him.

"I didn't know what to do," she tells me again. But it was clear she was watching an animal's final moments. "He was totally spent, exhausted. It was all he could do to just keep going."

Then he disappeared from her headlights.

"He was saying goodbye, maybe," I offer.

"No," Joy says, "that's not it. I think that fox knew, deep down, those wolves—they'd get him eventually. So he crossed my path because he knew the noise of my truck would buy him another minute—I mean those wolves, *they* were scared of it—and that's all he wanted, maybe. Just a little more time on earth."

I feel my heart heave beneath my chest.

"Did they?" I ask finally. "Did the wolves get him?"

Joy just looks at me. She grimaces.

"I had to pull away," she says. "I mean, who can say for sure. But that's just kinda life up here. That fox? He was in a pretty sorry state."

I press my head against the window, feel the cold glass against my skin.

"The world," Joy says, "up here—and certainly down there, too—it can be grossly apathetic."

In the rearview, I watch our taillights blink against the fog.

"Everything wants to live," Joy tells me. It is as if she senses my discomfort. "I mean, driving up here? I see it all the time. More than anything, things want to live. And what I was saying earlier—about those scary nights on the road? That's God allowing us to reinvent. He's allowing us to get deep-soul clean. You think you're going to die, so you forgive everyone for their wrongdoing; you forget the hurt, the pettiness. You let go of all your worldly grudges. You surrender yourself to God. You become more finely tuned for loving. And then He decides to let you go on living."

She reaches across the cab. I feel her soft hand above my elbow.

"This road is a way to reinvent," she repeats. "This highway is an act of living."

Then, as if on cue, we get a staticky call from the radio: there's a dead caribou up ahead, a carcass bleeding out in the snow, and a wolf pack that has found its dinner.

"It's really something," the trucker adds. "Mile 33, if anyone's around. To your left if you're northbound."

"Watch for it," Joy says. "Or don't watch for it? I don't know."

I squint out the window and watch as shadows move along the darkness. We can barely see the road in front of us, much less anything that swirls beyond. We creep slowly past mile 35 and mile 34, and Joy taps the brake lightly until finally we both see the caribou, no more than thirty feet off the highway.

The wolves look up momentarily.

"Look," Joy says. "That right there, that's not something you see every day. In fact, this is a first for me. Must've got the young one separated from his herd. But what a meal in a storm like this."

"Poor caribou," I say.

"It's how you think about it," she says.

She motions at the wolves.

"We all *want to live*, Spice Girl," she says, as they lower their heads down to eat. "This world is just all of us, fighting for a little more time to live. Some of us get it, some of us don't. But it's God's job to decide which is which."

11.

When Prudhoe Bay emerges, it is like heaven, all white light among the clouds. God is the first structure to appear on the horizon—in this case, a modular trailer set on stilts, proof of heat and food and shelter but also, Joy jokes, a smoothie bar.

I roll my window down and let the wind pass through my fingers. Snowflakes cluster around my cuticles.

"Get ready for it," Joy says.

Then suddenly, a chorus, a cell phone chiming with the sounds of love: from Samantha and James and everyone. We are still twelve miles out with only two service bars between us—not enough to send a single word, *safe*, much less a photo of us together—but it's enough to receive the text messages that have accumulated, each beep another dispatch drawn from a distant world.

"Would you?" Joy asks. She makes a show of wrapping her hands around the wheel. "Safety first," she says.

I grab her phone. She has received dozens of messages—from everywhere, from everyone—and now they flood and flash across her screen.

"Ignore those," Joy says, swiping left in the air with her thin finger. She tells me she only wants to hear the ones from family.

"Hope you made it safely," I read aloud to her. "That one's from Samantha. And, *Don't stay away too long.*"

"That's James all right." Joy grins.

These messages remind Joy of her place and value in this world, of the binds and ties that tether her to it. She tells me it's so dangerous to drive and text, but sometimes—she grins—*sometimes*, if she can see what's up ahead, if the weather's okay and the sun is up, sometimes she allows herself to read one text.

"One little love!" she shouts. "One tiny little message to help me make it the last few miles."

I smile, imagining the way the sky breaks blue along her hood after all those miles of darkness and fearing death, and how much James's words must mean.

His *I miss you, little lady.*

I listen for my cell phone, but it's quiet in my backpack.

Stupid, I think. *You're stupid.*

My parents know not to message—I told them I'd have no service and any dispatch I might send would come only after my safe return to Fairbanks. But I never told Dave as much, in part because I wanted him to miss me and wanted him to tell me so.

I wanted him to tell me that he's sorry—he is so sorry. He knows his abusive outbursts are unhealthy and unhelpful. I want apologies and acknowledgment and a list of all the steps he's taking to right his many wrongs. Therapy, and anger management. I want to believe—this, despite everything—that he will still find a way to make things right between us, and that my absence these past few days has made him want it even more.

But there are no messages on my phone. No promises or proclamations. There are only the edges of America all around us and its glow of industry. The buildup is abundant, and so is the loneliness.

"Do me a favor, won't you?" Joy asks. "Now that we have some service, call the Prudhoe Bay Hotel. The number's on speed dial. Ask for Joelle at the front desk, and ask her to save us some prime rib."

It is Sunday, after all, Joy reminds me: the Holy Day of Meat.

She explains it's a Prudhoe Bay tradition that every hotel and work camp serves the exact same meal on Sundays—"the biggest cut of meat you'll ever see."

I picture the hot gleam of juices, red, shining over beefy flesh.

But the line just rings and rings.

"That's okay," Joy says. "I guess we don't particularly need a huge, undercooked piece of meat."

Except now I'm imagining the beef, the buttery whipped mashed potatoes. How I could make a little moat. How I'm hoping there are peas.

"I can try again?"

Joy allows me to make three more attempts.

"Joelle must be busy. This is probably God's way of telling us there are better things for our bodies."

"Maybe God is just testing us?" I try. "Maybe we must prove ourselves worthy? Maybe He wants us to surrender to the holy, restorative powers of—"

"Meat?"

"And its mysticism," I say.

"That's some sense of God you've got."

"I'm told He works in mysterious ways."

Joy narrows her eyes and smirks. "You make me laugh is what you do."

"Do you think at least there will be some leftovers?"

"Of the best and biggest meat you've ever seen? In a cafeteria of mostly men?"

"Okay," I say, "okay."

I try to suppress my meat-moat fantasies. But all I can imagine is gas station convenience food: a soggy ham-and-cheese sandwich and its pillow of leafy lettuce, its mustard, a little spicy. I imagine a bag of corn chips and two cold, hard-boiled eggs packaged in single-serving plastic.

I keep returning to my mashed potato moat, my prime rib castle, my green pea fortress.

I force my thoughts to move along. Tomorrow morning, I'll strap on my teal bikini and wade out into the Arctic Ocean. The energy—the excitement—of our experience will peak, right there on the Arctic shoreline, where I'll dip my whole head under and throw my neck back against the cold sky. It will be the ultimate Arctic surrender, and I'll ask Joy to document all of it. It'll go on her Instagram and mine. Maybe in the first photo I'm just shocked, my mouth spread open from a full-body chill. In another, my arms are up, my pose triumphant, jubilant. Maybe I'll ask Joy to take a series—a stop-motion animation I can splice together with a little music on my computer. It's a video I'll show my children. How I was a young and determined woman. How I didn't take any shit. How I waded out into that Arctic Ocean, at last check twenty-two degrees, and I wore a teal polka dot bikini to do it, my whole body showing how to be tough, how to say *yes* to life.

"When we get up there," Joy says, "there's a couple other women I want you to meet. Proof I'm not the only one."

Because don't get her wrong, she tells me. She's honored I found her. But she'd be dishonest if she didn't introduce me to some additional women who have built careers in this place, have endured the harsh climate and isolation, have found ways to provide. Joy is the only female big-rig trucker, sure, but the North Slope employs a handful of other brave, intrepid women.

"Being a woman up here," Joy says, "you stick out like a sore thumb. But that only makes it easier for us to find each other."

And it's important that I meet them, she tells me, because their stories matter, too, and it's important that people expand their ideas of the type of people who brave Arctic Alaska.

"I'm sure you've heard of"—Joy pauses, thinking—"what's his name? That runaway bus boy? And Mr. Bear?"

Runaway Bus Boy and Mr. Bear are two American men best known for enduring remote Alaska. One—Christopher McCandless—fled his materialistic, dysfunctional family, toured the country by saying *yes* to hitchhiking and drugs and everything before finally settling down in an abandoned school bus in the wilderness outside Fairbanks. He died a few months later from starvation, or perhaps poisonous berries. But now he lives in the popular imagination of Americana: our forever boy, Peter Pan in flannel, pocketknife at his waist. He was naive, but he was idealistic. He was searching for something more.

McCandless is so popular, so beloved, that a number of tour groups outside Fairbanks offer sightseeing packages promising a similar remote adventure through woods and over rivers to McCandless's old school bus and the place they found his body.

A Trip to Bus 142, Denali Backcountry Guides exclaims. *See Chris McCandless's Last Resting Place!*

The tour earned five stars, last time I checked.

Mr. Bear is known more properly as Timothy Treadwell—the *other* American male made famous for his death in remote Alaska. Treadwell abandoned life in the Lower 48 to spend each summer among the grizzlies in Katmai National Park. He believed the bears were family, believed their protection was something he alone could ensure.

To most, he was a narcissistic lunatic, but he was also the subject of my favorite film, *Grizzly Man,* by Werner Herzog, who captured Treadwell's particular brand of bear-loving crazy but also shined a spotlight on the humanity that caused Treadwell to retreat: a deep-soul, deep-seated loneliness.

"Loony bin," Joy tells me. "I don't care what that man thought. Bears will kill you. In fact, they won't even think twice about it."

The bears did kill Timothy Treadwell. They did not think twice about it. But I know something that Joy doesn't, in no small part because of Herzog. I tell Joy that Treadwell was not up there alone. He died beside his longtime girlfriend, Amie Huguenard, the only person who ever loved Timothy enough to follow him to Katmai for a summer, despite her great fear of bears and her belief that they would kill them.

Amie was tall with long blond hair. In one photo, she wears an olive sweatshirt, mosquito netting around her neck. But in the hundreds of hours Treadwell filmed, Amie appears for only seconds. Treadwell was so insistent in propagating the narrative that he lived alone among the bears that he refused to have Amie appear alongside him.

At the end of his film, Herzog meditates on Amie's insufficient presence in his documentary—an apology, of sorts—and speculates on her presence, more largely, in Treadwell's life.

I tell Joy that Amie died not concurrently, as one might expect, but only after the bears mauled Timothy, which implies, to me, that she stayed beside him, was loyal to the very end.

"We should know about her," she says. Her voice is getting loud. "We should know about all the lunatic things good women do for love."

I recite to her the final line of the film, which I've memorized. They are the last words from the coroner. "Amie stayed with her lover," I repeat to Joy, "with her partner, with her mate—and with the bear. Ultimately, she stayed with the bear in the situation."

Joy is silent for a long time. "He's not fooling anyone," she says. I can tell she's angry. "Make no mistake," she says, "she didn't die because she stayed with the bear. A woman like that, like us? We die because we stay with the brute."

But we're going to make it right, Joy tells me, even if we can't redeem Amie Huguenard. We're going to rewrite the Alaskan narrative. From now on, she explains, the tour she provides will be one of women.

"I will show you who I can show you," she announces, "and the first woman I'm going to show you is Dawn. She works in the cafeteria, and she's my go-to gal."

Dawn has big, round eyes and a laugh like a cartoon character's.

"Memorable," she clarifies. "You see Dawn and you just grin. Of course, I can't be sure she's up here. Depends upon her shift."

The workers of the North Slope, she explains, all rotate on a rigid schedule: two weeks on and two weeks off, or two months on and two months off. Because while the conditions can be unbearable—especially in winter—the biggest advantage of a job on the North Slope is how frequently you can leave it.

"Everyone," Joy says, "they make their money and they go home. They see their kids, they go on dates. They connect with stuff that matters. And then they fly back up to the Arctic to do it all again. So if Dawn isn't up here, there are others. Michelle, for example, and Jen."

Michelle, Joelle, Jen. These are the women, she tells me, who make Prudhoe Bay possible, who make Joy's trips meaningful, who—while they may not drive a big rig, may not tie down thousand-pound loads—possess the same independent, dogmatic spirit beneath their cherry ChapStick or their cross charm or birthstone necklaces.

"They make this place *fun*," Joy says. "Because you're gonna see this soon, but life up here is only industry. It is work and work and work."

Every morning, employees wake and rise to eternal summer, or they wake and rise to eternal darkness. Oil rig workers work a twelve-hour shift, noon to midnight or midnight to noon. While their two-week shifts sound short, they are dominated by loneliness, by isolation and absolute exhaustion. And these shifts repeat ad nauseam.

"They even work Sundays," Joy tells me. "And Christmas. And Thanksgiving. Only holiday Prudhoe Bay workers get?" She laughs. "They get the Super Bowl."

There's a big buffet, she tells me. Crab legs, steak, and shrimp.

"Now, some of these work camps you'll see," she says, pointing out along the horizon, where distant structures twinkle like Christmas lights, "they might look small. But looks can be deceiving. One has an enclosed glass atrium and a waterfall. A waterfall!" She laughs. "And most have tanning beds and basketball courts and movie theaters."

We look out into the distance.

"Popcorn and everything!" Joy adds.

All distractions designed to stave off the grip of loneliness—the remembrance of children and spouses and families, thousands of miles and many time zones removed—and the endlessness of winter, which here spans October through May and is marked by whiteout conditions and temperatures that dip, more often than not, to a frigid and nearly unlivable negative sixty. The area sees only six weeks without frost, and snow can fall even in July. Then summer comes with its endless daylight, its Arctic flora bursting through cracked, dry earth: the blue of forget-me-nots and the pocked pinks of small-flowered paintbrush, the muted red of fireweed and the purple violets of bog laurel. At the height of summer, Joy tells me, the tundra is as green as prairie grass, the air mild and temperate and sweet, clouded by mosquitos and the occasional gull, looming inland in search of trash.

"You'd think you're in the Midwest," she says. "You'd think you're about to be sucked up by Dorothy's twister."

But you're not in Kansas—you're in Alaska—and the earth is over-whelmed by constant flux.

"The very ground we work on?" Joy asks. "It's constantly sinking back into the earth."

Before being constructed, every building must first be set up on concrete stilts, lest the warm air radiating within thaw the exterior, creating, in turn, a bog, which would threaten to suck the whole building back into the earth.

Joy's truck rumbles ever closer, and I can sense, even in the shroud of nightfall, the vast, noisy network of industry, buffered on every edge by roaming musk oxen and caribou, bears, and a skulk of red or arctic fox.

"Tomorrow," Joy says, excitedly, "I'll take you out on the tundra to get some real PBS-kinda shots. Not the kind that we saw earlier. Not blood, not gore, not *guts*. I mean musk oxen and grizzly bears. The kinda photos you print and frame."

I look out into the distance, at the oil rigs blipping red along the horizon. We cruise into town slowly, pass our first structure set on stilts. Men mill beside warehouse doors and the beds of pickup trucks and unload crates of evaporated milk from the hulking interiors of 18-wheelers. It's April, and it is dark, but parking lot lights shine as if from heaven. I crack my window to hear their sounds, and Joy tells me it's her favorite part: audible proof of other people after so long on your own.

"Isn't that just the most gorgeous sound?"

It is. The men around us are talking, laughing, boasting, drinking coffee from Styrofoam cups. They smile as we roll in. One extends a hand and waves. They have goatees and crew cuts and cell phone holsters on sturdy belts. They don ball caps and heavy industrial clothing that protects their bodies from the elements. They smoke cigarettes in company rain jackets that bag around their hips, the sleeves rolled up at the elbows, and they squint up at the sky, taking bets on the last day it will snow. For as little as we share between us, these men and I are here in this night together in the northernmost corner of America.

Joy puts the truck in park in front of the Prudhoe Bay Hotel.

"I believe there is a plan," she says. "What God gives, He takes away, and I'm just happy to be a part of it, whatever timeline He has in mind. Every time I'm up here, I say a little prayer. I thank our good God for keeping me safe and well, and I say thanks, too, to my body, because it's not easy, all that sitting."

She folds her hands together. She bows her head and prays.

"Dear Father," she begins, "thank you also for my good friend Amy. For bringing her to me, and for bringing us both here safely."

I look out at the world, milky and magical as a snow globe. The moon hangs low in the sky. Our world of ice and metal shines.

"Amen," she says.

"Amen."

We unbuckle our seat belts and move to get out of the truck, but Joy pauses, reaching for me, and says, "I'm so glad Jesus loves us."

I look at her face in the moonlight. Again, the crushing thought, the same as the first moment I ever met her: that I have never seen anyone more beautiful.

"Me too," I say. "Me too."

She smiles. "Ready to scrounge up a little dinner?"

"Prime rib leftovers?" I try, hopeful.

"No!" She laughs. "That's gone! But if I know these guys—I do—I promise they've saved us salad. And let me tell you this: there is nothing like a salad at the top of the world."

~

I refuse to make it to the top of the world and celebrate with salad.

So here is what I'm eating: a T-bone steak and garlic mashed potatoes and a sliver of a half-limp fish stick. Green beans sautéed with almonds, and custard-colored macaroni and cheese, the kind made with evaporated milk and chunks of freshly shredded cheddar. I marvel at the sight of cheesecake and a machine that pumps soft serve. Meanwhile, in the corner, in small white porcelain ramekins, the delicacy of my youth: chocolate pudding dirt cups, their neon gummy worms half-buried in Oreo dust.

"Jesus," I say aloud.

"No, honey, this is *man*," Joy corrects, grinning. She slides her tray down beside me, and I eye her plate piled with fresh romaine, canned peaches, cottage cheese.

I swig from a carton of chocolate milk. I contemplate key lime or cherry pie. I halve a slivered fish stick, dip it in a dollop of Dijon mustard.

Joy looks down at my tray and frowns.

"That's okay," she says, as if consoling herself. "You're young, I guess. Young *enough*. We'll work on you—you've still got time."

This isn't what I expected when I considered dining options in the Arctic. There are rosemary-basted pork chops. There are meatballs rolled by hand. Along the wall, a carousel of condiments, featuring three varieties of vinegar and four kinds of hot sauce in sticky bottles.

"This is wild," I say.

Joy tells me Dawn isn't here, so she'll have to facilitate my tour of the cafeteria. She leads me to a wall-length fridge full of nonalcoholic beers and sparkling waters, paper cartons of chocolate milk, grab-and-go bottles of V8 V-Fusions and energy drinks. There are more varieties than I knew existed, not only Red Bull and Rockstar but brands called Beaver Buzz and Venom, NOS, and something called, boldly, *BAWLS*.

"It's corporate policy that Prudhoe Bay remain dry," Joy explains. "I mean, like, *any* alcohol and you lose your job. Can't take any risks in a place like this. So they try to make it special."

Behind her, on a mounted television, *The Fantastic Mr. Fox* plays on mute.

All around us, men graze, spooning heaping forkfuls of buttered noodles and asparagus onto their plates. There seems to be a hierarchy among them, and Joy confirms this hunch. She nods at a table where an even mix of men and women are all dressed in navy-blue rain jackets.

"Pilot drivers sit with pilot drivers." She points. "Their job is to go ahead in pickups to warn of oncoming big-rig wide loads. And then truck drivers congregate together." She motions. "And oil hands sit with oil hands."

There is a myth about oil field workers, and it is important that I dispel it. The men I meet over the next hour in the cafeteria are the same men as Rich and Donald. These men want to show me photos of their oil rigs, or the worst of the North Slope's blows, want to buffer grainy videos of how they stepped outside one night to see the northern lights, electric. They want to talk to me about the good women—the wives, the girlfriends, the moms—waiting for them back home, how they make all of this possible. *Holding down the fort.* How they are their *stones*, their *rocks*.

I had expected these men to be dismissive: of Joy, of her work, of my presence there beside her. I'll admit that I expected men who grew exponentially more disrespectful the farther north we made it. I imagined a landscape of men who'd self-selected to live in America's last great playground precisely because it was lawless and unregulated. I expected ridicule and vulgar jokes. I imagined comments about my tits, my lips, and harassment I'd have to ignore.

This is the difficult truth of being abused: you come to expect abuse everywhere, and certainly from any person who resembles your abuser in any way. The generosity flees; the kindness inside you flees. There is no benefit of the doubt, no opportunity for pleasure. The mind tries to anticipate, to outwit, outsmart, and flee. It is a fight-or-flight behavior that encourages an antagonistic approach to the world, and it is not fulfilling, not empowering.

It makes me feel, instead, very small.

But all around us, in neat, benched rows, these men tell me about the Little League scores of their young children, or the fish their sons and daughters caught down in Colorado, Mississippi, Maine. These men have beards and big round eyes, and as they hold out their tattooed arms to fill cups with Coke, they describe their children's tenth birthday parties in bouncy castles, and the surprise romantic getaway they've got planned—a Sandals Resort all-inclusive—to make up for the anniversary, the Valentine's Day they always miss.

Here in the Prudhoe Bay Hotel, we are all hungry and fatigued and lonely. We are comforted by ravioli. We miss our familiar world within driving distance, the ability to order shrimp lo mein. It's so tough up here, they tell me. It's so lonely and remote. But Joy is always the friendly face, the woman with the electric smile. They say her name with great affection. They all tell me the same thing: that any friend of Joy's is a friend to them, absolutely.

One man offers to take us up in a plane, or to go gold-panning along the Yukon River. I feel embarrassed for my prior judgment, ashamed by my expectations.

I smile and tell him maybe, but my intention is to stay with Joy—not because I feel unsafe, or because I feel like an interloper, as I'd expected—but because I don't want to lose any time with her.

Joy grips my shoulder, and a few men clap. "You made it," Joy says. "You made it to the edge of the world." Then, "This is Spice Girl," she says to them. "She's going to be a name to know. This is my friend Spice Girl."

Spice Girl and Mothertrucker. We raise plastic tumblers of milk in tribute—one chocolate, one unsweetened almond—and the men beside us raise them, too, in a moment of celebration. We clink plastic against plastic, say "Cheers" and "I'll drink to that."

Joy smiles, satisfied. "We should get some rest," she says.

"You holler at me if you gals change your mind," an oil field worker says as we turn to leave, gesturing enigmatically with his right hand. "I'll gas up the ol' four-wheeler, take you ladies out on the tundra."

"Is that a euphemism?" I whisper into Joy's shoulder, but she only looks at me, disappointed. We're exhausted, deep bone-tired, but as we turn to make our way toward the lobby, Joy pauses before the front desk, swiveling her body to peer around the shelving. Michelle appears, and they squeal like teenagers while I await my introduction.

"Joy, Joy, Joy!" Michelle shouts.

"Michelle!" Joy shouts, rocking in their embrace. "Oh! Oh! Oh! And this is Spice Girl!" she cries. "Amy! My little professor friend!"

Michelle is warm, pink light. She has a soft peach glow along her cheeks.

Michelle welcomes me to Deadhorse, to the outskirts of Prudhoe Bay, tells me it's unlike anywhere else on earth, even if I can't see it in the evening's darkness. Michelle's job is to check people in, check people out, and run the gift shop, which sells candy and magazines, lavender bath beads and racks of neon sweatshirts. There are beer cozies and kitschy shot glasses and ball caps that read, *North Slope Militia: GOD & GUNS & OIL*. Another shows the outline of Alaska, Prudhoe Bay a starred blip on its northern edge, and below, *Yeah, I'd tap that!*

While Joy and Michelle are talking ice fishing, I browse the T-shirts, holding a green one with a cartoon polar bear up against my chest. He looks bored, or apathetic, unimpressed with this world. Beneath him, in big black capital letters, *PRUDHOE BAY*.

I put my T-shirt beside the register. Michelle turns and tucks it in a plastic bag.

"Oh," Michelle says, "I like green best, too."

Then she leads us down the hall, and Joy leans into me, giddy. She whispers, like it's some big secret, "I've never stayed the night!"

Normally, she tells me, she swings in for just two hours—an hour to eat and gab, and then an hour to work out in the fitness room, lift some weights, get "bikini-ready." She wags her finger in front of me. "I'm in and out! Easy peasy!"

"In the middle of the night?" I ask.

"Sure," she says. She laughs. "Gotta get home to my husband and kiddo."

Michelle turns and grins. "But you always fit me in."

"Always!" Joy says. She gives her arm a little squeeze. "The transport companies have strict policies about how long you can go. So I end up sleeping—I do!—but usually down at Coldfoot Camp. This is something new."

"Well, it's a sleepover," I say. "We can stay up late, maybe do each other's makeup."

"Do each other's nails," Joy adds. "Talk about kissing, talk about boys."

The room Michelle leads us to is just two twin-size beds and a couple cabinets, a tiny shelf for books and a television from the nineties—the kind shaped like a big black cube.

It is everything we need.

We set our bags down, and Joy turns to Michelle. They look at each other for a long time without saying anything.

"It's so good to see you," Michelle says finally. "Been a little while."

"Such a little while," Joy says. She lifts her leg for emphasis. "I've been out of work! I've been injured!"

"I know," Michelle says. "I'll be honest—I didn't know if you'd be back. That hurt my heart a lot."

I'm starting to see what Joy meant when she said there were women who make her life in Prudhoe Bay possible, who make her trips meaningful.

Michelle leans against the doorframe, beaming.

"Well, gotta finish up here," she says. "Come grab me before you leave?"

"Bright and early!" Joy says.

Once Michelle has left, Joy looks around the room and grins.

We sit on our beds and unpack our backpacks. I remove a pair of Carhartt overalls I bought especially for this occasion, a pair of Smartwool socks, a crew neck shirt that still smells clean, like flowers and Florida oranges. Joy unfurls a pair of neon-pink workout shorts and a Fort Knox Gold Mine hoodie packed like a Little Debbie Swiss Roll. She strips, pulls her neon shorts up over her hips, and snaps the elastic around her waist.

"I'm going to go bike in the exercise room for a little bit," she says. "My mind is tired, but not my body."

I tell her I'm going to shower.

"I smell like pee," I say.

The bathroom is down the hall—a narrow corridor with a few shower stalls, a few toilets, and an industrial-size drying fan to keep the place free of mildew. The water is hot, but the cheap fabric curtains blow and stick to my shins in the swirling air. I peel them off my leg with my ankle only to have the fabric swirl and fasten itself again.

It's nice to be here, I think—showering in a stall in the farthest edge of America, where I can savor what it feels like to be comfortable and clean, safe and dry and soft and warm. These are our most basic human needs, but it's been so long since I've had all of them met. So long since I've felt *safe.*

What I experience next is joy—unmitigated, uncomplicated, euphoria seeping through nerve endings and flooding my brain with serotonin. When did I become this woman, who feels joy at the rare occurrence of being alone and comfortable? When did I trade my strength and courage for a man who makes me feel weak?

I close my eyes, remember being seven, alone, and capable, casting my line out over shimmering green tree branches that reflected at the water's edge.

Then I think about being eleven, thwacking brush, milkweed, and cattails high as my forehead beside my brothers in the field behind our home.

At sixteen, I took illicit train rides into Philadelphia, to the Trocadero and the Mütter Museum, where I sorted through a filing cabinet of choking hazards, studied medical instruments and apparatuses used to poke and prod the body, perused a collection of human skulls aligned neatly in a lit-up bookshelf.

At twenty-four, I moved to graduate school five states away and stayed up late my first night alone, eating pizza and drinking beer, playing pop music and unboxing glasses.

I was that woman once—resilient, independent, seeking joy, even if alone. Now, at thirty, I wonder where all my joy went. I wonder how I can reclaim it.

I rinse clean, wrap a towel around my body, and stand before the bathroom mirror. My hands move over my lines and wrinkles, the curves that dip beneath my nose. The industrial fan blows, wicking the water away, and I feel suddenly certain of one thing over everything: that while I am a woman with plenty of regrets—plenty of missteps and wrongdoings—the biggest mistake I've ever made was allowing a man to decide if I was worthy, and then believing him when he said I wasn't.

When I return from the bathroom, Joy has her foot against the wall and is flexing and unflexing, listening to Duolingo pronounce Spanish words from a vocabulary unit on animals. Every now and then she pauses to flip over onto her stomach and press her fingers against her phone.

"Multitasking," she explains.

"I see that," I say.

"El oso," her cell phone chimes.

"El oso," she repeats.

I tell her the French that I know best comes from a seventh-grade camping unit—this despite years of study and seven months spent abroad.

"Raton laveur," I tell her. "It means *raccoon*."

Joy laughs and shrugs her shoulders. "France," she says. "I've always wanted to see it."

"You should go," I say, absently, as if that takes care of that.

"I'll go before I die." Joy laughs. "But that kind of trip is a lot of money."

It is a lot of money, something that escaped me at twenty-one, buying lavender soap to mail back home, and something that escapes me even in this moment.

I wish I could go back in time, wish I could give my trip to Joy.

"Oh well," she says, implying *different lives*. We live in different worlds entirely, but this is one of Joy's greatest strengths: she doesn't seem to mind these differences, doesn't seem to judge.

Joy rolls off the bed and pulls her toiletries from her backpack: a bar of facial soap, some floss, a tube of natural toothpaste that reads, in all caps, *FOAMING AGENTS*.

"What's a foaming agent?"

"I don't know," she says. "They promise no fluoride or glycerin, but I just liked the slogan. *Live your journey!* It's what I'm doing!"

"You're living your *joy*ney," I tease.

She whacks me with her pillow. I pull my bikini from my backpack—teal and polka dotted and cinched along my waist.

"Tomorrow," I tell her, "I'm going to swim in the Arctic Ocean. There are shuttles that depart at 8:30 a.m. and 3:30 p.m. You can get in with me, or else you can stand on the shoreline and take my photo."

The Deadhorse Arctic Ocean Shuttle is the only way for those of us who don't work among the oil fields to gain access to the water, is in fact the reason hundreds of tourists fly to Prudhoe Bay from Fairbanks or even Anchorage for a single afternoon. The tour is pricey—enough to cover the tour guide and the bus and the mandatory background check to circumvent the risk of terrorism—but the website promises an authentic Arctic experience. A glimpse at the reviews suggests the tour is especially convenient for aging tourists—recent retirees, mostly, couples who have saved for months or years so that they might finally see the northernmost edge of America.

"Oh, shoot." Joy shakes her head with regret. "That tour only runs May to August, Spice Girl. I'm afraid we're a whole month early. Must not have read the fine print, and those are strings even I can't pull."

I wanted that one brave moment, wanted to feel my body seize at the chill of the Arctic Ocean, wanted to feel cleansed and born anew. I had pictured it so many times. I wanted Joy to snap my photo, wanted to put it on my office desk. I thought it would mean something, would be proof that I'd reclaimed something I was afraid I'd lost.

"Oh, that?" I'd offer coolly when colleagues or students asked. "That's from my dip in the Arctic Ocean."

Instead I have to stop eight miles short of the Arctic Ocean.

"What was it like?" people will ask. And what will I tell them in response? That the world up here is surprisingly well manicured, comfortable, and quaint? That I paid more money than I earn monthly to fly to northern Alaska to eat my heart out on well-done beef, cheesy noodles, and potato casserole? That great time and consideration has been invested into the dessert options for the men, who are polite and curious and kind and want to talk to me about their children? That yes, sometimes, there are polar bears, and sometimes, yes, third-tier blows, but most of the time it is musty carpet, twelve-hour shifts, and plates of pie? Dunkaroos and *Maury*, Fox News and scratchy sheets?

For a second, I want to laugh at how silly it suddenly seems to have been so desperate for one moment. With or without any symbolic swim, privilege allowed me to lie here in a tiny room in northern Alaska, a couple twenties tucked in my boots beside the bed, in the same way that it helped me leave Ohio. I was able to book a three-leg flight and a hotel room where I felt safe, to spend a week away from work, to know that I'd be covered by health insurance if we encountered an emergency in the Arctic. It is privilege, for that matter, to trust the truth that a white woman like Joy, like me, would be searched for by trained experts, would be hauled out of the Arctic if things went suddenly wrong. That people would tell our story if the worst, indeed, happened.

I climb into bed and pull the comforter to my chin, feel my wet hair fan out across the cotton pillowcase and soak into the fabric. Outside our window, small lights blink from the mobile oil field camps. I close my eyes, feeling grateful that I've come to this place and put some distance between Dave and me. I'm grateful for our bed and sheets, however stiff, however scratchy. Grateful for Joy's friendship, grateful for our warm room. Grateful even for the night, like a rope released from heaven to finally draw us off the highway and away from all that danger.

Joy gets into her bed on the other side of the room.

"Can I say a little prayer for us?"

"Of course."

Joy pulls her Bible from her backpack. I hear her flip through pages. "The Psalm of David," she decides aloud.

With my eyes shut, with my mind quiet, I listen to her words. For years, with Dave, I have played the role of someone who attempts to mirror the faith of those around her so that they'll love her, won't walk away. But I don't want to pretend with Joy. She has allowed me to see her—all of her—and I want her to see me, too.

"*The Lord is my shepherd,*" Joy reads. "*I shall not want. He makes me lie down in green pastures. He leads me beside still waters. He restores my soul.*"

I imagine the girl I used to be, the green pastures she inhabited.

"*Even though I walk through the valley of the shadow of death,*" she continues, "*I will fear no evil, for you are with me; your rod and your staff, they comfort me.*"

I see the darkened valley, see the dog Dave and I share, her small tail wagging wildly. I see those nights when she felt a need to move between us, to become a buffer between our bodies. I see myself backing behind a toilet, see myself weeping openly in the street.

"*Surely goodness and mercy shall follow me,*" Joy finishes, "*all the days of my life, and I shall dwell in the house of the Lord forever.*"

I imagine goodness, imagine mercy, as if a coat I can slip on. I imagine wearing it everywhere. I imagine wearing it in a house where I don't feel threatened by a man's anger.

I hear the creak of Joy's mattress as she springs up to get the light, then the flip of the switch and the staticky sheets followed by all that empty silence.

"I liked that," I say into the darkness.

"Yeah?" Joy asks. She laughs. "God is good," she says.

I mouth the words *God is good.*

Outside, snow swirls and circles the lights. And maybe what happens next—maybe it is God, after all. Or maybe it is Joy, and it happens because we both feel safe, because our bodies are warm but weary, because we simply are together.

"My boyfriend, Dave," I say, "he screams at me, Joy. He backs me into corners. He screams until I'm on the floor."

The snow whirls, whips white against the darkened sky.

"I came up here, I don't know why," I continue. "Because I felt I had to? Because I wanted to put some space between him and me? I'm a smart woman, Joy, I am, but I just haven't had my head on straight about it. Something about coming up here, seeing how beautiful, how vast the world is—not just the Arctic, or Prudhoe Bay, but *everything*—I thought it might change something for me."

Joy is silent. I want to tell her that some part of me has started to believe we are versions of each other—like I am Joy from twenty years ago, or she is me in twenty years, if only I can get my life together, leave the bad man for someone better and do something with what I've learned.

Help other women, as Joy's helped me.

I feel ashamed, I tell her. My face burns pink in the Arctic darkness.

"Jesus, I don't know," I say. "I am trying so hard to do the right thing. Here, and then, and always. But I always align myself with men and surrender all my power, all my resilience, all my strength. And this time, I chose a partner who is especially reckless. And I don't leave him because I'm afraid I don't know how to stand alone anymore." I pause. "Jesus, is that the stupidest thing you've ever heard?"

Then I hear Joy's sheets slide along her mattress as she gets up. Her weight settles onto my bed as she scooches in to sit beside me. She draws her knees up to her chest and puts an arm around me, heavy. I feel her hand against my forehead. She feels for my hand in the darkness, tucks her small palm in mine.

"No," she says. "No," she repeats. "I don't think that's stupid at all."

She is the first person, beyond my therapist, I have ever told outright the things he does and says to me. We watch the snow accumulating outside the window. I wait for wisdom, but Joy says nothing, just moves her hands along my forehead and begins to hum a hymn I do not know. My body is warm beneath the covers. Her hand is warm against my skin. Outside, in that dark night, the snow spins and spins and we watch it until I feel dizzy.

I'm almost asleep against her when I feel Joy slip back into the darkness.

"The road heals in all kinds of ways," she says. "It's going to heal you, too."

I want so badly to believe her. I don't know what I'll do if we're both wrong.

"And anyway," she adds, "now I *know* He knew what he was doing. Now I *know* God brought you to me. Believe me when I say: we are soul sisters, all right."

12.

When I wake, Joy isn't in the bed beside me, and for a minute I wonder if the night before was just a dream, if any of our conversation ever really happened. I look out across our tiny bedroom. Joy's bedsheets are crumpled along the floor, but her boots are still sprawled beneath the mattress.

She couldn't have gone very far.

I roll the covers to my feet and feel the cold world come rushing in. I rise, stretch. It's then I hear her voice.

"Joelle!" she says. "Joelle! I kept my eye out for you! I prayed!"

Out in the hallway, she clarifies: she prayed, she explains, that their trips would overlap, that we'd arrive in Prudhoe Bay and stumble right into Joelle's schedule.

"God knew!" Joy says. "He knew! We needed to see each other!"

From the doorway, I raise my hand meekly and say good morning to them both before I realize I'm not wearing pants.

"Oh, it's okay," Joy says, fanning the air dismissively, pulling me to her. "It's okay, little sister. We're all family here."

I pull my T-shirt to my knees, trying to stretch the fabric farther. "Hi," I say. I wave.

Joy squeezes me around the shoulders. "This," she says, "is Joelle."

Joelle's from Mississippi, and I can hear it in her drawl. She cleans rooms, listens to music, and dusts. Turns over beds, scrubs the in-room sinks. It's her job to afford the oil field workers a little hospitality, a little kindness, the feeling you're in a place a whole lot fancier than you are.

"It's my job," Joelle says, "to put the *hotel* part in the Prudhoe Bay Hotel." She smiles dotingly. She's got her hair pulled back in a tight ponytail, one earbud out and dangling while the other plays what sounds like jazz. "And to save Joy some prime rib sometimes," she adds.

"We tried!" Joy says. "We tried!"

I ask Joelle why the Arctic. She tells me she always dreamed of being by an ocean.

"The *Arctic* Ocean?" I ask. "Of all the places with a coast?"

"Oh, I don't know," Joelle says. She flutters her hands in a way I understand to mean *nonsense*. "A job is a job is a job—it's a way to pay some bills. And here's the same as anywhere. I keep to myself all day, and I prefer it, truth be told. Just nice to know I'm close to water."

She looks at Joy and grins, then points to the closest window, which is partially obscured by an off-white curtain.

"Joy knows this," she admits, "but here, for some reason, I always feel the water in me, always want to get on a boat and get out there."

"You have to get out on that water!" Joy cries. It's clear this plea is not her first.

Joelle smiles, shakes her head. "I never do," she says. "I never do."

"This one wanted to get out in that water, too," Joy adds, nudging me. I try to smile, but my disappointment is still palpable. "Except not in a boat," she clarifies. "This one wanted to kick around with her own legs."

"A boat sounds a lot easier," I say. "Less dependent on an official tour."

Joelle laughs. "You'd be surprised," she tells me.

She explains that the oil fields and coast that stretch beyond are secured by a series of checkpoints and perimeter fences, and that access is restricted to employees who possess the highest-possible security clearance.

"Domestic terrorism," Joy interrupts. She looks at me and her fingers firework. "Someone lights a match, and everything—everyone—goes *BOOM*!"

There has yet to be a *BOOM*.

But there have been very violent booms elsewhere—West Texas and Texas City—so the oil fields remain off-limits. The only time workers are permitted beyond the secured perimeter is for seasonal socialization events, including something called the Deadhorse Dash, a two-mile walk around Holly Lake that includes a token at the halfway mark, redeemable for a burger and a handful of chips, a chocolate chip cookie wrapped in glistening Saran Wrap, and a choice of apple or banana.

"It's a lot of fun, honestly," Joelle admits. She tells me the earth is more mysterious out there than anywhere, so restricted and untouched, and the presence of people stranger still as they gossip and eat their hamburgers and swat away mosquitos.

"Sometimes we see musk oxen," Joelle says, "and always a lot of birds."

Joelle tells me a lot of the oil field companies have much-loved mascots, including Carlile Transport's cape-wearing polar bear.

"He's a hoot at events." Joy laughs. "He'll dance, you know, he'll *groove*."

I picture the gyrations of an enormous mascot, the bobbing puff of tail. I imagine the overlay of the Backstreet Boys, the crooning sounds of Nick Lachey.

"It's the little things up here," Joelle says. "You know?"

Joy smiles. "I do."

"It's a shame you're gonna miss the tour," Joelle says finally. "The water is great—it's gray—but the tourists are the real sight to see. They always come dressed the same: snazzy, swishy windbreakers and pairs of clean white Keds."

"Yup. They sit in the Deadhorse work camp, surrounded by oil field workers in their industrial work shirts and hard hats and dirtied denim, and there's really—what to call it? Quite the contrast?"

Joy and Joelle laugh and then turn their attention to the subject of summer. Joy tells me to return in August. She reminds Joelle once more to get in a boat.

"You *have to*," Joy repeats. "No excuse this year! We only live once!"

Joelle laughs, slaps her thigh. "You know I'm turning fifty-six this month?"

Joy turned fifty in December.

"We done lived over half a century!" Joelle laughs. "Well, it's good to see you. And nice to meet you," she says to me.

"This is God," Joy says, her finger swirling in a circle that sweeps the air. "God made sure you were on shift up here, and God is at work in the three of us."

Back in our room, Joy and I look out the window at the snow accumulating.

"We should get going," she says. "Forecast looks pretty bad. If we stay, we might get stuck, and you've got your flight." She pulls her mining hoodie over her chest, shimmying as she tugs it down.

I thought we'd spend the day, and for a moment I feel disappointed, even if I didn't know what a day up here might look like. But I also don't want to get stuck in Prudhoe Bay, and the idea of bad weather makes me nervous. Joy looks at me, studying my face. I can tell she's eager to get back to James and Samantha, to her horse and dogs and parents.

"Sure," I say. "Okay."

"When we get back, I'll make you dinner," she says, a consolation. "A moose roast and a salad. The moose that Samantha and I shot."

She looks at me. She smiles.

"I love you—you know? You're like my daughter. I won't give you iceberg lettuce with mayonnaise on it. For you? I'll do dinner right."

I smile and stuff my Carhartt overalls back into my bag. I thought I'd wear them here, attempt to achieve a look of North Slope authenticity, but they're too heavy to wear in the truck. I roll my socks, my heavy sweatshirt. Joy slings her backpack over her shoulder.

I'm struck then by the sense that I am on the downward slide, edging ever closer back to Dave and my old life. I follow her back down the empty hallways of the Prudhoe Bay Hotel, past the showers and the cafeteria and the reception area gift shop with its kitschy T-shirts and calendars. It's only then I realize that I've been looking to Joy for a miracle; I've also been looking to her to do my work. I am certainly not the first to have made a religious pilgrimage, Arctic-inspired as it might be, not the first to see God in a human, but I have come to her, heartsick and humbled, and in need of so much more than prayer.

The truth is I'd expected something *wild* to happen here on the North Slope, something life changing, something so profound and so downright holy that it would shake me from my reality, make me smarten up. Existing even temporarily in Prudhoe Bay, I'd thought, however naively, would usher in a surge of strength, maturation, or mental clarity, and while it might not be fair or reasonable, it's nothing if not the truth.

In Scripture, such miracles are instantaneous, divine change immediate. Fish swell into starved men's netting, and rivers part swiftly for the feet of God. Water is blessed into wine. The blind regain their sight. Demons are driven from the tongues of men so that suddenly those men can speak. The dead son of a widow, the dead daughter of a priest—they are touched and brought back to life. Lepers are cured of leprosy. Fevers lift and break.

But back outside in the parking lot, I lean against Joy's truck and feel the same uneasiness I often do. I have yet to experience the great epiphany some crucial part of me anticipated, the seismic shift in thinking, and now we are heading home.

My disappointment is not in our quick turnaround in Prudhoe Bay, not my prohibition from the Arctic Ocean, not even in this dull, gray day, already gusty and clouding over as we prepare to leave it. My disappointment is in myself: how little confidence I have that I can do what most needs doing.

Joy, after all, can only give what she can give me: a drive up the Dalton Highway, a dinner of moose roast and a salad, and then a ride to my flight back home, where I will reenter a life I hate, a life I don't know how to escape, or I do know, but still I'm terrified to escape it.

"Listen, honestly?" Joy says. She leans against her truck. "Up here." She pauses. "Up here? Honestly? It's not made for stories you tell. It's made for stories you *live*. You went north of the Arctic Circle. How many gals can say they did that?"

The problem, as I see it, is I've been waiting for someone else to do the hard work of changing me. If not with faith, then love, and if not love, then Prudhoe Bay.

"You have to remember," Joy tells me, "up here on the North Slope, and in life, sometimes another day is all you get."

"But your days," I say, "are remarkable."

I look at her, frustrated.

"Your Instagram drew me in, Joy, because it seemed such an authentic representation of your world, and here I am, now, living it: the snow, the highway, the North Slope, every visual like the ones you've posted. Your pictures are true to life, true to your ongoing daily reality."

I kick the dusty parking lot.

"But my photos tell a different story, and it's the story of a life altogether different than the one I live."

Joy pauses, key in hand, and we look out at the horizon, at trucks pulling in and out.

"I'm an idiot," I say, my voice softer now, "to think this trip might change something so profound as my whole life, my relationship to men."

"Come on," she says at last, gesturing me to follow her.

I look at her and blink.

"Come on!" she says again, so I do, I come on, as she traces the edge of the parking lot, kicks the dirt, and reaches toward the sky.

"You want to know a story?"

She turns so that we face each other. I look at her soft skin, her gentle eyes, her hair down to her hips. I feel my body stiffen.

"It's a story, and it is true, and it's a story you can share. You want to hear this one?"

The story is about Toby, a North Slope grizzly bear who for many years wandered in from the Arctic coastline to lumber around the oil fields of Prudhoe Bay. He moved from warehouse to warehouse, observing the workers, meandering. Over time, he became something of a town mascot. Everybody knew Toby. They radioed about him on dispatch. He was sort of a fan favorite. And he was dangerous, Joy tells me, sure, but for the most part, he kept out of people's way.

"There was a sense," Joy says, "of mutual respect, you know? Because we've all got to share this space."

Sometimes, she tells me, Toby made trouble, like the time workers found him out beside an oil rig, smashing boxes of coffee creamer.

Another day he fell asleep on the airport tarmac.

And once—the morning after the local Native community of Nuiqsut's whale harvest—he got into some tote bags of whale meat, of baleen and soft, white flesh. The village of Nuiqsut is located on a tiny island several miles out in the Arctic Ocean, Joy explains, so workers help store the whale inland until they need it, a small favor to combat the glowing lights and whirring noise of oil field industry.

"They probably had fifty or sixty totes full of meat workers were prepping to store," Joy explains. "I mean, picture it: all of the meat is in these totes, and you've got flippers hanging out, maybe ten or fifteen feet of baleen. Whale parts, whale meat—it's big. It doesn't exactly fit inside a bag."

But as workers walked out to check on it, they found an impossibly enormous bear, spread out, whale-drunk and woozy.

"That air? It was filled with a reek that was all its own." Joy smiles in recollection. "I was unloading some crates that day, and you really cannot even fathom the smell that is dead whale. Toby was sound asleep, didn't have a care in the world. And all the guys around me? Well, you know I don't curse, but they all looked around at one another, and they said, they said"—she looks around self-consciously—"they said, 'Holy shit, you big, fat whale-eating bastard!'"

I like the idea of this big, brown whale-drunk blob. I ask if we can see him. Maybe stay a little longer, drive around and look for him.

"See," Joy says, "in general, he was good."

She kicks to release a dust cloud, a yellow haze slowly rising. I look at her and wait.

"But then there was," she says, "this one time."

This one time was a few years back, when Toby broke into the Prudhoe Bay Hotel. It was evening, Joy tells me, and the workers were eating, preparing for shifts or preparing for sleep. There were a couple hundred people present, all milling about in the lobby, in the cafeteria, in the workout room. But someone had left a door propped open.

"There's an inherent risk," she says.

So the workers called the local policeman, a man named Don, who arrived and had to shoot him.

"Don loved that bear," Joy tells me. "He loved that bear more than anyone. But he also knew what he had to do. For himself, yes, and for others."

And it was heartbreaking, Joy tells me, it really was, but that's just how life goes.

"We are lucky," she says, "to get to love something without violence. But when violence enters the picture, the only question is how long love lasts."

I look at her. I'm gutted. I have no idea what to say.

"You want to know what life's *really* like?" she continues. "We make decisions all the time. Hard ones. Our lives are just decisions: one made after the next. And you can make a decision one day, and you can feel *so good* about it. But that doesn't mean a new day won't come when you'll have to make the decision differently."

I'm silent for a long while. I watch a truck pull in, move slowly, move carefully.

"I'm bringing you down," she says. "I know I am, but there's no point in pretending. It's beautiful up here, but it's difficult, too, just like the world down there. You can keep making the same decision, or you can finally do something different."

She looks at me with an expression that tells me she's not just speaking about a bear.

"What I heard?" she says, switching topics. "They taxidermized Toby's body. At first, they hung it up in the airport lobby, like a *Welcome to Deadhorse* sort of thing. But eventually, Don wrote a letter, or someone wrote it on his behalf, and he acquired Toby, arguing he belonged in a place of love. Don loved that bear," Joy repeats. "If anyone deserves Toby, it's Don absolutely, and that's the truth."

"Even though he shot him?"

"Maybe because he shot him—did what needed doing. Love," she says, "is all kinds of complicated."

We say nothing for a long while. She takes my hand, and together, we step out onto the tundra. She points to a patch of growth, where already the dry, cracked earth has given birth to a cluster of pink azaleas.

"This place," Joy says, bending, pointing to where roots of flowers have intertwined, where lichens cling to rock in this otherwise empty stretch of endless soil. "It's difficult here like it is anywhere," she says, "so everything has to stick together. Men and women, flora and fauna."

She kneels to part the petals of a rich purple Arctic flower.

"The Native people and hunters who inhabited these lands long before us—and the Inuits who still do—they understood things we never will," she says. "But most of all, they understood change. And what do I mean? The *need* for it."

Their lives, Joy explains, have been nothing if not a lived response to the ongoing fluctuations of the environment. Migrations and fishing and sustenance. They have survived only because they found a way to welcome this wild earth, the transitions this place incurs.

"You look at this landscape, right? And today it's all flowers blooming, beautiful. But four months from now?" Joy stands, dusts her hands on her jeans. "Everything you see here will be lost to ice. This is a place of change—and danger. The two go hand in hand."

A mosquito buzzes into my ear canal, and Joy pulls two netted caps from her pocket, holds one up for me. I dip my head into it, then tuck the netting behind my hairline.

"Listen to me," Joy says. "Nowhere on this earth is there a place more volatile than this. How to adapt is how to survive."

And there's a lesson in that, she says, for us.

"This place is cool," she continues, "it's different. And these folks work hard, they really do. The men that make up this place? They're among the nicest guys I know, will give you the shirt right off their back. But don't go thinking this place is everything. That it has special powers or something. Everything it is, you already have back home."

I look at Joy in this vast expanse, how small she looks, how fragile. She bends at the hip to touch the earth, rich and rippling blue beneath. I bend to join her there. The earth is softer than I expected, slick, the deepest shade of blue.

"Permafrost," she says.

My cell phone is in the truck, but I'm learning that a photo is not what matters. What matters is this moment, one that would undoubtedly fail even if I *were* able to duplicate it.

"It's beautiful," I say.

For these few seconds, these fleeting moments, I am touching permafrost beside Joy Mothertrucker in budding spring in Alaska's Arctic.

I think of the woman I was five months ago, three months ago, one month prior: a woman in her backyard, fluffing throw pillows for a man who screamed.

If I could say anything to that woman—or the thousands of women and girls just like her—it would be, very simply, "You are worthy of so much love, and it needn't take traversing an entire continent to remember."

I was strong, am strong, *will be* strong.

I smooth my thumb over all that blue.

"I say we hit the road," Joy says. "See what God has in store for us back out there."

"Okay," I say. I straighten.

We turn to make our way back, but Joy pauses, studying me. Then she lifts her arms out to her sides—a little Jesus on the cross in her Carhartt overalls and green-blue flannel.

"Listen to this landscape," she says. "We can be anyone."

She spins, and I watch her move. I am so dizzy with hope that I almost miss what she says next.

"You can be anyone," she tells me. Then, "You can leave him, you know."

13.

The road to Fairbanks feels shorter on the return, sleepier, as if the experience has peaked and now slopes back toward the familiar. Outside, the world is glossy, wet, the light like Christmas morning. I lean my head against the window and feel the glass beneath my forehead shift with every rock and gravel incline, every turn and twist of wheels.

Joy is silent in her seat, studying the skin around her thumb.

There are only ever two modes of sky in a place like this, she tells me: gray and gauzy, or the bright white light of sunshine. Today is the latter, all of winter's darkness lifting in a dizzying, dazzling shine.

"It's beautiful," she says. "There's a lot of hope in a light like this."

There is a lot of hope in a light like this. There's a truck ten miles up—a deep-blue dot against the slate of sky—and because Joy thinks she has so much time, because she thinks she has the world, we coast into a pullout, one of the last we'll have access to for miles, because he's headed our way, Joy says, and fast. She insists we give him the road.

"He's in more of a rush than we are. Probably got caught up in Atigun Pass and now he's running late."

She points into the distance, where the minor outlying mountains of the Brooks Range look like a watercolor.

Amy Butcher

"He's coming in at high speed from all those inclines, so we're just going to give him space."

I consider this idea of space, how subjective it can be, and thus how dangerous. Of all my friends back home, only two know what my relationship with Dave really looks like, and neither knows the full extent. Joy and my therapist are the only people to whom I've confessed everything, in large part because I feel shame and embarrassment for the role I've played in it—often calling him after our fights, begging him to come back, or accepting his apologies. Still, one friend calls what she knows of the life I've been living "the shadow of abuse's doubt"—the gray space that exists between what we think of as clear and identifiable abuse and a run-of-the-mill couple's conflict. The shadow of abuse makes it difficult, she explained, to feel validated in my fear or to ever claim those words: *I am in an abusive relationship.* They are words I've never said, because my relationship with Dave is not what I've been taught to believe an abusive relationship looks like. I know bruises from television, prime-time police crime dramas. Black eyes and busted fists. The victims live in the shadows, quiet, introverted, and shy.

Most of the time, I appear quite confident. I move around the world. I work. Dave and I present, generally, as well-adjusted and balanced equivalents, well-mannered.

Still, my friend insists, what I have been dealing with is abuse, though she admits she's never known this kind of abuse herself. Her ex-husband threw a ceramic bowl at her, and she had to walk around in a boot for a month until the bone reset.

"*That* was abuse," I told her.

"Abuse has many forms," she said. "Physical intimidation is just where domestic violence begins. It escalates, like everything. If you were scared—if you worried for your safety—that's not nothing. There was a reason."

Reason or no reason, for so long I've operated under the idea that abuse implies a bruise; domestic violence implies *physical* violence. It's a trick society teaches us, a sort of hierarchy of pain. But this hierarchy only exacerbates and serves to further silence victims; with so many ways in this world to conduct violence against women, it encourages the false impression that some forms of violence are more permissible than others. That only the worst can warrant worry.

"He's never hit me," I told my friend.

But sitting in the cab with Joy, replaying that conversation, I'm not sure it matters. It seems clear to me now that I will never again be a woman who hasn't spent a night in the desert, worrying the man she loved might kill her. I will never again be a woman who has not protected her head in a kitchen hallway. Cowered behind a toilet. Cowered behind a dog.

I feel my body tense, even in these memories. My toes curl inside my boots.

That day, with my friend, I told her more than I'd ever told her before, as if edging my way into a conversation I'd spent many months avoiding. I recounted my experience in San Francisco with Dave, the way he'd backed me into the bathroom, the way my body began to tremor, and she'd argued for the value of language.

"You have to give this experience its proper name," she said. "Once women do that, once they stop minimizing what they experience, we can begin to have a real conversation about what he is doing to your body, which—when we're talking about domestic violence—means of course your flesh, sure, but also your mind, your heart, your way of thinking."

She said, "You're terrified all the time."

She did not know about the knife I kept in my glove compartment, the pepper spray I'd tucked in a bedside table in case I had to get away from him—and fast. She understood mostly that he was whittling me down to nothing.

"Listen to me," she said. "Men break women in all kinds of ways that have nothing to do with flesh. To rebel against male violence, we have to rebel against the ideas that limit what male violence looks like. Say it: *this is abuse.*"

This is abuse. This is abuse.

It didn't feel right that day; it feels easier this morning. My head jostles against the window as I try to accept the words that will reframe the world waiting for me back in Ohio.

This is abuse. This is abuse.

Outside our narrow windows, Joy and I watch the blue truck advancing. Our cab smells like forced heat and what is left of the cilantro, wilted and browning in the back seat. I shift my feet around Joy's pocketknives and a six-pack of water-purifying tablets, her emergency flares and several flashlights and a reflective neon-orange hiking vest— the same one she will be wearing in the photo distributed at her funeral, four short months from now.

But this morning, she's alive and waiting.

There is hope in a light like this.

The blue truck is coming, coming, gone, and then Joy pulls us back onto the highway. I slump against the window, slip in and out of rest. Every time I wake, she's there, hands gripping firmly at the wheel. She's biting the skin around her finger, or braking liberally, waving to big men in bigger trucks who grin back at her and wave. She's peeling the corner off a granola bar's wrapper with only her two front teeth, or checking the dips in her bucket seat, trying to salvage a salted almond she tried to pop into the air and catch with her mouth but dropped.

"Here." She points to a single raven overlooking a river just off the edge of the road where every summer, she tells me, someone drowns. "It's not that deep, but it's fast-moving."

Caribou graze on the other side. We watch the river and the wilderness until we can no longer see it.

When I turn back to look at her, she's rubbing gently at her eyes.

~

We fall into an easy silence somewhere south of Atigun Pass, which the truck ascends easily. The sky is blue and cool. I don't look for sheep this time; I keep my eyes fixed straight ahead. When at last the road begins to flatten, Joy turns to look at me.

"You know what I think?" she asks, drumming the steering wheel with her palms. "This road, I think it's so *healing*, because every time I'm coming back down, headed on back to Fairbanks, it's like I get a whole fresh start."

I know what she is doing. She's trying to get us back to Dave. I fidget with a pack of Skittles, slip a wild cherry onto my tongue.

"That's such a bummer," I say. "I mean, isn't that such a bummer? Doesn't it bother you when it's the same? When you get home and you jump out and you just step back into your same old life?"

"I like my life!" she tells me. "And anyway I think we've all got to find ways to like our lives. If you're not liking life, that's God telling you to make some changes."

I roll my eyes, though I know she's right. It doesn't take God to see I'm unhappy.

"What will you do when you get home?" she asks.

"I don't know," I say. "Summer's almost here. Plant a garden, maybe. Drag the grill out from the backyard shed."

Joy doesn't look at me, does not break contact with the road.

"With Dave?" she asks.

"I don't know. I guess. I don't know. I love him, like you said."

"Sure," she says, "I said that."

I can tell she is treading lightly, but still I feel my body stiffen. I feel uncharacteristically defensive. Joy had little when she started over—and she also had two young sons—and I have friends, and family, and community. Still, the idea of finally separating from Dave—and edging closer to that moment—has incited a primal rise in me, a panic, a feeling of overwhelm. For years, I have been nothing if not his partner, and if I'm not his partner, what remains?

The landscape shifts and shifts again. Mountains move and magnify and then disappear in our rearview. Hours collapse and fold, and trees gradually reappear—short at first with muted branches, their growth stunted from so little sun, but then the broader trunks from ample daylight. We hit a snow-glazed valley, and Joy whistles as she looks out.

"Look!" She points out the window to a patchy pad scorched by forest fires. I think of what it would feel like to have my whole life leveled, to walk through that ashen wreckage and feel everything I knew suddenly sooty underfoot.

"Forest fires," Joy says, "are God's way of starting over."

Where the fires burned years ago—Joy points—the new trees grow rich and dark.

I imagine a future of all-new growth, of trees grown deliberately and with purpose. I imagine what it might feel like to be a woman without a man, to be a woman self-satisfied. Or what it might feel like to be that woman many months or years from now, how good, how right, it'd feel to meet a new man and let him touch me without my bristling from fear. I imagine his skin warm against mine each morning, how a day could start with hope.

Joy straightens, tells me the only way women can ever truly be happy is by exorcising all that has its terrible claws in the thick trunks of our identity.

"Men love to hurt women," she says, "and society more or less tells us we deserve it. But you have to dig all that stuff out. Every day, you just have to dig."

I tell her she's mixing metaphors. I'm a smart-ass, fifteen years old.

"You want fire imagery," I say.

Then she does what I never expected her to: she brakes hard and looks at me. We sit, stopped, still, in the middle of the Dalton Highway—the one thing we are not supposed to do.

"Enough's enough!" she shouts, angry. "I mean, cut the shit. I don't know this man—what he's capable of, or what he's doing—but there's no hope for you in a love like that. There's no reason to align your hearts. I see what's inside of you, and it is beautiful, and he's killing it, of that I'm sure. You want this trip to change things for you? Well, you have to put in the work. You have to believe in change. You've got to make the past the past, and you've got to leave this man behind you."

She's yelling, and I start to cry. But she doesn't yield the way most would. She's angry and right to be. I'm angry at me, too.

Joy is right: it is my task to extract myself, and I am one of the fortunate few who has every resource to do so at my disposal.

Finally Joy eases off the brake, confident her words have reached me, and we roll, slowly, past a forested mountain. She's intentional in her silence; she wants me to stew in my discomfort. She wants me to understand this trip could be my forest fire if only I will let it. Arctic Ocean or no Arctic Ocean. Climactic moment or no climactic moment. Alaska could be the moment that I finally start anew.

"Did you mean what you said earlier?" I ask her. "Do you really feel this is God's land? That you feel Him most when you're up here?"

She taps the window to the world, the wind sweeping down from the mountains a sheet of soft, white flurries.

"Absolutely," she says. "How could I not? Don't you feel Him at work here? Don't you feel Him at work between us?"

She moves the air in the truck cab, swirling it around with her pinkie.

"And especially right *here*? *Right now*? This is God's country, yeah. When it's just me, in this truck, alone? I can hear His voice a whole lot clearer. I can hear Him perfectly, because there's nothing in the way."

"And it's still that way with me?"

"He's louder with you here," she says. "You've got a good spirit, and God loves it. I hear Him trying to talk to you, absolutely. And I hear Him talking to me, too. He wants me to protect you."

"What's He saying?"

"That you're my soul sister. And that I was right—*you know* I was right—when I said God brought you here to tell my story. He wants you to tell my story."

"I don't know your story."

"Sure you do. You're living it."

She looks at me, says nothing. I fold my arms and look out the window. She's talking the way Dave does—like when he claimed to hear God behind a dumpster, when he rode his bike around San Francisco, craning his ear to California's sky—but her words don't feel manipulative, exploitative, or like attempts to further harm. Her words—her faith—feel genuine.

"But maybe?" she says finally. "He also wanted me to tell you my story because He knew you needed it."

Suddenly I realize how wrong I was to feel disappointed by Prudhoe Bay. I wanted to trace the Dalton Highway, wanted to stand against the Arctic Ocean, because I thought the trip, the water, would make me strong. But it was my own strength—all along—that brought me to join Joy here in the first place.

All that matters is Joy's story. Her words alone can be my lightning.

Her love, her vulnerability, has the power to help me burn my whole life down.

Joy sees something in me—something worth salvaging—and she wants me to see it, too, so that I can salvage myself when I get back home: to Dave, and to our life, and to the thirty-year-old story I've been writing about who I am.

"Honestly?" I say. "I don't know what I believe anymore. God, or no God. I think you have this sense."

"I do."

"I've spent so long trying to force it, or to pretend, because I felt like being loved—being accepted—was contingent on it. It's been like this for so long that I don't know what I feel. But you say these things, and they comfort me. You say you hear Him, and I believe you."

Joy looks at me and smiles.

"What do you think *makes* this God's land?" I ask. Ice crystals clink against the window, sparkle like diamonds in the morning's sun.

And it doesn't matter what Joy says next.

It doesn't matter to me at all, because, for the first time, I have the answer.

God's land is a place where women are talking, where they are confiding, where they are free.

~

The Fairbanks we find waiting for us is cracked in half like a yellowed yolk, the rich light of orange dusk spreading wet over the mountains and the city there beneath. I marvel as we pass fast food chains, gas stations and their neon lighting, America again in rich abundance. We slip back into it easily. We pass Joy's favorite Korean restaurant, an orange building with Christmas lights. I watch the women inside fill glasses with cold water, look out at Joy's truck and smile, wave, the lights shining wildly against their windows.

"I love that little waitress, and the owner—I love her, too."

"You love everyone," I say.

We descend farther, and Joy points out more buildings that house more people she loves: the man who works the register at that gas station, a man who used to "drive truck" like her, and the hostess at a corner diner.

"Creamer's Field," she says, pointing. "This is a resting stop for sandhill cranes. Those giant, velociraptor-looking birds? They park here every year, a little respite after flying thousands of miles from Mexico to the Arctic."

She loves those birds, she tells me, too.

The field is wet, brown mush, empty, no dinosaur birds in sight.

"You'll have to come back at the end of August," she says, "and see."

"We'll take the big rig," I say.

"We'll take the big rig." She smiles. "That's right."

Finally, we reach the SpringHill Suites, and Joy parks, kills the engine, and throws up her hands.

"I got you home safe," she says.

"A marvel. My mother will be so relieved."

"I bet you're tired," she says, "yeah?"

I nod and exhale deeply.

She sighs, shrugs. "Well," she says, "we've still got that moose. You'll come over for moose tomorrow?"

"Of course I will," I say, "but on the early side, because I fly out at midnight."

"Right. You know," she adds, as if an afterthought, though something about her words feels rehearsed, "you're welcome to stay with me tonight."

But I've got my hotel room booked, and perhaps more importantly, some part of me feels I owe it to Joy to give her a break. From me, from everything. I owe it to her family.

"I should probably spend some time alone," I say. Her words have sunk their teeth in me, and I need to think about what they mean: for me and for my future, for whatever steps I'm about to take. "I appreciate it, though," I add.

"Okay," she says, "but moose supper? Tomorrow night?"

"Absolutely, yes."

I tell her I'll bring dessert.

"No, no, no," she says, "no way. We've got ice cream up to our shoulders, and I bet you Samantha will bake up something."

"Okay," I say. "Okay." I move in and clamp her shoulders. "Bye," I say. I squeeze.

"Bye, Spice Girl." She starts the engine up. "But I'll see you tomorrow, and tomorrow's not so bad!"

And she's right, it's not so bad.

Except upstairs in my hotel room, I feel like I don't belong—not there, not anywhere. The bedsheets, the towels, the pillows—everything is white and clean, and all the clothing I own is dusty, yellowed, and smells of sweat and pee. I lay a perfectly laundered towel along the carpet, then unpack my backpack, conducting an inventory. Everything is steeped in memories from my life before Alaska.

I take the elevator to the lower level and buy a mint-green sweatshirt and pair of sweatpants from a souvenir store playing nineties pop. Back in my hotel room, I take the world's longest shower. I towel off and apply some makeup and again look in the bathroom mirror, resembling for the first time in a long while the woman I was before I arrived in Fairbanks.

I don't like the way she looks. I wash my makeup off.

I ask the woman in the mirror what it is she plans to do.

"What are you going to do?" I ask.

She doesn't seem to know. I move around my room, reorganize my toiletries, read from a welcome pamphlet that there's a laundry room in the lobby and a restaurant beside the hotel.

There is no time like the present for a steak.

But upon entering the adjacent restaurant, I realize Lavelle's Bistro is the fanciest restaurant in all of Fairbanks. Votive candles blink on the linened tables. But I refuse to be ashamed of my new sweatpants, which read *ALASKA!* across the butt. I take my seat at the wine bistro's bar, tuck *ALASKA!* onto a stool.

Tonight's special is crispy duck layered over pilaf with a side of roasted asparagus. I order the black-and-blue-cheese salad with seared steak and a glass of their house white wine. It comes cold and crisp, and I try to forget about the road and my expectations that two days on a highway in remote Alaska could transform me into someone else:

someone braver, smarter, *stronger*, more willing to walk away. That two days with Joy Mothertrucker might make me more of a Mothertrucker myself.

My phone hums as I reach the elevator. It's a text from Joy, and she misses me, and I tell her I miss her, too.

Let me tell you about the puppies! she says.

TELL ME, I write.

They all look good—they've grown—except one of them, she writes. Three dots appear and blink, proof of Joy's mind in motion.

But I'm worried about the runt. All the rest have doubled in size, but this one, he seems to have gotten smaller? And all their eyes are almost open, and he's still squeezing his so tight.

Maybe he's just built smaller, I write, hopeful. Maybe he's just fine?

Maybe, Joy concedes. Except he was born bigger than he is now.

She asks if I can come early tomorrow.

I can come help, I say, of course.

Thanks, she says. I need it! Samantha and James are laughing—I finally get home, I hug them, and then I disappear down into the basement to try to help this puppy! But I'm afraid he'll die without me!

I picture her alone in her dark basement, the other puppies crawling against her leg. I picture the small one tucked against her sweatshirt, his little warm heart beating against her chest. I imagine the prayer she's said for him, and how I know without really knowing that she's singing, swaddling him.

~

The morning of the moose, Joy calls to tell me she'll pick me up at my hotel, and when I meet her a few hours later, she's standing in the lobby, tapping her fingers at the check-in desk.

"You're not going to take an Uber to my house," she says as we make our way outside. "That'd be some hospitality, my gosh."

I'm wearing clean jeans and my new green T-shirt—the tiny cartoon polar bear standing up and waving. He's Toby and he's alive.

"Nine years before I met you," I tell Joy as we climb into her truck, "I lived in Iowa, where the sky regularly went this color each summer. Storms. People called it God's machine—the way the clouds went green and swirled in the moments before a twister dropped clean and churning from the sky."

"God's machine?" she asks.

"Because you look up, and you see what's happening, and you know that He's in charge," I tell her. "Or that's what one man told me, my first summer in that state."

"Well, sure," Joy says, "I can see that. I feel that way all the time."

"Right," I say. "But then I met this woman. Kathleen Rash, this artist. She paints these beautiful, enormous canvases—what she does, she drives her car out into the prairie to paint Iowa's fiercest storms. They're beautiful—full wall-length acrylics, a rush of blue and black and gray above a blip of yellow field. I visited her studio all the time, just to see her works in progress. Finally, after a few years of visits, I asked her: Why do you do it?"

"Paint?"

"Paint those images, specifically. Those storms. And do you know what she told me?"

"What?"

"She told me that she began to paint midwestern storms after losing her partner of many years. Her wife, or maybe wife. I don't remember the story exactly—either the Supreme Court legalized gay marriage and they were finally able to get married and then she died, or she died before it was legalized—but the point is, society changed, and they lost each other in the midst, regardless."

"People should love whoever they want."

"People *should* love whoever they want." I tuck my hand in hers. "Her work—it was so moving, so powerful, and so expensive, you know?" I laugh. "Not more expensive than it should be, and not expensive for most people, but for a graduate student, a *teacher*? I've always wanted to buy one, but I never have. Still, I visit her studio every chance I get. Every time I go back to Iowa, I visit. And I email. I'm always asking: What are you working on? What now? What *now*? She's been so generous with me, and with her story, you know? She always emails me back. She sends me these enormous image files. And when I return to Iowa, she just lets me stand there in her studio and admire."

"She sounds like a wonderful lady."

"She is," I say. "And do you know what she told me once? She told me that she knew by people's preference for her work that that person was awash in grief. Once, she even asked me outright, said, 'What hard thing happened to you?'"

"What did you say?" Joy asks.

"That my friend had murdered a young woman a few years before, and that I'd been in volatile relationships with men ever since, and that I felt like, in some ways, I was still fumbling my way from one act of male violence to another."

I tell Joy how I felt struck by this artist's astuteness, by how thoroughly she saw me. How she could tell in just a minute all the things I tried hard to hide.

"She saw me like you did," I say. "You saw me in all my fullness, and you didn't reject me for it, and she saw me in all my fullness, too, and she didn't reject me for it, either."

"Women know," Joy says. "They know."

"*You* knew."

She squeezes my hand in hers. "When you called me?" she says. "I wasn't certain. I thought maybe you were crazy. But then God spoke to me—He did—and He told me I had to meet you."

She nods, tucks her hair behind her ear, and checks her teeth in the rearview mirror.

"You'll own one of those paintings someday," she tells me. She puts a hand on my shoulder. "And I want you to send a photo of it when you do."

I smile at her. I nod.

"Okay," I say, "I will."

"I mean it," Joy says. "Women support other women. It's the most important thing."

I nod, and I agree, but I'm still hung up on the recognition that Joy has offered to me in one week what I've spent three years looking for from Dave.

I think of Kathleen, of Joy.

Thank you, I think, *for seeing me.*

14.

If there's a stigma about being a female trucker, Joy tells me on the drive back to her cabin, there's an even bigger stigma about being a female who hunts moose.

"Oh, some men? They don't like it," she tells me. "Think we're a buncha girls, trying to play with grown men's toys. But Samantha and I? We love it. We take it as some sort of challenge. Just wait until she tells you the story of how we bagged this moose."

"The moose we're going to eat?"

"The moose you're going to *love*," Joy says, pounding her palms on the steering wheel emphatically. But she stresses that it's important she let Samantha tell it.

"She's better at it," Joy adds. "Telling that story? She's—how do you say it? She gets *animated*. She honestly comes alive. What *I* can tell you about? I can tell you about how I've prepped it." She rolls the sleeves up on her sweater, one arm at a time. "It's been in the slow cooker now for hours."

The light on the trees this afternoon is a pitchy orange sap. Joy lives fifteen miles up the Dalton Highway, and I savor the light, the fields, the wilderness, the return to adventure.

Her driveway is gravel and steep, her house a cabin tucked beyond a wall of woods. Joy puts the truck in park, and two dogs rush out and run in dizzy circles beneath the truck bed. They bark as we open our doors. The land is a naturalist's heaven, complete with a greenhouse and a small, open pasture. Her old horse whinnies in the distance, and I imagine the small white horse beside it, neighing softly, a purchase Joy deserves.

"This moose!" Joy exclaims, leading me up the steps and through a small screen door to an interior that is all wood and family photos. Everything smells like rosemary, like thyme and ground parsley. James is in an easy chair, the newspaper folded across his lap.

"Well, hello," he says, folding the paper in half and setting it on his knee. "In fresh fashion from Prudhoe Bay."

I Vanna White my T-shirt. "Ain't it something?" I ask.

He rises, hugs me. I feel my face flush against his flannel.

"I'm glad you guys had fun," he says, standing back to study me.

"Your wife is something else."

"She is," he says, nodding.

We sit in the living room, Joy's exercise bike front and center. Joy herself takes a seat beside her parents, who flank both ends of an uphol-stered couch. Her mom wears a hot-pink Kenworth hat and a floral but-ton-down. Her dad is in green flannel. They both sit perfectly upright, staring out a window that overlooks blue mountains. Above and all around us hang ribbons of every color: white and yellow and red, all pinned to walls or behind glass or hanging from the knobs on corner cabinets. There are whole shelves full of golden trophies, each sporting the rounded head of a metal child glinting in hard-won triumph.

"That's Samantha," James says. "She was a youth dog-mushing champion. Could've gone pro if she wanted."

"But I *didn't* want," Samantha says, emerging from the hallway. She's wearing an AC/DC T-shirt and jeans ripped at the knee. She offers a sarcastic, I-do-what-I-want kind of smile, something I've seen Joy do more than once, as we look at proof of all her winning. I reach out and touch one of her awards, the blue ribbon cool between my fingers.

"Too many big dogs," she tells me.

"Isn't that good?" I ask.

"Sure, but I'm just a skinny bean," she says, again the spitting image of her mother. "When I was younger, I could control the dogs—*most* of the dogs—but the one we got last was wild. I couldn't. He was just so big."

Joy moves into the kitchen behind us, touches my shoulder as she passes.

"I was good," Samantha says, nodding.

"She's like her mama," Joy says, slicing a loaf of bread.

Samantha rolls her eyes. From his place back on his recliner, James calls, "Samantha, get her something to drink."

She turns to me, annoyed. "Can I get you a drink?" she asks.

I tell her water is fine.

"One of the last races I raced?" She takes a glass from the shelf. "I put my lead dog in the middle. That's a big mistake for a dog that's been leading his whole life."

"I see," I say. I don't. But I love the nuance of this sport and how easily she accepts her shortcomings without shame.

"So you're a writer?" she asks, handing me the cool glass of water. "We're reading *The Great Gatsby* in English."

She tells me *The Great Gatsby* is very stupid.

"I thought a lot of people your age like that book?" I ask. "And plus there was that movie?"

"If people like that book, they're stupid," she says. "What a dumb book. That book is all like, 'Build your romantic and life hopes up, and then crush them. *Shank*.'"

"What is *shank*?"

"The crushing of dreams!" Samantha says. "The crushing of what we still think is possible!"

According to Samantha, the problem with *The Great Gatsby* is that it's selling a false premise. And often selling it to young people, at that.

209

It's dangerous, she says, to make young people believe they can be in love, be happy.

"Just stupid," she says again.

"I hear you like to hunt? Your mom tells me you've got a story about this moose."

Samantha grins. She's a perfect little Joy, and I have talked her into a place of comfort.

"My mom, she helped me memorize the rules of moose hunting when I was young. Like, you can't shoot across the highway. You have to step off the road—and by road, the state means any drivable service road, so even goat trails, for example. And you need a hunting license. That's thirty, forty bucks. And a moose-hunting permit fee. Luckily there's no lottery in this state or whatever, because there's not that many people in Alaska."

"She was ten," Joy tells me over her shoulder, "when I took her to a laser-shooting range and she shot every target perfectly."

"There's a reason," Samantha says, still grinning.

"We didn't know"—Joy laughs—"but she'd been practicing shooting with her brother's rifle."

"An Alaskan girl has to know how to fire a weapon!"

Joy hands Samantha a stack of place mats.

"People think hunting is savage," Samantha continues, "but honestly, it's much more humane. This year, moose hunting went from September first to the twenty-first, so it's not like there's a ton of time. And three of my moose were one-shot kills, and others would've been, but I was too fast and I scared them."

"Twenty-two years ago," Joy says, "I was the only woman allowed at a friend's hunting lodge. Now I've got a daughter with a one-shot kill. I mean, that is some kind of capacity. And it's true, you know? More and more women hunt. But some folks, they're still resistant."

"Did Mom tell you," Samantha asks, "about the men who tried to steal our moose?"

Samantha winds up, the same way Joy does, ready to make her story a work of art.

"We saw this moose," she begins, laying her fingers down on the air, setting an atmosphere. "And *it was ours*, and we pulled off the highway. But these two men saw us do it, and so they pulled up, parked right behind us. Now, something you've got to know: it's illegal to hinder a hunt. And not just because it sucks to hinder someone's hunt, but because if they miss the moose, and it runs, that moose becomes a danger."

"Moose on the loose!" Joy squeals.

"It's frantic, right? And it's scared? And it weighs, oh my god, *so much*. Well, these two guys," Samantha continues, "they didn't want two girls to get that moose."

"They were dicks!" Joy adds. "Dicks! But Samantha had a moose caller—this little whistle—around her neck. Wears it all hunting season. It was a gift from a family friend who gave it to her when she was four."

"Four!" Samantha says. She rolls her eyes. "So yeah, right, was I going to let some men get my moose. I've been training for this *forever*. And those men were so stupid. Thought we were just two dumb girls. So Mom? She stepped off the highway and fired."

"I wanted to let Samantha get it. But most of all, I didn't want *those men* to get it."

"It was *our* moose!" Samantha agrees.

"Hey," James calls from the easy chair, "you two ever think maybe they just wanted to help you out?"

"*Bullshit* they wanted to help us," Samantha says. "I was mad about that for like a month."

"And me!" Joy says. "That was my moment with my daughter. That was my moment to pass a torch."

"You passed a torch," Samantha says, turning to her mom in appreciation.

"But you girls still got your bull!" James says. He rises from his chair, places his hands firmly on Samantha's shoulders. He kisses the top of her head.

"Well, the story doesn't end there, because it turns out those guys were camping up the road." Now Samantha is laughing. "So Mom and I, we drove by, and we just started honking, honkkkkking—making all kinds of noise, having, like, a little victory party right there on that highway!"

"We hope they saw us and they knew," Joy adds.

"Oh, they saw us and they knew."

Joy steps over to side-hug her daughter. Samantha lowers the oven door for Joy as she pulls a tray of roasted potatoes out.

"Well, anyway," Joy says, "it's our moose now."

Samantha shakes her head, whispers under her breath, "Stupid men."

Joy retrieves the meat from the slow cooker, carves it, ladles the vegetables into bowls, and tells us to take our seats. The table is big and wooden, and Joy occupies the head. I lower my chin on instinct.

"Lord, thank you for bringing us together," she says, and then we eat our moose.

The meat is perfect, fragrant and fork tender. It tastes of mushrooms, herbal and earthy. I almost taste the sweet Alaskan grasses the animal pulled from wild earth.

"This is so good," I say.

Joy beams, proud to take care of me again. She looks at Samantha and grins, proud to show her off, as well.

"It is good, Mom," Samantha says. "You did a good job cooking it."

"Well, like I said, I'm glad you two made it home safely," James says, reaching across the table to take Joy's hand in his. "It's good to have her back."

"I bet," I say. "Now I miss her."

"You two have to share!" Joy laughs. She grins at me, takes a bite of moose, then turns back to James. "We're going to try to help the puppy after we eat."

Then she turns to me and whispers, "I bought that little white horse, did I tell you? We pick him up next weekend."

She looks at James and grins.

"She gets everything she wants," he says, "plus all the stuff she doesn't."

"She deserves it," I say. I think of Jake and Joy's marriage, all the stories she relayed to me. *You have to make peace with the past,* she'd told me, *or the past will follow you.*

But the past is never a neatly closed chapter; the past is not skin you shed. The legacy of history remains. I look at James and love him. He supports her, is kind to her. Still I know that tricky past remains wedged somewhere inside her ribs. Her world is an American diorama: the good wife and the good mom and all the violence she's endured and squeezed love and beauty from regardless.

Someday, I hope to be her. To leave this past behind. To begin a second life myself. I feel grateful for her white horse, the slate mountains outside the window, Atigun and all its sheep, their legs like pinwheels against the sky.

"She does deserve it," James says at last.

We eat the rest of our moose in silence, then, James holding Joy's hand across the table. We finish, and Samantha stands to clear the plates.

"Can I help?" I ask.

"I got this," Samantha says. I watch Joy take her palm from James's and rise to stand beside the sink and ladle warm rhubarb pie—still steaming from the oven—on top of scoops of vanilla ice cream.

"Can I stay with you forever?" I ask when she sits down.

Everyone looks at me and smiles, except James, who seems slightly uncomfortable. I place another spoonful of pie into my mouth.

"Only kidding," I say.

I'm not.

~

In the basement an hour later, Joy sits cross-legged beside the dog crate and tells me I'm about to be up to my ears in so much cute that it might feel unmanageable.

"*Major* cuteness," she warns. "Frankly, you might never recover."

"I can handle it," I say. "I've spent my lifetime building up my tolerance."

She laughs. "Okey dokey."

One by one, she scoops the puppies from their crate, each a tiny black cloud she deposits into my lap. The puppies crawl along my shin, mouths open, yawning, then tumble onto the carpet to move slowly around my feet. One lifts his head to howl, but it's mostly air passing beneath his teeth.

"Now this one," she says, reaching in for the runt.

But when she pulls him from the cage, her face goes slack, and we both know.

"He died," I say.

"He died."

She holds the small animal up, his body stiff in the light of an old floor lamp. She doesn't like what she sees and pulls him close against her chest. She swaddles him, tucking the loose fabric of her sweatshirt over his head, as if to thaw him.

"I'm sorry."

"It's not fair," she says. "He was so young. He didn't even get a chance."

I reach my hand out to stroke his head. His fur is cool and oddly stiff.

"What was it you said to me? Up in Prudhoe Bay, during the blizzard, when we saw the dead caribou? How it's a matter of perspective?"

"That was about wolves eating caribou. Or wolves chasing down a fox. Nothing is going to get to live differently, live *better*, because he died," she says. "This poor guy suffered for no one and for nothing."

I look down at the other puppies, fumbling around her lap. I count nine: nine separate balls of fluff, nine pairs of blinking eyes, nine small sets of puppy teeth gnawing gently at my ankles. I pick one up and hold him, nose to nose, against my face.

"But these guys," I say, "these ones get to live."

The puppy squirms beneath my fingers.

"And they'll have good lives, rich lives," she says. "But this one should've had one, too."

I put the puppy down, watch him wiggle back into formation. She's talking about a dead dog, but she's talking, too, about her friends, about the people who disappear in snow or sleet or rain on the highway or in bars or bedrooms. All the deaths she can't prevent, all the hurt she cannot heal.

She reaches for another blanket, lowers the dead puppy, and gently burrito-rolls it. "Just rotten luck is what it is."

She looks at me and nods, as if acknowledgment is all she needed. I nod, too, and then we stand and are quiet for a moment, our eyes on the unmoving blanket. At last, Joy sweeps him up in her arms and carries him up the stairs. In the foyer, she lowers him into a plastic bucket and places the bucket beside the door.

"James will take care of this," she says. "He always takes care of the stuff I don't have the heart to."

Samantha pops her head into the hallway and peers over our shoulders into the bucket. "Oh, she can drive the deadliest highway in America," she says, "but she can't bury a dead puppy."

"I'm sorry," I say again. I put my hand on Joy's shoulder. "I really thought I could help him."

"I should get you home," she says, distracted. She sighs, stretches.

Back in the pickup, the trees glow blue beneath the moon until the headlights click on and flood the yard in light. The highway unravels beneath our wheels as we make the slow descent back to Fairbanks, but something feels different now between us. I can tell that she is hesitant, that Joy has something she wants to say.

"If this is about the puppy," I start, "I mean, we can say a prayer for it, absolutely. I don't think it's silly. I've come to find comfort in all your God talk—I mean, it doesn't bother me."

"It isn't that," she says.

I think maybe this is about remembrance, maybe she wants me to take one of the remaining puppies home, something to commemorate our time together. A living, breathing souvenir. Twelve to fourteen years of built-in memory, black fur and fluff and cuteness, solidifying our connection. I decide that I can do it. I can accept her puppy, absolutely.

"I'll take a puppy," I say, "if that's what this is about."

"No," Joy says. "No. Just listen."

The moon has slipped behind the forest so that I can't see her face, can't study her expression. I can't even see the space between us, though it feels larger than it's ever been.

"So the thing you said to me back in Prudhoe," she begins, "about Dave."

Immediately, I think I know what's coming: how she's sorry she only listened, how she didn't know what more to say, how I deserve better but how I have to know my worth before I can deny a man who denies my value.

"I know," I say. "I *know*."

"No, I don't think you do," she says, "because there's something I haven't told you."

~

The story is the story of many women, and for the most part, it goes like this: the marriage was good except when it wasn't. They were happy except when they weren't.

According to Joy, James drank, and often he hid it, but people knew, because people always know.

"People who drink?" Joy tells me. "They think they're getting away with something, that it's a secret, and if you don't bust them, they get *bold*."

James drank and they fought, and James drank and he fought with himself. Joy tells me his was the very real, very palpable anguish and anger of most who drink, and for much of their marriage, Joy says, it felt as though he took this anger out on her.

"You remember what I said back on the highway?" she asks me. "How I was so convinced I was getting a second chance when I met James? How I thought James was God's reward after Jake?"

I nod.

"Jeez," she says, "you know, I love him, I *so* do. And I was so convinced he was my gift from God that I ignored all those warning signs, all those early red flags I should've seen. I mean, I'm not kidding. When we first met, he was a *mess*."

But he was a mess she tethered herself to, and quickly, because she was a single mother with two boys in Alaska, and because her first husband had tried to control her, and because she wanted the safety and familiar comfort so often couched in the idea of family.

"I think a lot of women," she tells me, "they have this idea that all the world's bad stuff—you know, all the harm the world can do— it won't happen to you if you're married. Almost like a husband will protect you. And I thought I could help him. When we met, his first wife had just left him, and James was one of those guys who, when they get divorced, you know, their whole world just falls apart. He was hell-bent on destroying himself, and I didn't want to see that. I mean, no one does."

The truck dips down through a valley, tall trees on either end, looming big. Fairbanks glows orange in the distance beneath the sky's deep, darkening blue.

"But he was just a *mess*," she repeats.

I remember James admitting the same thing to me. That day at Golden Heart, when he'd leaned in and whispered, "That little lady is a legend," as we watched her arrange communion crackers. "But she fixed me up," he'd said, "she really did. I was a bit of a mess back then."

"A bit of a mess" makes me think of people who have vices because the world has made those vices feel necessary, a means to cope with something painful, with whatever hardship the world has dealt. I think of people—angry, struggling—who harbor deep and personal pain. But it also occurs to me that, by extension, this language might function as a coded way to say that their pain manifests in ways that cause harm to other people.

Coded language for inflicting harm.

Still he was a mess, and she loved him. So they married, they hunkered down, and then they got pregnant and had Samantha.

It was good, so good, they were *family*.

Joy and I are warm and safe and sharing, but still I don't expect what comes out next: how once, Joy tells me, James held a gun—no, he *pointed* it—at her and their newborn baby.

"He was drunk," she says, "and he held the gun to our faces."

I don't know why or how it happened. What happens next is only what I've imagined, all the ways I have pictured that scene unfolding in the days and weeks and months after Joy told me, because it's the kind of story that doesn't go away. The details change a little bit every time, the setting, but in the version that prevails most frequently, Joy is on the kitchen floor. Brown linoleum, the pattern vintage, sticky spots beneath the cabinets from where the kids spilled apple juice.

The boys are watching television in fleece pajamas. A plush couch, or a recliner. They've got sippy cups and Goldfish crackers.

Samantha is just an infant, fussing in Joy's lap.

Joy and James have been fighting over something.

Doesn't matter what.

James points the gun, and Joy goes quiet.

In my imagination it is always night, a clear dark sky, no northern lights, though it is winter. The big dumb moon is all aglow. Are they in the cabin that burned down, or the trailer they were in when Joy first met him, or something in between? I don't know the answers, and in the most foundational sense, they do not matter.

What matters is what Joy tells me. That she thought she might die that night. How she held her crying baby, glanced at her two young sons, then she looked at the man she'd married and thought they might not make it to see morning.

"I've never been so terrified in my whole life." Her hands wrap tightly around the steering wheel. "I felt the air go out—I felt it leave my body."

Obviously, she did not die that night. She told no one for quite some time. Then she told her best friend, Debbie, then no one else for almost twenty years.

Now she is telling me.

"I didn't want to mention it," she says, "because I didn't want it to change your opinion about James. He's a good guy—he is—and it was important to me that you like him."

I have no idea what to say, so I say nothing. I certainly do not ask questions; I can tell that already the few words Joy has offered me feel like a few too many.

Perhaps it is worth noting, then, what I *do not* think about, considering all I do.

I do not think, *That monster.*

I do not think, *No way.*

I think that it makes sense. That it aligns with what I know, the duality of our America, the performance and then the reality behind so many domestic scenes. I think about James's button-down, and his neatly combed brown hair, and the way he smiled as Joy pulled me into his truck in the hotel parking lot for my first Saturday Sabbath. The way he wrapped an arm around her in the damp parking lot. How he held open the door for her. How he told me she was good.

"The best woman," he said, "there is."

I don't say anything. The air is getting colder, darker. The wind rushes through the trees. Each time our truck dips beneath a streetlight, I glance over to glimpse small, wet crescents forming and pooling beneath Joy's eyes.

"One time," Joy whispers to me, "I was up here, trucking—I always seemed to be trucking during the worst of James's drinking—and our buddy called me, said he'd spotted James out around town and he could smell the liquor on his breath. Told James if he could smell it, the cops sure could."

She pauses.

"And I mean, what do I do with that kinda knowledge? And with our daughter? And that's the thing—our daughter? She doesn't get why I work. She doesn't get why I'm always gone. She's seventeen, so she just knows I'm never home. I think she thinks it's selfish, what I do. She doesn't get it. She *does not get it.*"

She looks to me for sympathy. I think about my own mother, the ways we fought when I was seventeen. How we fought about anything, really. How any chance to express disdain seemed reason enough then for me.

"She ribs me for it!" Joy continues. "We argue about it all the time. Finally I get home from the road, and I am so glad to see her, and I just want to hold her in my arms. She's a teenager—of course she doesn't get it—but I do this work *for her*. So I can support her if I have to. I mean, if it comes down to that."

She rubs at her nose meekly, and I want to reach out to her across the cab, but we both know I can't offer her anything she doesn't know already. Instead, I push my head into the seat rest until the back of my skull begins to ache.

"We always love these men," she tells me, "and we think that we can fix them. We think our good love will be their remedy."

"That's what you said about Jake," I say.

"And it's what you say about Dave. And I mean it about James, too. I love him so much it hurts. And women? We have so much love to give. But it often puts us in harm's way."

"But you left Jake," I say. "Why have you stayed with James?"

"Because I love him," she says. She doesn't hesitate. "And because it's not easy, being a woman with three kids all alone, and because I love him—I love him, absolutely, yeah. I mean, isn't that what we do?"

We're idling at a red light. Her wedding ring glints on her thin finger. I can see her hands are shaking and how, this time, it has nothing to do with the engine.

"And I didn't want to do it," she tells me, "wake up in ten years' time and say I didn't try. Three babies and I didn't try." She flutters her hand. "I used to know how to do it. Be a woman and make it work. But I don't know anymore. I do not know. Should I have left him?"

I can't tell if it's a rhetorical question. I let it float in the air between us.

"I mean, probably?" she says. "But women are taught to love. What do I think? Women are taught to love too much. We prioritize men's pain in this culture when what we really need to do? We need to prioritize the lives of women."

We need to prioritize the lives of women.

Joy exhales through her teeth, punches the wheel with her fist. "Listen. I believe we were put on this earth to love," she says, "and I believe we love until we can't love any longer. But the woman I was then, when we first married, when all this started? I so desperately wanted James to break the cycle, to get sober. Had I listened to Dr. Laura back then, I would've walked away. And I would've saved myself a lot of pain. A lot of heartache. But I believed I could love him out of it. And I believed it was my job to make him better."

"I have spent my whole life incarcerated by that idea."

"Of course you have!" she says. "I have, too! I think most women do! I have spent my whole life shackled to this belief, and it's a bunch of garbage."

"But James?"

"I told him," she says. "I told him that was it, enough was enough, that was the last time. I said, 'No more, no more, no more.'" She pauses. "And maybe it would've been different if James thought what he did was okay, but you know, he was sorry. He said he knew that wasn't love. Said he was committed to being better. Said he'd work on getting sober."

"Yeah?"

"He has one full year under his belt."

"A year is no small feat."

But there are almost twenty years shared between them, and almost seventeen years since that night.

What gray area do I not know about?

I think, *I don't know how she does it.* But I know it all too well—the mercy we afford our men because they did not pull the trigger.

Would I leave Dave if he bought a gun? Would I leave if he pulled that gun on me? I want to think I would, but so often, his words have felt like weapons, and I haven't left him yet.

"So James is a year sober now," Joy repeats, "and I am so proud of him."

Which is not to say that life has not been a struggle since that evening, but James has worked to make it right. And she's stood by him all this time.

"We've had our ups and downs," she says, "but I think this is it. We are finally up."

I want so badly for this to be true. Joy deserves to be up for good.

"I hope so, too," I say.

She tells me about the ring she purchased for him last year: cold, hard metal inscribed with her favorite line from Scripture, which I do not ask about on this night, and therefore, I will never know. The ring was a celebration of their marriage, she told me, of everything they'd been through—a reward for his sobriety—but it also functioned as a warning.

"Oh, it's a threat, absolutely," Joy tells me. "It's a promise, sure as day, that if he picks up that bottle again, I'm leaving him. Listen." She pulls into the hotel parking lot. "I don't want you thinking that I'm weak. But I also don't want you thinking I've got some superhuman strength."

I look at her and nod.

"This story." She shakes her head. "I am telling you this story because it's a part of me. I am the highway, but I am also this. I think most women are. We have to take turns being one and then the other if we want to get ahead in life."

"You told me you drove the highway because you love adventure."

"I *do*," she says, "love adventure. But I also love the freedom of making my own money. Of being a woman who can pay her way. And support her family, herself, her children. This job—I make more money than I ever would here in Fairbanks. So much more, *so much* more. So that if I need to, I can do it. I can take my daughter. I can *go*."

I intuit all she's not saying: that the risk is worth the reality, that she forgives him but she can't forget, that the truth—what it all comes down to—is that sometimes she feels safer on the deadliest road in America than in the living room of her own home.

"Listen, this story? It doesn't make me weak. I'm not weak," she repeats. "You were right about that from the start. But more than that, what *matters*, I don't think *you* realize you're not weak."

In a moment of brief levity, she reaches across the cab to poke me, firm, in the rib cage.

"What I'm saying to you, honestly, is that we're more alike than you realize. I've been you most of my life. Which is to say, I guess: I understand what you're doing, and I understand the impulse to stay. I know what it means to love a man so much you can't imagine any other way. But I don't want you to be me—twenty, thirty years down the line."

She unbuckles her seat belt, pulls me in. I begin to cry.

"Listen to me," she says. "I told you about all that because I need you to understand. You look to me as a role model? Look to me as *a warning*. Do not stay with a man like that." She runs her fingers through my hair. "A man like that does not get better."

The truck beneath us is idling, the world around us waiting.

In this moment, in her truck cab, I make a commitment to myself. I will fly home to Ohio. Dave will pick a fight and I will let him. He will leave and I will let him. If I am lucky—and many aren't—I will watch him back out of my driveway and it will be like watching him back out of my life completely.

This time will be different. This time I will not take him back.

I will close the door to all of this.

And I will have Joy to thank.

In the truck, our final moment, Joy holds me in her arms in her sweater laced with dog fur. She smells like moose and carrots. She feels like all that's holy.

"I love you," I say gently.

She pulls away to look at me, the last moment we will ever share as two women alive on earth.

"Do not stay with a man like that," she repeats, whispering, and then again her mouth is on my head, her breath hot against my ear. "I am telling you, you have to leave him. I am telling you, it does not get better. A man like that? I am telling you, it will just get worse."

15.

I flew back to my Ohio. I flew back to my old life.

But the truth is—and I think Dave and I both knew this—something had changed in me, become emboldened by Alaska. I would not become his Christian woman; I would not become his Christian wife. Not if Christianity, if faith, looked the way it did with Dave.

I landed late in the afternoon after twenty-two hours of travel. He did not pick me up from the airport, and I drove back exhausted, delirious. When finally we saw each other, his face looked different, somehow, older. The shadow of a beard had begun to grow along his jawline, and it made the softness I remembered—those first months, that whole first year, those evenings spent on the beach outside San Francisco—feel like moments spent with a different man entirely.

Those first few days, I found myself waiting for an inciting incident, another moment to ignite his anger, but the moment came quietly, and without escalation, when one morning—out of nowhere—his old school in San Francisco called to offer him his job back.

"You should take it," I said.

He agreed.

We had been presented with an easy out, and I think we both were all too happy to welcome it. He left without incident a few days later, almost as if he'd heard Joy, her words.

As if she'd spoken to him, too.

Or maybe it was God putting an end to our escalation by placing an entire country between us.

I didn't know—I still don't know—what I did to deserve such easy closure. Most women are not so lucky. But in many ways our relationship—and all our love, and all the fear and beauty housed inside it—ended as quietly as it began.

Somehow I knew this as it was happening, as I watched him pack his things and load them into that navy-blue sedan and get in the driver's seat and disappear. I knew with unfathomable certainty he would not be coming back. I could feel his grip loosen, could feel an easiness as I pictured his car moving down the highway, as he drove clear across the country and far away from me.

Still, I think of Dave sometimes, and never in the ways that I expect. I think about his plastic miniatures, the long, clean curls of his eyelashes, his wide smile, those perfect teeth, how I wanted to make a home inside his laugh. Always that sound of him laughing, laughing. I think about our sleepy mornings, our Sundays at noon in bed, our dog as a little puppy and his fingers tickling up her sides, tracing the fur that coiled and lightened along the soft flesh of her pink belly.

I think about his hands, his wrists.

How, often, he'd return to our summer kitchen with his palms full from all we'd planted. He'd stand in the white light of morning with our red peppers and our summer squash and the delicate orange film of zucchini blossoms, the leafy stalks of sage and basil.

He still exists in my mind, handing me perfect red orbs of cherry tomatoes. I am still pouring creamer in his coffee.

There was beauty in our love. There was tenderness. So often, there was light.

I loved him, despite his violence.

16.

I found out about her death from a text message from a student. It was Saturday at 8:00 a.m. I was painting my first-floor bathroom. In Dave's absence, the world was quiet, and I was working to adjust to its lack of noise. Any chore I could think to do seemed like a chore worth doing. So I'd rolled up my sleeves that morning, had beige paint on my arms and wrists, when the text message came in:

Tell me this isn't Joy?

But of course it was.

The image was a screenshot of her son Daniel's Instagram. The photo he had captioned contained Joy's face in the center, her sunglasses tucked up on her head, Daniel and his gorgeous wife sandwiching her petite body beneath a Hi-C-orange Hawaiian sunset.

Today has been the saddest, most devastating day of my life, Daniel wrote.

And then I stopped reading.

~

Only God, Joy believed, could make a person disappear, and on that first cool evening at the end of August, when already the sky in Prudhoe Bay suggested snow, God took Joy, made her disappear.

The sky was obscured that evening by a thick fog that crept in over the Arctic Ocean. The sun was going down. Joy wore blue jeans, a sweater. She had just finished loading and gassing up her truck before the long drive back to Fairbanks. She was eager, Rich would later tell me, to get a head start on the drive, to get on home to Samantha and James. With a few things left to do themselves, Rich and Donald agreed to meet up with Joy at the nearest pump station, some several dozen miles south, where the men had errands to take care of and where Joy wanted to swing in to say hello to friends.

"She was like that," Donald told me. "Every reason to show warmth was reason enough for her."

It was nearly midnight in Alaska, the world a fluorescent pink. Joy stopped along the shoulder of the highway to roll down the window and take a photo. I can imagine her giving thought to what to say, what she'd write for the photo's caption once she was home with Samantha and James and her parents and had enough connectivity, again, to upload it.

Summer is, ostensibly, the safest time to drive on the Dalton Highway, truckers would later tell me. After all, it is always light, and there is no ice, no snow, no darkness to hide the sharp curves or steep summits that wind between the mountains. In Prudhoe Bay's summer, truckers tell me, you can see everything, *protect* yourself from everything. But more truckers die that time of year than any other, because when we talk about safety on the Dalton Highway, we are always talking about *illusion*.

We are talking about *delusion*.

We are talking about what is and *always* is the most dangerous highway in America.

The story, as it was first relayed to me, was as simple as a children's fable: Joy was on the highway, and then suddenly, Joy vanished.

The longer version came only with time: Donald and Rich reached the pump station, where they agreed they all would meet, and they didn't see her truck. They knew it was not like Joy to break a promise. And they knew there was no other place she might have gone except off the road, *down*, *over*—into thin air, into thick air, into rich, lush tundra, into God's great world.

With no cell phone service and no call box, Rich and Donald got in their trucks and circled back, making their way once more north toward Prudhoe Bay, the fog thick enough to slice.

"And that's when we saw it: a terrible, descending pathway winding, wildly, into tundra," Rich recounted.

There, several yards from the road, they saw Joy's fifty-three-foot tanker overturned, the cab crushed, folded, and flattened by the weight of over 9,700 pounds of diesel fuel. In photos I would later find on the internet, the vehicle is a snag of metal sunk into the moon.

The last time I'd heard from her was one week earlier, a hi and a photograph from Paris—the first time Joy had ever left the country, the first time she'd traveled alone with just her daughter. In the photo, she and Samantha lean into each other from a sightseeing boat on the Seine River, the Eiffel Tower glinting gray in the waning, dusty light behind them.

The trip, she'd told me, was a bribe.

"Pull your grades up, and I'll take you to Europe," she'd told Samantha.

"She wants to go to Europe because she can drink," she'd told me before they left. "And she thinks she's pulling one over my head, but I know all about their drinking age over there, and here's the thing: I'm going to let her do it. 'Indulge,' I'll say. 'Get wasted.' And then I'll be there to make sure she's safe and that she never wants to drink again. Better now with her mom in Europe than in college with some boy!"

That was August 14.

Ten days later, she was dead.

"Heaven on earth," she'd called it just four months earlier, slowing the truck between rows of spruce, swirling her hand out the driver's window, snowflakes catching between her fingers.

"Heaven on earth," she repeated. "Don't you let anyone tell you we can't have both."

~

In Ohio, I drove to the nursery, a little garden shop on the edge of town lined with forsythia and daylilies and ceramic fountains carved in stone, tiny ornate birds with scarlet marbles in their beaks.

It was late August, but already hay bales and pumpkins lined the parking lot, and parents in buffalo-checked flannel hoisted chunky toddlers up for a thirty-second photo op, the suede of children's moccasins blending into the hay.

In the aisle dedicated to annuals—those temporary, fleeting joys—I crouched low among the mums and their black plastic shelving, pulling pots from their shallow divots. I moved carefully, plant by plant, checking for tight, green buds, surveying flower coverage, inspecting for signs of disease.

The rule of gardening is simple: you look first for healthy plants, and then you pinch and pull the yellow stems, which threaten to overwhelm. On tomatoes, on peppers, on burly zucchini plants and mums, if it's yellow, the stem is sickly and sucking nutrients. You pinch and pull what is weak so as to restore energy to all that's working.

God was supposed to pinch and pull my yellow parts—not my vibrant, healthy stem.

In the parking lot, I lined my back seat with fifteen pots: pink and peach and yellow sherbet, the colors of a sunset. The pots rattled as I drove them home over train tracks and past churches Dave had made me hate before Joy had seized that hate from my heart.

In my front yard, I got down on my hands and knees, dug holes, and heaved the heavy mums into the ground. I wanted the routine of physical labor: the digging out and putting in and mulching around the roots. I didn't want to think. I didn't want to grieve or process.

What was a world without Joy? Ostensibly, the world I'd known before her.

But I wanted no such world. I wanted to go *back, back, back.*

She gave me the best days of my life and all the strength I needed to give myself a better life each day after. How do you thank someone for that?

At my quiet desk, in my quiet house, I booked a week at the SpringHill Suites.

~

The Fairbanks I arrive in a few days later is a city slowly wading into winter, the trees gold and red like freshly lit matchsticks, branches burning against the clouds' low ceiling. Back in the airport lobby, beside the dueling taxidermized bears in their glass displays, I rent an economy vehicle and ask for premium coverage.

"Are you heading south to Denali?"

"Maybe," I say, distracted. "I'm here for a funeral."

"The woman who drove the Dalton Highway?" The woman's face puckers gently. "I'm sorry," she continues. "I'm just so sorry—so many people have been flying in to mourn her. I've sold five or six car rentals today already."

A map of Alaska spans the wall behind her. My eyes follow the single black line tracing the only route through the state's northern interior, where I got to know her, where I grew to love her, where she taught me to love myself.

"I didn't know her," the woman adds, "but is it weird to say I feel like I did? Because she seems like quite the woman. So much coverage on the news. So much coverage everywhere. Honestly, her death has really shaken all of Alaska. Lot of men drive that road. Never knew a woman did."

The woman clicks her pink nails against the counter. She squints into her computer.

"I tell you what," she says. She hands me a set of keys, says, "Second row, spot eight." She's bumped me up to the next class of vehicle, a Jeep Cherokee, all-wheel drive.

"You should go to Denali," she says. "A woman like that . . ." She swallows, nods. "A woman like that would want you to."

Outside, in the parking lot, the neon-orange Jeep glistens in the sun, glossy as a Jolly Rancher.

I look up at the sky and squint. Is it Joy or is it God or is it the kindness of a stranger that makes me feel what I feel next? As I climb into the Cherokee, as I sit high in that front seat, as I pull out of the airport parking lot, it is almost as if I'm with Joy, sitting beside her in her truck. It is almost as if I am Spice Girl and she is alive and proselytizing—about God, about wilderness—and we are riding clear across Alaska.

Time to do this, mothertruckers.

But the drive to the hotel is short and gray, and imminent winter is everywhere. I pass drive-up trailers selling coffee and crudely made lean-tos advertising thick bundles of firewood for three, four dollars a stack. Men and women shuffle along sidewalks in insulated fleece, the fur-lined collars of their parkas drawn tight around their necks.

I am looking around for Joy, and I am seeing her everywhere: in the grocery store where we bought tempeh, air-puffed green beans, and arugula. In the gas station where we filled up. In the Korean restaurant she loved so much, the string of rainbow Christmas lights still twinkling in the window, though it is August. I park the Jeep in the hotel parking lot and recall meeting Joy here for the first time.

I think, *I'm a woman without a mother*. But of course that's not true, of course that is ridiculous. I have a mother—a very good one—but Joy was something else. In Fairbanks, I feel her absence, feel everything about me, and this place, flicker.

I am far from the only one. Already, I have fielded calls from Debbie and Shannon, Joy's best friends since childhood, who—from their places in recliner chairs many miles removed—wanted to tell me about their friendship, about their early life in Arizona, when it was just sun and sweetness and red dust caked into heat-baked hair. Between tears, between laughter, each woman created a portrait of a Joy who was young and fearless, who rode horses that bucked and kicked, who sought out relationships with everyone.

"I don't know why I'm calling you," they both told me, but I knew exactly why, because I shared the impulse, too. We loved Joy, we *needed* her, and we did not yet know how to not have her with us.

So I sat on my couch and listened as they recounted memories and told stories and devolved into an inventory of inside jokes they, more than once, vocalized they feared I'd mind.

"I don't mind," I said.

They asked about our trip, asked if I'd send them photos, told me Joy had told them how much she liked and trusted me.

"She said you were like one of us," Debbie said. "Like she met you and she knew."

"That means the world," I said.

Shannon couldn't afford to take time off from work to fly up to Alaska, but at the end of my call with Debbie, she asked about the funeral.

"I've never been up there," she said. "Why did I wait until she died to see the place that she loved most?"

I didn't have an answer. But I told her I'd be there when her plane got in. I'd meet her for lunch and take her out and show her everything Joy showed me when my plane first touched down in Fairbanks.

"I'll be your guide," I said.

It's what Joy would have wanted. It would have delighted her beyond belief.

But Debbie doesn't land until tomorrow. Upstairs in my hotel room, I sprawl across my bed to watch the sun set on a darkening Fairbanks, on the little chapel beside the river that glows cool beneath angled spotlights. I slide my thumb around my phone, replaying videos, listening to Joy, who is always laughing, calling me Spice Girl. In one video, she is cackling so wildly I cannot hold still as I squat to pee beside her truck in the white-hot light of the northern Arctic. I've written *JOY!* with my finger in the dust on the side of the pickup truck, and the camera wobbles with the wind as I try to focus on the word.

"Coolest pee," I narrate, "I've ever taken in my life!"

I play it once and then again, and something in my heart pulses. The chapel waits outside the window, and because I feel so open, because she's filled me with something sweet, I open the pages of my electronic Bible. I scan the passages I'd highlighted because Joy had told me to.

The last passage we'd discussed: Ecclesiastes 7.

With all my wisdom I have tried to find out how everything fits together, I read, *but so far I have not been able to. I do know there is one good man in a thousand, but never have I found a good woman.*

The first time she'd sent this to me, I'd told her I found it ludicrous.

It means men and women often ensnare each other, she'd explained. *They ruin each other, which is why we always have to keep God at the forefront!*

Our trip had changed something in me. In those days and weeks following our drive, I sometimes felt what I thought was Him. Sometimes, in Ohio, at dusk, I stood on the sandy, empty banks of the nearby lake, watching my dog float across the surface of the water, her paws gliding through thick brown reeds, her tail buoyed and bobbing, and I felt the kind of calm people often claim is God. Dave was gone, and the world was quiet. But it was a quiet I preferred to any of the noise I'd known before. It was a strong feeling of self-assurance.

But I'm not convinced, I'd told her, *this is God.*

Perhaps this was simply how it felt to be a woman alone and independent for the first time in my adult life. Was it God, or was it Joy, or was it simply finding myself untethered? Was it knowing that all the good, and all the time, and all the love I put out into the world would not be ruined, would not be squandered, by the temper of any man?

I told Joy I was the happiest I'd ever been.

I felt pretty again, and young. The lake foamed beneath my feet.

After everything? I wrote her. I just want to be alone forever.

That's not what He has planned for you, she wrote. Her message came very quickly. You're meant to meet someone kind. And he's going to afford you love easily.

My dog was circling the reeds for minnows, and I watched as she looked back to me.

Can I get that in writing? I joked. Will you vet every man from here on out?

Of course I will, she wrote. I'll be right here when you need me.

She's not, I think in Fairbanks, pulling the blinds closed on the church and God. But back in bed, with the covers pulled to my knees, I remember how the conversation that day had ended.

I'd told her the passage might be misunderstood, but it was still dead wrong about good women.

Just wait, I wrote, till He meets you.

She'd replied with a smiley face. Can't wait!

She'd meant it.

~

The next morning, after she lands, I meet Debbie at the Korean restaurant. We order club soda with a slice of lime and two heaping bowls of bibimbap. Joy loved this place, I tell her.

"She called baby bok choy 'baby lettuce,'" I say.

"Never met a vegetable Joy didn't like," Debbie tells me.

Debbie is middle-aged with big eyes, light-red hair, and cheeks that flush the same soft amber. She is beautiful but sad and does her best to smile at me. We are both trying to make this normal, but mostly, we are waiting, anticipating the heaviness that will be Joy's funeral, and quietly peeling back steamed edamame, salt granules glistening along the pods.

"I've heard so much about you," I say.

"Same," she says.

Debbie wants to tell me about Joy. She wants to tell me about everything. She says life was made meaningful because she had Joy, that the two were inseparable. As a teenager, Debbie tells me, she spent a whole year living with Joy and her parents because her family had to move, and no one could see the two torn apart.

"We were like that," she tells me. "We were good apart, but we were better together. There was a kinship, like bloodlines, like family."

Along with their friend Shannon, the three spent summers culling adventure from Arizona's arid desert. Already Debbie has told me about the pranks the three committed—the homemade Reese's Peanut Butter Cups filled with cornstarch and green food coloring, which had made their teacher gag. The coordinated lies they'd told their parents to stay out late into the night. The typing class they ditched after finding a tape recorder and recording the sounds of spastic fingers pressed to keyboard keys.

"The typing teacher, he had this little utility closet set up just for typing," Shannon told me on the phone a few nights earlier, "and we set up the recorder by the door and went outside to enjoy the sun."

In the Korean restaurant now, Debbie squeezes lime into her water and asks what I was doing the moment I found out Joy was dead.

"Painting," I say.

She tells me she was shopping: the cleaning aisle of Walmart.

"James didn't have my number," she tells me, "so it was only when Joy's phone was recovered from the accident and returned to him—two days later—that he could call and deliver the news."

She tells me her phone lit up as she was surveying different Swiffers.

"Her name popped up, and I thought, 'Oh good, there she is,' like she could help me pick. I must have looked like a crazy person after I answered and heard that news. I fell to the floor, right there in Walmart."

But now, in our shared booth beside the window, Debbie tells me Joy's not dead. She reminds me that Seventh-day Adventists believe that people who pass on from this world remain in a state of unconscious rest. Like sleeping, she clarifies. The Resurrection will occur, she tells me, and then Joy and the resting others will join Him, followed by the faithful living.

"What happens to the rest?" I ask.

Fire.

I eat my edamame and say nothing. I don't believe in a Resurrection. I don't believe in a fiery earth.

But it doesn't matter to me, the way it might've only a few months before. Debbie is here and grieving, and I am here and I am grieving, too. I imagine there are sharp differences between us—of faith and ideology, of viewpoints and political beliefs—but our connection to Joy is paramount. It eclipses everything.

If Debbie believes Joy is sleeping, then let her sleep.

"You know, it's funny," she continues. "The last time Joy and I spoke, a day before"—she waves her hand around the restaurant—"all this? It was a Friday. She was in Prudhoe, was about to lose service, she said. She told me she was hurrying on back to be home for Sabbath."

At the table across from ours, we watch as a mother lowers her daughter into a cherry-red booster seat.

"I know what this sounds like—*crazy*—but I think she was ready. God knew Joy," Debbie tells me, "and He knew her heart was right. He took her, but she was ready."

It's a wake-up call, she says. We need to ready ourselves, too. She clears her throat as our dishes arrive: vegetables glistening on sizzling-hot rice.

"Our time will come soon, too," she says.

I see Joy's face, then, in Debbie's. I see the same softness and love and light. I have no way to tell her this. Instead I squeeze her hand and reach for the Sriracha and a glass jar of hot chili oil, drizzle it over my food. Debbie looks curious but refrains.

"She called me 'Spice Girl,'" I say, and Debbie looks confused, but I don't clarify.

We eat our food mostly in silence, suck the flesh clean from the complimentary orange peels, and pay our tabs. In the parking lot, beside my Jeep, we hug, and Debbie turns toward her rental car.

"See you tomorrow at the funeral," she says.

I repeat the words back to her. It doesn't feel right—any of it— but we get in our separate cars and return to our separate hotels, walk through separate lobbies, unlock separate rooms.

In my room, I draw the shades, get in bed, google Dr. Laura. I find her children's book, *Where's God?* I think to myself, *Good question.* The sky glows blue behind the blinds as I read it doesn't really matter where God is located.

If you are talking to Him, He's listening.

I love you, I say to Joy.

~

The next time I see Joy, it's in the faces of her children—the ones I'd yet to meet.

Andy and Daniel share her features, the freckles that frame her nose. Their pretty wives stand by their sides, solemn and composed. Samantha is every bit as beautiful, a Joy in intrepid youth.

I find the five of them together in the front row of Golden Heart, where, four months earlier, Joy arranged the congregation's communion wafers.

Now Joy's face extends the length of a giant ceiling-mounted pull-down projector screen, part of a slideshow Daniel made: Joy in a teal bikini; Joy leaning against a van; Joy as a young woman, a cooing Samantha in her arms.

Outside, it rains and rains. People don't know what to do with their umbrellas.

"Joy would have delighted in this," one woman says. She tells us Joy always felt happiest when she believed her God was expressing exactly what He thought His earth needed. She says, "And we needed a sad day of rain, all right."

The men and women all around her nod.

I stand there amid the strangers, uncertain of my hands. The last funeral I attended was sixteen years ago, the death of my grandmother, and I was still a child then. As an adult, grief is so much harder. Everyone wants to talk and offer testimonials to her character: how she brought clothing to the homeless who would gather on Steese Highway in downtown Fairbanks, how she accumulated dogs and horses and stray anythings with heartbeats, how once, she drove from Arizona to Alaska with a 9mm pistol tucked in a hollowed-out Skippy jar.

"She didn't have a permit," one woman explains, "but she said she wasn't going cross-country alone as a woman without a gun."

One haul road veteran named Duane tells me about all the times Joy snuck extra groceries in her truck to deliver to people in need along the way, how it was illegal, technically—you can only carry the load you've been authorized to truck—but Joy couldn't see the harm in a few extra pounds, especially when those pounds sustained a few people through a harsh winter in northern Alaska.

I take great pleasure in these stories, how the woman I knew and loved was the same person to everyone.

"She helped me a lot, too," I say. I don't enumerate how, exactly.

"Well, Joy had a sense about people," Duane says, nodding, "and she used that sense to help them."

This, perhaps, was Joy's greatest legacy: a network of people she was helping who are now helping one another. The depressed and the addicted, the wheel-spun and newly divorced—Joy was a woman who spent her days placing little antennae feelers out into the world, feeling for pain or suffering, feeling for the people who needed her. And in the hours and days since her passing, we've all done our best to self-identify, commenting on her Instagram account and tagging one another via separate and concerned dispatches: *Are you okay? Are you okay? And you, are you okay?*

In the church, before the service, James is all but shadow. I find him by the water fountain. Looking at his face, the hair thin across his forehead, I am surprised by the warmth I feel for him: a hard and tiny bud of compassion for a man who did much wrong but worked for love to make it right.

He is one year sober now, I remember Joy telling me, and I see his *sorry* in everything.

"She loved you," I say at last.

It takes longer than I wish it did for his face to rise up to the surface.

"Thank you," he says, but his eyes float over me and to the projector, where a Joy bigger than both of us is riding a brown horse on a beach.

"Thank you," he repeats, but somehow I have the sense that these words aren't meant for me. They are meant for the woman floating above us—larger than life and now only memory.

~

The funeral service itself feels like an exercise in communal weeping.

The pastor announces he'd like to begin the service, and people take their seats among the pews but quickly spill out into the aisles. Joy's funeral becomes standing-room-only; latecomers congregate quietly in the back. Everyone Joy knew and loved is here, except the ones who couldn't make it because their work is in Prudhoe Bay, those two weeks on and two weeks off, where not even the death of a haul road angel can slow the roll of industry. But they're mourning up there, too, someone tells me.

"Make no mistake," one man says from the podium in the front, "this was *all of Alaska's* loss."

In ways, I know, I'm lucky: that I knew her, that I met her, that we bonded as immediately and intimately as we did. But after the testimonials and prayer, I stand along the back wall beside Rich and Donald and show them pictures from the second half of our trip, and something about me seizes. I tell them we saw wolves, the corpse of a caribou. I tell them I touched the permafrost. I tell them now that she's gone, I might finally go to Hilltop, maybe eat that Fatman cake. They laugh and say I should, tell me it's better with vanilla ice cream, tell me Joy won't be there to scold me, say Joy would've gotten a kick out of that— past tense.

Joy's death, they tell me, should not have happened. It is the only thing we can all agree upon.

One trucker shakes his head and tells me, "Joy did as *she was trained to do.*"

In fog, in snow, in ice, truckers are taught to ride the shoulder— skirt, and slowly, those occasional metal delineators thrust upward in the earth, which are the only way up there to know what is road and what is tundra when the landscape and snow and ice make the distinction indiscernible. I tell them I remember; I tell them Joy told me the same thing.

"Why," someone asks, "aren't drivers trained to ride the middle of the road in those kinds of circumstances, where the ground is indisputably more solid?"

The veteran drivers scoff.

"Head-on collision like *that*," one says, snapping his fingers for emphasis. "You can't see the road in front of you in fog, in snow? You can't see the *hauler* coming at you, fifty, sixty miles an hour, hauling long pipe or a tank of oil."

We tell him: Joy was the safest driver anyone knew. She rode the shoulder as she was taught.

Which is why—when the fog crept in, and the delineators grew scarce—her front truck tire bit into the soft shoulder, and she flipped off the steep embankment, just parallel to Franklin Bluffs, the same stretch of tundra where mere months earlier we'd seen that pack of wolves feasting on the bloody carcass of a baby caribou.

It's how you think about it, she'd said to me. *This world is just all of us, fighting for a little more time to live. Some of us get it, some of us don't. But it's God's job to decide which is which.*

One minute she was here, and the next minute she was gone.

One trucker leans down and whispers into my ear that this is the price of capitalist greed.

"The delineators are supposed to be every fifteen feet," he says, "but they're every hundred in spots to save money."

"She told me that, too," I say. I remember the blow, the fox, Joy's brake tapping gently as she traced the shoulder.

"Cutting costs," another trucker nods. "Cutting *corners*," he amends.

"Put it this way," the first trucker tells me. "There are seven maintenance camps on the Dalton Highway, and each camp covers about sixty-five miles. We're talking maintaining potholes, maintaining washouts, maintaining avalanches—we're talking maintaining *every-thing*. You think they care about delineators? You think that makes any sense to them at all?"

"No," I say abruptly. I find that I am angry.

"And let me tell you something else," another trucker says. He asks if I have a notebook. He wants me to write this down. He thinks I am a journalist and that my words mean something. I don't want to be the one to tell him that I am no one, really, that I have no power here whatsoever, that I can't bring Joy back or keep others living.

"The road's not supposed to be so high," he tells me. "Two years ago, the Alaska Department of Transportation built the road up some five feet or more in places—it took 2.4 million tons of gravel—as a means of expediting travel. Now the Dalton Highway can be traversed in nearly any condition, but at the risk of truckers' safety. Used to be that when the Sag River flooded, truckers were stranded, because the road was impassable."

"She told me that, too," I say.

"Good," he says. "Good! The whole world should know that! The whole world should care, goddammit. We make the whole world pos-sible. Where would this country be without Alaskan oil?"

Another trucker, Chet, tells me he was once stranded on the side of the road for nearly a week because Prudhoe Bay needed what he was hauling, but the road was washed out entirely.

"It's something else," he tells me, "spending a whole week inside your truck cab, or climbing into someone else's, playing Uno or soli-taire, eating cold Pop-Tarts and reading books, just waiting on someone to radio in that, after six days, you can finally *move*."

"That built-up road and lack of delineators is why Joy flipped," the first trucker tells me. "Make no mistake. That sharp drop-off? She stood no chance. None of us do."

Still, no one expects to die in August; no one expects to die in fog.

"The illusion of safety," one woman tells me, tapping her finger against her head. Her name is Jessie, and I know from stories she's Joy's best Fairbanks friend. "The same way they say most accidents happen thirty miles from home."

But to Joy, the highway *was* home, *was* safety; she knew it better than she knew anything. And she knew how to handle her truck. Jessie tells me that footage retrieved from the inside of her cab shows Joy was hugging the road, like she was taught. She was driving slowly, as required. Her tire bit into the tundra, and she turned into it, as she was trained to do, and as she had done for thirteen years, maybe a hundred, several hundred times before. Still, the truck overturned, all nine thousand pounds of it, and with it our friend Joy, who—paramedics reported, to great relief—died an instant death.

"It should've been me," Debbie tells me later. We're idling in the funeral service's buffet line, which someone called "potluck row," and now we all repeat it, laughing, trying to find a little lightness in what makes this day so hard. We tong our wet croissants and say, "Potluck row, potluck row." We scoop a cube of melon, a wedge of golden pineapple, separate bratwursts that have stuck together, whispering, "Potluck row." Potluck row is just a series of seven card tables aligned to make a long buffet, a varied offering of sustenance in this day that depletes our spirit. It is lined with blue vinyl tablecloths, staticky and clinging to our funeral slacks. Bowls and platters glisten with perfectly rounded deviled eggs, scoops of pasta and chicken salad, hot dogs already enveloped in potato buns to allow for easier consumption. Her favorite waitress from the Korean restaurant unwraps layers of thick Saran Wrap from a bowl of glossy glass noodles with slices of red roast beef. Her vegetarian spring rolls go quickly. Joy's father croons about the chocolate cake.

"I'm technically older," Debbie clarifies. "Four months, but who's counting?"

"It shouldn't have been you," I said. "It shouldn't have been *anyone*."

Debbie is angry and right to be, and I tell her I'm angry, too—angry because Joy is dead and angry because she shouldn't be and angry because I don't know what else to be. How do I explain the way Joy gave me all her stories, told me she wanted me to tell them, and then left me so that I would have to, regardless of what the act of telling those stories might mean?

"I'm not angry at Joy," I say, "but I am so angry with how this shook out."

Debbie plucks a Vienna Finger from a silver tray.

"Yeah," she says, acquiescing, "but we have to accept that this was God. We have to accept He's got a plan."

I pluck a Styrofoam plate and fill it with Oreos. "I guess," I say. "Maybe."

But I see no God in this. I see no plan here whatsoever. I see the lesson of male violence, which once again has a cost, and that cost was Joy's whole life.

"God is in this," Debbie repeats, "and He'll come for us, too, in time."

I absent-mindedly tong a slice of cheesecake. I don't know how else I should respond. I don't believe in the Rapture, do not believe in the Second Coming. Sometimes, if I'm being honest, I think the end times are already here. For while it is true we inherited a world that is better than our mothers'—and better, still, than *their* mothers'—it is not enough for women to simply feel *safer*. We deserve to *be safe*.

An absolute.

I want to be safe; I want to know safety. I want to walk and jog and run through American forests and American sunlight, down American sidewalks and suburban streets. I want the backyard swimming pools without the men who assault, who murder; I want the backyard barbecues without men's guns. I want, someday, to have a daughter, and I do not want to spend my whole life worrying about all the ways the world will know to hurt her before she is even born.

Outside, puddles collect in the parking lot, threatening to suck us back into the earth. I make my way to the Jeep, where I find Jessie leaning against a headlight. Debbie walks out to join us, pulling a hood over her big hair.

"We need to spend more time together," Jessie tells us. "Just us girls," she adds, eyeing all the men she knows and works with still milling around the exit.

We stand in the rain for a moment, quiet. Jessie suggests a soak in Chena Hot Springs, the neighboring sulfur baths, and asks if we're free tomorrow. Yes, we say, we're free. I tell them I will drive, that this Jeep is good for nothing if not a caravan of weeping women.

"This is good," Jessie says, tucking her hair behind her head in a wet makeshift ponytail. Tendrils wisp along her forehead, and she exhales to blow them back. "A soak will help us out."

"Joy would like this," Debbie agrees.

"She would *love* this," I amend.

~

In the morning, on our drive to Chena, Joy shows up as a moose and Debbie tells me to pull over along the shoulder so she can step out to take her picture.

"Hiya, best friend," Debbie says. "I think that's you in there."

I stand against the berm, my boots sinking in the soil. The world around us is uniquely golden, summer's lush foliage burning up into shades of orange amber, and Debbie stands cooing in her blue jeans and sneakers. She steps closer, grins, snaps a photo, tells me—tells Joy—she regrets the circumstances that brought her here, but she's so glad to finally see Alaska.

"I love it here," she says.

Joy the moose is largely indifferent.

Standing there, watching them, I think of how the universe throws us lifelines when we don't yet realize we are drowning.

Joy was my long rope, the life preserver around my neck.

The moose is Debbie's comfort, and I understand the impulse; never is the world more vacant than when it is drained of someone we love.

"You sure are pretty, big girl," Debbie says. Then she swivels her head around to motion toward Jessie and me, now leaning against the Jeep. "And I love these gals, just like you did."

She gestures. "Come here!" she calls to us.

I am hesitant to join her. But then my hesitation gives way, and I step forward. I tuck my hand inside her palm, and Jessie falls in line beside us. Together, we cluck, we coo, we coax the moose like foolish tourists to lift her head and enormous antlers from the shallow pond beyond.

"Come on, girl," we call, and she snorts, shakes the water from her body, huffs, and stumbles forward.

~

We should crave music for this moment—three women on a road trip across rural America in an orange Jeep—but instead we savor silence and the introspection it permits.

Finally, Jessie exhales.

"She helped me *out*," she says. "I've fucked up once or twice in my life, you know? And she was always there for me, no judgment. Even when I did stuff that was *really* dumb."

"She knew everything," Debbie says. "All the struggles I ever dealt with—with my ex, and with my kid. All the hard stuff that really hit me."

"She saved my life," I say, then realize immediately how melodramatic my statement sounds. "I know that sounds silly."

"Doesn't," Jessie says. "She had a way about her."

"She had a way about her, all right," Debbie agrees. She puts a hand on my shoulder. "You say she saved your life? I believe you. But whatever you were going through, some part of her was saved by you coming up here, as well. She said so. You changed some part of her life, too."

"What are we going to do?" Jessie asks. "What are we going to do without our Joy?"

"We take a minute," I say. The answer comes out cleanly. "We take a beat. We think, 'What would Joy do?' *WWJD*," I say. And I start laughing. "We should get that on a bracelet. We should have someone put that on a shirt. WWJD?"

"For the women who walk with Christ," Debbie says.

"Or the women who walked with Joy."

Outside, dark gates announce we have arrived at Chena Hot Springs. The grounds are immaculate, marigolds and foxgloves and lilies overflowing in freshly mulched above-ground planters. Neat rows of brown rental cabins flank the parking lot, and beyond, the restaurant with its greenhouse greens, its homemade vinaigrettes, its king crab legs with hot drawn butter. Debbie snaps a photo of the ice museum, a giant igloo-shaped dome that houses carvings of naked figurines and furniture, animals and vases and even a tiny ice xylophone.

In the women's changing room, steam envelops our bodies, and we strip down to our bathing suits. We are not embarrassed of our anythings. We put our hair up with elastic ties and then wade into the milky water via a ramp that extends from the locker room until, inch by inch, we are submerged.

"Look!" Debbie says. She's down to her shoulders, the loosest hairs from her ponytail dipping into the water. She rises slow, the tendrils frost covered and sharp and white.

Jessie laughs and plugs her nose, dips, disappears. She emerges, and within seconds her whole head is ice, each strand stiff and silver along her forehead. She grins, batting frost-covered eyelashes, each one rimmed in white.

We bob along the edges of the hot springs like deities, our features softened by the healing water. It is early morning still, and the springs are nearly empty. The mountains are still green. Our laughter rises in the smoky steam.

For a moment, it is as if this morning was made for us, as if the flowers and the day's quiet and the moisture rising in thin clouds beneath the mountains were awaiting our arrival. Fountains in the center of the springs spray water that sparkles in the clean sunshine, freezes midair, and lands with a soft *thwack* as it breaks the surface. Debbie laughs, leans back, extends her legs out from under her. She floats easily. We are buoyant, light as air. We slap the water with our palms firmly, and our hands glide across the smooth, clean surface, forming dense, cascading fans that disrupt the reflection of this Alaskan heaven—all its pink and yellow flowers and the neat clouds of rising steam. We are void of grief, void of fear.

I float, feet up, in a canopy of stillness. For so long, I worried that God eluded me, that what others heard as His voice I heard only as stubborn silence. I've spent so much of my life searching for a faith that aligns with my lived experience, and of course I haven't found it, because I've been looking in all the wrong places. I have been looking for God in men. It's no wonder I can't relate to a faith or an ideology that holds at its center a figure who resembles all the men who've ever hurt me.

I look at Debbie, at Jessie, their bodies buoyant in the milky water. There's a very special place in hell, Madeleine Albright claims, for women who don't help other women, but what I want to add is this: there is a special part of heaven that peels open against all odds when a woman helps another woman.

It is a better heaven altogether.

There in Chena Hot Springs, I close my eyes and remember: the truck, her laughter, her incantation. Joy insisted it was God's miracle that brought the two of us together, but I don't believe in miracles. I believe she did this. I did this.

We.

Debbie calls me over, and I paddle until I am upright and nestled beneath her armpit, Jessie beneath the other. We grin, and Debbie snaps a photo, and then we lower our bodies together, heads and all, underwater.

There are angels on this planet, yes, and they fan out and float beside me.

17.

There are four days separating Joy's funeral from the memorial trucking convoy that will be held in her name, so I take the Jeep south to Anchorage. The morning is clear and bright. The rest of the world drops out, and I am often the only car on the highway, a luscious orange dot moving through Alaskan foliage. A few miles north of Denali, I pull over along the shoulder to watch a moose ford a river. I stand in the shadow of a mountain as asters and goldenrod bob their heads.

In Whittier, I buy a ticket for an afternoon glacier cruise and lean against the guardrail to count the jellyfish below, their bodies pulsing, wild with life. An hour later, the ship parks beside a glacier, which glows turquoise beneath the sun. Sea otters chitter and churn in dizzy circles, their bellies soft and white. Everyone clamors for a photo while the crew scoops the remnants of a glacial iceberg and divvies it up into ice cubes for cocktails.

In Anchorage, I meet a retired pilot who offers to take me up to Mount Marcus Baker, the highest peak in the Chugach Range. We take off in his yellow plane in late morning. Thick and luscious rainbows hug the plane's thin yellow wings, and I think of halos, of Arctic sun dogs. We skirt so low along the bluffs that I can see elk and grizzlies running.

They crane their necks to the sky at the mechanical sound of the plane as we skim the orange crust of earth.

Everywhere there is color, and everywhere life abounds. In these moments, these afternoons, I swear I feel Joy flicker inside me. She is in the yellow brushstroke of turning foliage, the gray and green of mountains. I feel her drawing me through the days, through nights, through the questions that have no answers, through the decisions that do not come easily.

I am one woman, I realize, whose life has changed profoundly because another woman made it so.

"Did you get what you wanted?" the pilot asks into his headset.

"All of it," I say.

~

When I show up at the Colville parking lot a few days later, every truck is washed and polished, every hubcap plastered with a memorial sticker—*Find Joy in the Journey!*—and every big rig's antenna carries a cranberry ribbon that waves wildly in the wind. Everyone knows I want to ride in a truck, and they've discussed how to make this happen.

"Technically speaking," Donald tells me, "you're not allowed to ride with us."

"Liability," Rich adds. "You're easy grounds for termination."

No one wants to risk their job, their livelihood, Rich says, but they know how much I meant to Joy, how much her life meant to me.

"Oh, I can squeeze you in," Donald says, finally. He scuffs his boots into the earth, kicking up dust and ashen gravel. He's already bringing his wife and son. And besides, we acknowledge silently, he's one half of the two men who found her.

Who's going to question or penalize?

"A tribute like this," Rich says, raising his hands to encompass the whole parking lot, "it says a lot about who Joy was."

"I don't think I've seen anything like it," Donald agrees. "Lots of parades in my lifetime. But never have they been this big."

The math, in fact, is staggering: sixty trucks and several dozen pilot drivers, their pickup trucks blue or white or red. I climb into Donald's truck with his wife and son just as the convoy is about to begin.

"Here is what you do in a memorial trucking convoy," Donald instructs, as if I'll be him one day. "You go slow, you turn on your moose lights, and you get liberal with the horn. Folks want to hear your honking. They want a lot of noise as you pass by."

Convoys like this don't happen often, he tells me, because death is a part of the job description. But for someone special, you make time.

He points ahead to the line of trucks.

"James is up front," he says, "with Samantha and Joy's parents. They're riding in the pickup."

The trucks begin to rumble, and we pull out of the parking lot, heading slowly into downtown Fairbanks.

"Here we go," Donald says.

Everything is in motion, metallic and gleaming in the sunshine.

Police and pilot cars block the intersections, and Deb Baker—our lead pilot driver—speaks clearly into the radio, giving us all the go-ahead.

"All clear," she tells us. "Let's do our friend Joy right."

Our convoy lurches, slowly, through Fairbanks. Drivers, stopped and hunched over their steering wheels, snap photos excitedly and wave. The elderly sit in lawn chairs, and children stand along the shoulder, thrusting their small arms into the air and drawing them down abruptly, as if to yank invisible levers.

Donald knows what they want. He is liberal with the horn.

Over the dispatch, on the staticky CB radio, the truckers take turns voicing a chorus of their love.

"New guardian angel watching us," one says.

"I miss her big smile," says another.

"You know she's lookin' down at us," one jokes, "laughing at us, dragging our sorry behinds on this road."

"This is Joy's last ride: 9-8-18 at 2:23 p.m."

"Safe travels, Joy. It was good trucking with ya."

"God bless ya, Joy. We're gonna miss ya."

Then the CB radio goes quiet. I want to ask Donald if I can say something, but don't. I am not a trucker; I was Joy's friend.

An hour later, just south of Hilltop, we park in wide, neat rows. There's a picnic down the hill: hot dogs and hamburgers and chocolate sheet cake topped with sprinkles. Children swing from heavy metal swing sets and leap off into the air. James puts an arm around my shoulder.

"Do you know what the last prayer she sent me was?" he asks me. He pulls his phone from his pocket. There, in a text: **Where there is joy, give them continued joy.** "How do you reconcile something like that?"

"It means she's with us," I say to him.

The heat of the day swells, and everyone begins to congregate beneath the wooden shelter. Daniel thanks everyone for coming. He's written some words down, and as he reads them, I feel Joy.

"Pursue adventure," he reads, "love easily, treat strangers like friends—that's how we keep my mom alive."

I think about how I might honor Daniel's wish, how I might keep Joy's love alive with all the resources I have at my disposal. I know exactly what I will do. Because the truth—what it comes down to—is that I didn't fear for my safety on that road or those steep Alaskan mountain overpasses. I didn't worry about my body taking days or weeks for crews to find. Sitting shotgun next to Joy—two days spent tracing nearly five hundred wild miles I was told I'd be lucky to see intact—I'd watched wolves track a herd of caribou, tear flesh clean from bone. I watched musk oxen claw the dirt, kick up a thick cloud of hot mosquitos. And I thought about the little fears women give in to every day, and how men—despite some trying—can't really ever know any of them.

I thought about how often and how many women in this world are made to feel small or weak or dumb, helpless or afraid.

I think of all the men I've allowed that luxury.

I won't do it anymore.

The luckiest people in this world are those who manage to reinvent, to live so many lives in the one life that they are given. Joy is one of them. And I want to be one, too. I think of what Joy believed: our bodies are just a vehicle. We can do good with them, or we can harm. And while I have no way of knowing, I have to believe that because of Joy, I am bound to do much good, because Joy believed that I deserved it—that every woman does.

It will be my life's work to remind others.

~

The flight attendant is kind a few hours later when she collects my ticket and invites me aboard. Tourist season is over, and the plane is quiet and empty. I get a whole row to myself. I kick off my boots and gloves, peel my body from its many layers. The plane ascends easily, and I unbuckle my seat belt and stretch out, wrap my jacket across my torso, and slip, gratefully, into sudden sleep.

When I wake an hour later, it is to lime-green lights flickering overhead. I think it's the flight attendant, come to offer me ginger ale. But in the oval window of Alaskan evening, I see stars and then something else—something I'd waited my whole life to see, something wild and well lit and dancing, something some people believe is God.

Is that you? I ask.

Of course it is.

AFTERWORD

In researching and writing this book, I made every attempt to verify details as they were relayed to me, including allegations. When asked to comment on Joy's story, James declined. As is often the case in incidents housed within romantic relationships, there are no witnesses other than those who were a part of it, so I do not know his side. I have no reason to believe Joy would lie.

ACKNOWLEDGMENTS

This book—and the years that led me to it—would not be possible if not for women.

Thank you first to Samantha Shea, for your brilliance and your encouragement and the way you championed this project from the very beginning. You are a fierce defender and advocate of my words, and I feel like the luckiest to be represented by you. Thank you to my incredible editors, Laura Van der Veer, Carmen Johnson, and Christina Henry de Tessan, for being so smart, so gentle, so committed, and for helping me share this book with the world. It feels like love, what you three did. Thank you to the entire team at Little A, most especially Emma Reh, Merideth Mulroney, and Kristin Lunghamer, and thank you, too, to Hafizah Geter, for all the smart thinking you helped encourage even well beyond the page. Thank you to Suzanne Williams. Thank you to Nicole Caputo and Merideth Mulroney for giving this book a very beautiful face; you are both talented beyond belief.

Thank you to Addison Duffy and Jasmine Lake, whose presence I enjoy every bit as much as I enjoy your good news, and to Mirabel Michelson. You have all been such a delight to work with. Thank you to Joey Soloway, Julianne Moore, and Beanie Feldstein—a ludicrous thing to be privileged to write—for believing in this project and seeing some part of yourselves in it. I am in such admiration of the art you make.

This book benefited in innumerable ways from the careful reading and consideration of a few very key and thoughtful players. Thank you to Martha Park first and foremost for your thoughtfulness, consideration, and time—our friendship is quite frankly one of the best things to come out of these past few years. Thank you to Frances Jo and Jessie Mathews—I am a stronger woman, and this is a stronger book, because I have you in my life. Thank you for reminding me what I am capable of, both on the page and off it. Thank you to Adam Stiffler for your unprecedented kindness, your intelligence, your friendship, your perspective, and all those head-clearing summer woodsy walks and emergency peanut-butter-banana smoothies. I am very grateful for you. Thank you to Mieke Eerkens: truly so much of this book, and my heart, is bound up in our conversations. Thank you, finally, to Maura Atwater, whose friendship—and fierce wisdom, and intellect, and heart—arrived just in time.

I am the lucky beneficiary of incredible women's wisdom, insight, perseverance, protection, time, love, and energy. Thank you from the bottom of my heart and most of all to Lisa Ho—I don't know where I would be without you and the time and compassion you afford every-one and everything. Thank you to Ellen Arnold for more than I know how to express here in writing; you were my first and remain one of my very best and most loyal friends here in Ohio, and so much of this book exists because you talked and walked through it with me. Thank you to Colleen Byers for seeing me through so many difficult days and for your patience and love and wisdom that a brighter future awaited me. You weren't wrong. Thank you for all things big and small to Lauren Vermilion—you have made my life so much fun to live lately—and to Jay Waldron, Karen Poremski, Maggie Smith, and Kelly Sundberg. Our conversations are why this work exists. Thank you to Rebecca and James Yates for your quiet home in Alabama, where I worked on many of these final pages. Thank you to Michael and Molly McOsker for your friendship and your porch sits and your pasta. Thank you to Luong Ho, Chris Hinshaw, Tammie and Rich Edwards, Jennifer and

Chris Wolverton, Julie Fink, Sarah Reimer, Chris and Nancy Walker, Zebbie Pettit, Amy Wright, and Jason and Kristen Allison for many things unnamable but all bound up in love.

Thank you to the Ohio Arts Council, whose generous support and early encouragement made so much of this book possible. Thank you for seeing the value in a project like mine.

Thank you to the Vermont Studio Center for providing me with an artist's residency and the space (and bread and cheddar) necessary to begin the very early pages of this book.

Thank you to the faculty, staff, and students of Ohio Wesleyan University and my supportive colleagues in the English Department, in particular, for giving me ground upon which to root. Your support has meant so much. I am especially grateful for the support this book received by way of the university's Katherine Boles Smith '71 and Alton Smith Endowment for Scholarly Leave and the Thomas E. Wenzlau (TEW) Presidential Discretionary Fund. Thank you for affording me the time and resources necessary to commit to such an undertaking as this.

Thank you to brilliant women writers whose work inspires my own: Leslie Jamison, Cheryl Strayed, Rebecca Solnit, T Kira Madden, Cathryn Klusmeier, Chelsea Bieker, Lacy M. Johnson, Kerry Howley, Jennifer Percy, Mary Miller, Alissa Nutting, Melissa Febos, Mira Jacob, Lidia Yuknavitch, Blair Braverman, Rachel Yoder, Sarah Menkedick, Sarah Viren, Cameron Dezen Hammon, Kristen Radtke, Terese Marie Mailhot, Maggie Smith, Tressie McMillan Cottom, and Kelly Sundberg, among others. Your words are always banging around in my brain.

Thank you to my Alaskan family: Roger Schmidt and Jeanine Brooks, Rhiannon Guevin, Kenley Jackson, Tracy and Mat Turner, Michael Hudock, Brendan and Rachel Jones, Cassidy Russell, Ed Littlefield, Abel Ryan, Javier Barboza, WT McRae, Drew Sherman, Susan Wingrove-Reed, Zeke Blackwell, Colin Roshak, and Elle Campbell. Thanks especially to Merrill Gehman for planting this seed of love for the Alaskan interior and for your kindness and your friendship; I think you and I are kin. Thank you to Melanie Gehman Coar and Andrew Coar for sharing your home and your sweet babies and your love of the Alaskan wilderness with me. Thank you to Duane and Linda Emmert, Charity Lorraine Timm, and the greater trucking community of Alaska for letting me dip a toe into your world.

Thank you to my students, whose work reminds me what a gift new words can be. Thank you especially to Chase and Ashley Montana, Ariadne Will, Serena Alagappan, Stephanie DeSoto, Katerina Barry, Lily Callandar, Dmitri Ashakih, Emma Neeper, Anna Edmiston, TaTyana Payne, Carody Wise, Cuckoo Gupta, Anja Brooks-Schmidt, Jonas Banta, Merrigan Horn, Nicole White, Anna Davies, Molly Berrey, Meredith Neff, Acadia Caryl, and Adriana Rodriguez, in particular.

Thank you to Joy's children for their belief and trust in me. More thanks than I could ever express to Joy's friends, most especially Candace De Witt and Susan Jones. Candace, especially: I am so very glad the world brought us together, even if I hate the circumstances.

Thank you finally to my family and most especially my parents, John and Heidi, to whom I owe everything.

SOURCES CONSULTED

Alaska Public Lands Information Centers, "The Trans-Alaska Pipeline." Accessed August 8, 2017, www.alaskacenters.gov/explore/attractions/trans-pipeline.

Bartosch, Jamie. "Why Are So Many Indigenous Women in Alaska Coming Up Missing and Murdered?" A&E, February 26, 2019, www.aetv.com/real-crime/missing-murdered-indigenous-women-native-alaska-other-states.

Bass, Rick. *Caribou Rising: Defending the Porcupine Herd, Gwich-'in Culture, and the Arctic National Wildlife Refuge.* San Francisco: Sierra Club Books, 2004.

Brown, Alleen. "Five Spills, Six Months in Operation: Dakota Access Track Record Highlights Unavoidable Reality—Pipelines Leak." *The Intercept*, January 9, 2018, theintercept.com/2018/01/09/dakota-access-pipeline-leak-energy-transfer-partners/.

Collins, Michael. "Congress Moves to 'Drill, Baby, Drill' in Alaska's ANWR. Here's What You Should Know." *USA Today*, November 19, 2017, www.usatoday.com/story/news/politics/2017/11/19/congress-moves-drill-baby-drill-alaska-anwr-refuge-heres-what-you-should-know/874187001/.

Daly, Matthew. "Oil, Gas Drilling in Pristine Alaska Refuge Takes Step Ahead." *AP News*, April 19, 2018, apnews.com/article/4285b7d4e3b945d2a3e73bcafb8ecba3.

Fairbanks Daily News-Miner. "The Trans-Alaska Pipeline, Then and Now." June 25, 2017, www.newsminer.com/gallery/featured/trans-alaska-pipeline-then-and-now/collection_4176d3e6-56e9-11e7-b69e-b3511429b2d8.html.

Fleischman, Lesley, and Marcus Franklin, "Fumes Across the Fence-Line." NAACP. Accessed April 27, 2018, www.naacp.org/climate-justice-resources/fumes-across-fence-line/.

Gardner, Kianna. "Savanna's Act Advances to Senate Vote." *AP News*, November 16, 2018, apnews.com/article/5452afe3429a4f97aefc8cf72d95bc6d.

Hedgpeth, Dana. "'Jim Crow, Indian Style': How Native Americans Were Denied the Right to Vote for Decades." *Washington Post*, November 1, 2020, www.washingtonpost.com/history/2020/11/01/native-americans-right-to-vote-history/.

Himrod, Corey. "Congress Seizes New Opportunity to Restore Arctic Refuge Protections." *Alaska Native News*, May 1, 2019, alaska-native-news.com/congress-seizes-new-opportunity-to-restore-arctic-refuge-protections/41719/.

Jeltsen, Melissa. "Domestic Violence Murders Are Suddenly on the Rise." *Huffington Post*, April 11, 2019, www.huffpost.com/entry/domestic-violence-murders-rising_n_5cae0d92e4b03ab9f24f2e6d.

Jeltsen, Melissa. "Who Is Killing American Women? Their Husbands and Boyfriends, CDC Confirms." *Huffington Post*, July 21, 2017, www.huffingtonpost.com/entry/most-murders-of-american-women-involve-domestic-violence_us_5971fcf6e4b09e5f6cceba87.

Langdon, Steve. *The Native People of Alaska*. Anchorage, AK: Greatland Graphics, 1993.

Lee-Ashley, Matt, and Jenny Rowland-Shea. "Arctic National Wildlife Refuge 101." Center for American Progress, October 10, 2017, www.americanprogress.org/issues/green/news/2017/10/10/440559/arctic-national-wildlife-refuge-101/.

McCann, Carole R., and Seung-Kyung Kim. *Feminist Theory Reader: Local and Global Perspectives*. 5th ed. New York: Routledge, 2020.

Morin, Philippe. "'We're Not Giving Up' Say Gwich'in Despite Start of ANWR Sales." *CBC News*, January 6, 2021, www.cbc.ca/news/canada/north/arctic-national-wildlife-refuge-advocates-not-giving-up-1.5863103.

National Coalition Against Domestic Violence. "Domestic Violence in Alaska." 2015, assets.speakcdn.com/assets/2497/alaska.pdf.

Ortiz, Erik. "Lack of Awareness, Data Hinders Cases of Missing and Murdered Native American Women, Study Finds." *NBC News*, July 30, 2020, www.nbcnews.com/news/us-news/lack-awareness-data-hinders-cases-missing-murdered-native-american-women-n1235233.

Ridgley, Heidi, "Where the Wild Things Are." *Defenders*, Fall 2016, defenders.org/magazine/fall-2016/where-wild-things-are.

Rosay, André B. "Violence Against American Indian and Alaska Native Women and Men." National Institute of Justice, US Department of Justice, May 2016, www.ncjrs.gov/pdffiles1/nij/249736.pdf.

Rowland-Shea, Jenny. "Measuring the Loss of American Wildlife If the Arctic National Wildlife Refuge Is Drilled." Center for American Progress, December 11, 2017, www.americanprogress.org/issues/green/news/2017/12/11/443964/measuring-loss-american-wildlife-arctic-national-wildlife-refuge-drilled/.

Ruskin, Liz. "Can Congress Squeeze $1b from ANWR?" *Alaska Public Media*, November 1, 2017, www.alaskapublic.org/2017/11/01/can-congress-squeeze-1b-from-anwr/.

Solnit, Rebecca. "A Rape a Minute, a Thousand Corpses a Year." *Mother Jones*, January 25, 2013, www.motherjones.com/politics/2013/01/rape-and-violence-against-women-crisis/.

Urban Indian Health Institute. "Missing and Murdered Indigenous Women & Girls." Accessed November 27, 2019, www.uihi.org/resources/missing-and-murdered-indigenous-women-girls/.

Vagianos, Alanna. "30 Shocking Domestic Violence Statistics That Remind Us It's an Epidemic." *Huffington Post*. Accessed December 7, 2017, www.huffingtonpost.com/2014/10/23/domestic-violence-statistics_n_5959776.html.

The Wilderness Society. "Trump Administration Undermines Environmental Review for Drilling in Arctic National Wildlife Refuge." September 12, 2019, www.wilderness.org/articles/press-release/trump-administration-undermines-environmental-re-view-drilling-arctic-national-wildlife-refuge.

ABOUT THE AUTHOR

Photo © 2021 Adam Stiffler

Amy Butcher is the author of *Visiting Hours* and an essayist whose work has appeared in the *New York Times*, *Granta*, *Harper's*, *The Iowa Review*, Lit Hub, *Guernica*, *Brevity*, and others. Excerpts of *Mothertrucker*, which is currently being developed into a major motion picture, earned a 2020 Individual Excellence Award from the Ohio Arts Council, and Amy's additional work has benefited from awards and grants from the Vermont Studio Center, the Kimmel Harding Nelson Center for the Arts, the Stanley Awards for International Research, and the Olive B. O'Connor Fellowship in Creative Writing from Colgate University. She earned her MFA from the University of Iowa and presently serves as the director of creative writing and an associate professor of English at Ohio Wesleyan University. Amy teaches annually at the Iowa Summer Writing Festival and the Sitka Fine Arts Camp in Sitka, Alaska, and she lives in Ohio with her three rescue dogs, beautiful beasts. For more information visit www.amyebutcher.com.